'He was one of those Englishmen Kipling delighted to picture. Nothing daunted him; he lived for enterprise and rejoiced in the handling of men; the more difficult and dangerous the job, the better it pleased him. He bore an English name not easy to add glory to, yet he succeeded.' – THE WORLD, *February 23rd, 1915*

Captain Shakespear is at once a portrait of an extraordinary man and a portrait of two distinct cultures in a bygone age – the British Empire in its heyday and the fierce desert tribes of Arabia.

H.V.F. Winstone was born in London in 1926 and was educated at the University of London. For most of his working life he has been a journalist – a Fleet Street financial writer and editor – and has contributed to the *Guardian*, *Connoisseur* and many other journals. He is also an expert on pottery and porcelain and has written extensively on the subject. He first became interested in Arabia when commissioned to write a book on oil, and later wrote (with Zahra Freeth) a history of Kuwait – *Kuwait: Prospect and Reality*. He has also published *Explorers of Arabia*. He is a fellow of the Royal Geographical Society.

CAPTAIN SHAKESPEAR

A Portrait

H. V. F. WINSTONE

QUARTET BOOKS
LONDON   MELBOURNE   NEW YORK

Published by Quartet Books Limited 1978
A member of the Namara Group
27 Goodge Street, London W1P 1FD

First published by Jonathan Cape Limited, London, 1976

Copyright © 1976, 1978 by H. V. F. Winstone

ISBN 0 7043 3169 1

Printed in Great Britain by litho at The Anchor Press Ltd
and bound by Wm Brendon & Son Ltd
both of Tiptree, Essex

The following provided invaluable information and assistance:

   Foreign and Commonwealth Office: India Office archives: Political and Secret
(1905–19), Persian Gulf and Kuwait Agency files, Bushire Residency diaries
(summaries of Political Agency and Consular reports 1911–15), military
records. Foreign Office library; *Arab Bulletin.*
   Public Record Office: Documents in Turkish Arabia and Najd files.
   Royal Geographical Society: Shakespear's travel notebook and photographic
negatives.
   Ministry of Defence: Astronomically determined positions in northern and
western Arabia, from Shakespear's notes, published by Geographical Section
of War Office, 1918.

Contents

Note to this Edition   7
Author's Note   8
Maps   11
Principal Arab Participants   15

1   Desert Politics   17
2   The Man in the Making   28
3   Preparing the Way   36
4   The Open Road   40
5   History Lesson   55
6   At the Court of Shaikh Mubarak   65
7   First Steps in the Desert   72
8   Arrival of the Warrior King   80
9   Conflict and Competition   86
10 Diversion and Invasion   94
11 Among Friends   100
12 Lord Morley Regrets   106
13 Dorothea and the King Emperor   113
14 Time of Trial   120
15 Interlude   134
16 Across Arabia   147
17 The Hot Summer   187
18 War and Death   195
19 Aftermath   211

Selected Bibliography   229
Glossary of Arabic Words   231
Index   233

Illustrations

between pp. 96 and 97

1 Shakespear in the dress uniform of the Indian Political Service (*courtesy Mrs Joan Wright*)
2 Dorothea Baird, later Mrs Lakin, 1908 (*courtesy Mrs Joan Wright*)
3 Shakespear in the Rover in which he travelled overland from the Arabian Gulf to England, 1907 (*courtesy Mrs Joan Wright*)
4 The British Political Agency at Kuwait, 1909 (*courtesy the Royal Geographical Society*)
5 The Shaikh of Kuwait's palace (*courtesy Major-General J. D. Lunt*)
6 The future king of Saudi Arabia (*courtesy Major-General J. D. Lunt*)
7 Shaikh Mubarak of Kuwait with Ibn Saud and members of the Saud family (*courtesy Major-General J. D. Lunt*)
8 Ibn Saud with brothers and sons near Thaj (*courtesy Royal Geographical Society*)
9 A desert execution, 1911 (*courtesy Major-General J. D. Lunt*)
10 The main street of Riyadh, 1914 (*courtesy Major-General J. D. Lunt*)
11 Ibn Saud distributing camels to his fighting men (*courtesy Major-General J. D. Lunt*)
12 Ibn Saud's army on the march near Thaj, 1911 (*courtesy Major-General J. D. Lunt*)
13 Breakfast with Ibn Shaalan and the ruling family of the Ruwala at Jauf (*courtesy Major-General J. D. Lunt*)
14 Halt on the Labba road (*courtesy Major-General J. D. Lunt*)
15 Shakespear's escort in the Kuwait hinterland, 1909 (*courtesy Major-General J. D. Lunt*)

On page 102
One of the stones of Thaj, found by Shakespear in 1911 (*courtesy Royal Geographical Society*)

On page 190
A letter from Shakespear to Ibn Saud

On page 200
Shakespear's last letter, to Lieutenant-Colonel Grey (*unpublished Crown Copyright material in the India Office Records, reproduced by kind permission of the Controller of Her Majesty's Stationery Office*)

Note to this Edition

Inevitably the publication of a biographical study gives rise to information which escaped the author in the compilation of the original text. I am greatly indebted to Mr Seton Dearden, Brigadier Lord Ballantrae (otherwise writer Bernard Fergusson), Mrs Christine Kelly the archivist of the Royal Geographical Society, and Lt. Colonel D. R. Smith, for bringing to my attention some useful additional facts and for correcting a few errors. This new edition provides an opportunity to incorporate their observations, parts of a letter from Shakespear to Gertrude Bell which Mr Dearden rescued from the old Chancery at Baghdad, and some small amendments of my own.

August 1977

Author's Note

I have called this a portrait, rather than a biography, because the passage of time has left gaps which can only be filled by guesswork, hearsay and circumstantial detail. But I hasten to assure the reader that the essential facts of time and circumstance are as accurate as intensive research and thorough checking can make them. Most of the stories relating to the brief but eventful life of Captain W. H. I. Shakespear were told to a few European travellers in Arabia and the Persian Gulf between the two great wars, by which time they had become part of the legend of the desert, handed down from father to son and perhaps coloured a trifle in the telling.

When someone has been dead for more than sixty years and the facts of his life buried so deep in official files that even his closest surviving relatives, no more than two generations removed, have not so much as heard of him, it is difficult to pick up the threads. I was fortunate. In the course of writing a history of Kuwait in collaboration with Zahra Freeth I needed to delve into the files of the India Office relating to the period when Captain Shakespear was Political Agent in that gulf state. From the political files I was led to the probate records of his family and, eventually, to the few relatives still alive. The search began with Mrs Judith Key, my subject's great-niece, and her mother, Mrs Barbara Carew, wife of the author Tim Carew. She was previously married to the late Major Richard Harry Baird Shakespear, the son of my subject's brother, Lieutenant-Colonel Henry Talbot Shakespear. It was with some disappointment that after so promising a piece of detection I drew a blank. Neither Mrs Key nor her mother had ever heard mention of my quarry. However, Mrs Carew was able to direct me to Major-General J. D. Lunt who was at Sandhurst with her late husband and remained his closest friend until his death in the Second World War. General Lunt, Bursar of Wadham College, Oxford, gave renewed hope to a dispirited searcher. He had inherited the documents left by Captain Shakespear to his brother in 1915, had written a lengthy article on Shakespear for the *Quarterly Review* and had considered writing a biography. When he learned that I had the same notion he most generously handed over to me the documents in his possession, and put me in touch with the Baird family into which Henry Talbot married and among whose daughters Captain William Henry Shakespear found the single romance of his life.

I have to thank virtually all the surviving relatives of both families for helping in one way or another, but most especially Lieutenant-Colonel Niall Baird for pointing me in the right direction, and Mrs Joan Wright, daughter of Dorothea Lakin (*née* Baird), for devoting so much time and effort to my persistent enquiries; and, on the Shakespear side, Mrs Carew, Miss Madeleine E. Worsley and Colonel R. P. Shakespear of Melbourne, Australia.

I also owe other debts of gratitude along the line. Mr G. R. Rees-Jones, present-day Principal of Shakespear's old school, King William's College in the Isle of Man, and two old boys of the college, Mr Neil Donaldson and Mr Ralph Thomson; the Curator of the Montagu Motor Museum at Beaulieu, Hampshire, and Mr Michael Sedgwick, the distinguished motoring historian; Mr Robert Austin who, at the age of eighty-five, recalled to me some of the personalities and colour of the gulf in the early years of the century and who remembered Shakespear's last sea journey from India; Mrs E. Clarke-Williams who knew the Shakespear family; most especially Zahra Freeth whose close family ties with the badawin of Arabia provided the impetus for my own enthusiasm and whose knowledge I have leaned on greatly. I was helped and encouraged, too, by Colonel Gerald de Gaury, distinguished traveller and chronicler of Arabia and its princes; he has always been close to the Shakespear legend and I am grateful for his help and advice. For information about my subject's friend Brigadier-General Sir G. S. G. Craufurd, my thanks are due to Mr M. C. Spurrier and Lady Rosamond Hanworth.

The biggest single handicap to a full-scale biography of Captain Shakespear is the disappearance of the Kuwait Agency diaries for the entire period of his office as Political Agent. Despite the most thorough search, these documents could not be found and it must be assumed that they were weeded from the records of the Indian Government by mischance, though it is surprising that the diaries of less important periods survive. All the same, I leaned heavily on the resources of the India Office, whose expert staff make light work of the most devious research; and on the Royal Geographical Society, without whose help few accounts of British-inspired expeditions or voyages of discovery would see the light of day. The latter institution holds Shakespear's photographic negatives and his travel log books and I take this opportunity of expressing my gratitude to the director, Mr John Hemming, for permission to use and reproduce them. My good friend Saad Allam of Cairo and Qatar helped with the translation of Shakespear's Arabic correspondence, for which I thank him.

There was one major problem in the telling of the story: the breadth of my subject's activities and the extent of his travels in the course of his short life. He made several long motoring journeys at a time when the automobile was still in its infancy and a journey of any distance demanded careful planning of fuel supplies and spares, and nerve. He also made six journeys of exploration in eastern Arabia in addition to his major expedition across the peninsula. In both cases I have had to telescope events, for to describe each trip in detail would test the reader's patience and make too great a demand on space. Unless otherwise acknowledged, quotations are from official records or surviving correspondence.

Lastly, a word on the vexed question of Arabic-English usage. Most writers use their own conventions, and many regard the whole matter as being beyond hope of rational or systematic treatment. I am inclined to agree with them. I have tried to be consistent with common words like 'shaikh' and 'amir', even in quotation. But I confess to instinctive preference in the case of *Ibn* and *Bin*, 'son of', which to the keen observer and the literal minded will look slapdash. Generally, but not always, I have used *Bin* when spoken and *Ibn* when written, such being the Arabic convention. As for the wandering people of the desert, I have avoided 'Bedouin', which cannot be justified in reason or usage, and plumped for 'badu' (collective) and 'badawin' (singular and plural). Not correct, but the nearest I can get to sense and intelligibility.

March 1975   H.V.F.W.

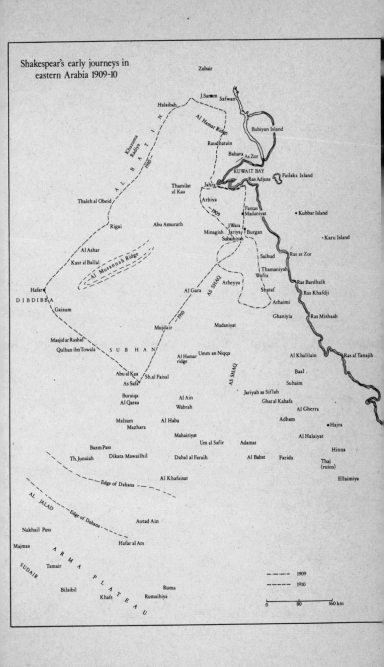

Shakespear's early journeys in
eastern Arabia 1909-10

Zubair

J. Samm
Safwan

Halaibah

Al Hamar Ridge

Bubiyan Island

Raudhatain

Bahara   As Zor

KUWAIT BAY

Thamilat
al Kaa

Ras Adjusa

Failaka Island

Jahra

Arhiya

Thaleh al Obeid

1909

Fantas
Madaniyat

Kubbar Island

Rigai

Abu Amurath

Minagish

J.Wara
Jariya   Burgan
Subaihiyah

Karu Island

Al Ashar

Saihud

Ras as Zor

Kasr al Ballal

Thamaniyah
Wafra

Ras Bardhalk

Hafar

Al Gara

Arheyya

Shataf

Ras Khafdji

DIBDIBBA

Gaisum

Athaimi

Ghaniyia

Ras Mishaab

Mujdair

Madaniyat

Masjid ar Rashid
Qulban ibn Towala

SUBHAN

Al Hamar
ridge   Umm an Niqqa

Al Khalilain

Ras al Tanajib

Baal

Abu al Kaa
As Safa

Sh.al Faisal

Suhaim

Buraiqa
Al Qaraa

Al Ain
Wabrah

Jariyah as Siflah
Ghar al Kahafa

Al Gherra

Malzam
Mazhara

Al Haba

Mahairiyat

Um al Safir

Adamat

Adham

Al Halaiyat

Hajra

Bazm Pass

Th.Junaiah   Dikata Mawailhil

Dahal al Faraih

Al Babat   Farida

Hinna

Thaj
(ruins)

Edge of Dahana

Al Khafaisat

Ellaimiya

AL JALAD

Edge of Dahana

Nakhail Pass

Aotad Ain

Majmaa

Hafar al Ats

SUDAIR

Tamair

Bilaibil

Khafs

Ruma
Rumaihiya

1909

1910

0   80   160 km

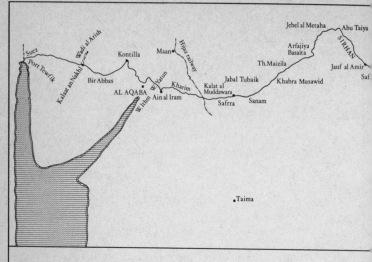

Capt. Sadlier's route 1819

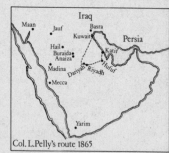

Col. L. Pelly's route 1865

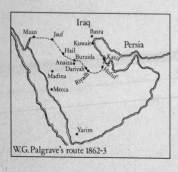

W.G. Palgrave's route 1862-3

B. Raunkiaer's route 1912

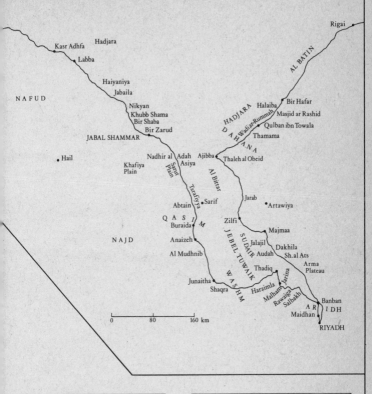

Shakespear's 1914 journey

Rigai

Kasr Adhfa
Hadjara
Labba

AL BATIN

Haiyaniya
Jabaila

NAFUD

Nikyan
Khubb Shama
Bir Shaba
Bir Zarud

JABAL SHAMMAR

Hail

Nadhir al Adah
Asiya

Khafiya
Plain

Sanr Plain

Tarafiyya

Abtain
Sarif

QASIM
Buraida
Anaizeh
Al Mudhnib

NAJD

Halaiba
Bir Hafar
Masjid ar Rashid

HADJARA
Wadi ar-Rummah
Qulban ibn Towala

DAHANA
Thamama

Ajibba
Thaleh al Obeid

Al Bitar

Jarab
Artawiya

Zilfi
Majmaa

JEBEL TUWAIK
Jalajil
Dakhila
Audah
Sh.al Ats

SUDAIR

Thadiq
Arma Plateau

Junaitha
Shaqra
Haraimla
Jattin
Malham
Rawaiga
Salbakh

WASHM

A R I DH
Banban
Maidhan

RIYADH

0   80   160 km

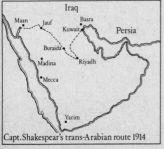

Iraq

Maan
Jauf
Basra
Kuwait
Persia
Buraida
Riyadh
Madina
Mecca

Yarim

Capt. Shakespear's trans-Arabian route 1914

Anaiza   Shammar   Muntafiq
Howaitat   Mutair   Ajman
          Hutaim   Sbai
          Harb   Nayban   Dawasir   Manasir
          Hadhail   Buqum   Suhul   Murrah   Ghafiri   Duru
                    Sbei   Dawasir   Shahran   Awamir   Jaalan
                    Qahtan   Yam   Manahil
                              Amalisah
                              Wayilah

Tribes of central and eastern Arabia

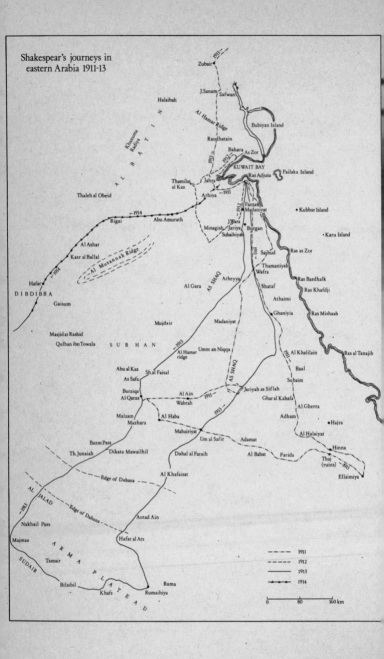

Shakespear's journeys in
eastern Arabia 1911-13

Principal Arab Participants

THE WAHHABI HOUSE OF SAUD AT RIYADH

Faisal ibn Turki   Faisal the Great. Amir of Najd
                                            1835–1865

Abdullah
Saud   sons of Faisal ibn Turki
Abdur Rahman

Abdul Aziz ibn Abdur Rahman   Ibn Saud. Amir of Najd from
                                            1902, King of Saudi Arabia
                                            from 1926

Muhammad
Saad   brothers of Abdul Aziz ibn
Abdullah   Abdur Rahman

Turki
Saud   sons of Abdul Aziz ibn Abdur
Faisal   Rahman. There were many
Fahad   others.
Muhammad

Ibn Jiluwi   kinsman of Ibn Saud

THE HOUSE OF SABAH AT KUWAIT

Muhammad ibn Sabah   Shaikh 1892–1896

Mubarak ibn Sabah   'Mubarak the Great'. Shaikh
                                            1896–1915 (half-brother of
                                            Muhammad).

Salim
Jabir   sons of Mubarak

THE HOUSE OF RASHID AT HAIL, CAPITAL OF JABAL
    SHAMMAR

Abdullah ibn Ali ar-Rashid	Amir of Hail and Viceroy of Faisal the Great from 1835
Ubaid ibn Ali	brother of Abdullah
Muhammad ibn Abdullah ar-Rashid	son of Abdullah
Abdul Aziz ibn Mitab ar-Rashid	nephew of Muhammad
Saud ibn Abdul Aziz ar-Rashid	son of Abdul Aziz
Hamud ibn Subhan⎱ *Zamil ibn Subhan*⎰	regents for Saud ibn Rashid, cousins

SHARIFITE (OR HASHEMITE) HOUSE AT MECCA

Husain ibn Ali	Sharif of Mecca from 1908
Ali *Abdullah* *Faisal* *Zeid*	sons of Husain. Abdullah and Faisal became kings of Transjordan and Syria and Iraq respectively, after the First World War.
Shaikh Khazal	ruler of independent principality of Muhammerah between Mesopotamia (Iraq) and Persia
Nuri ibn Shaalan	Amir of the Anaiza tribal federation and chief of the Ruwala
Nawaf	son of Nuri
Sultan	grandson of Nuri
Audah abu Taiya	Shaikh of the Howeitat
Dhaidan ibn Sadun	Shaikh of the Muntafiq
Faisal ibn Dawish	Shaikh of the Mutair
Dhaidan ibn Hithlain	Shaikh of the Ajman

1

Desert Politics

A benign sun shone on the rash of tents that covered the plateau
of Arma. Left and right, the black tents of the badawin tribes; at
the centre, the great white marquee of the amir, the *majlis* tent,
and around it the dwellings of the princes of the blood. Nearby,
another group, a white tent and six or seven black ones. A canvas
and goat-hair armada, stretching as far as the eye could see along
the western edge of the flat desert. Serried rows of black, and
here and there a pocket of white, obliterating the gravelly
ground except for a bare irregular patch where a band of nomads
gathered to bang their war-drums and dance their war-dance,
working themselves up to a state of fevered belligerence. But
most of the men sat quiet and immobile under the awnings of
their open tents. Distant camel herds grazed disconsolately, for
they had eaten greedily during the past few days and there was
little fodder left. A few riding animals crouched outside the tents
of their masters, a foreleg bound in folded position so that they
could not roam, stretching their serpentine necks and sniffing
the evening air.

Behind, to the north, the fertile villages of Sudair, their groves
and gardens irrigated by subterranean waterways. South, the
straggling townships of Al Aridh, leading down to Riyadh, the
walled, mud-brick capital of Najd; the settlements watered by
fingers of the Wadi Hanifa so that now and again a clump of
vegetation sprouted defiantly.

As nearly as they could be counted the men of the black tents
numbered six thousand. Bare-footed and bearded men, chequered
kaffiyas tied to their heads with rough goat-hair strands, bandoliers
across their chests. Wild, unkempt men with wiry bodies, aquiline
noses and serious countenances. The townsmen of the white

tents looked askance at them and kept their distance; they were
fewer in number and wore clean frocks and tidy headdresses.
They used water to wash with, which the wild men deemed an
unholy waste.

It was a scene common enough in the desert regions over which
the Amir of Najd kept vigil, from the border of Jabal Shammar
in the north to the 'Rub al Khali', the Empty Quarter, in the
south, from Hijaz in the west to the coastal shaikhdoms in the
east. Abdul Aziz, son of Abdur Rahman son of Faisal, 'Bin Saud'
to the people of Arabia, was on the warpath, preparing for battle
with his old rival Ibn Rashid of the upstart royal house of Hail.
Rashid, ally of the Turk, moved across country with a well-
armed force of comparable size and Ibn Saud's desert scouts
reported that they were camped north-west of Zilfi, 150 miles or
more from Camp XXI.

The Arab warriors made so much noise it was hard to detect
the anachronistic sound that came from the white tent among the
half-dozen or so black tents. But those who wandered by could
not help but hear the *clack-clack* that came from it, and they
stopped and inclined their ears. It was, said the best-informed
among them, a writing machine at work, a weird device surely,
even for the strange nasrany in their midst. The tent flap opened,
and Captain Shakespear stood at his front door, the tallest man
among them, moustache drooping below the line of his mouth,
high forehead and penetrating eyes challenging the eastern scene.
His khaki field-dress, complete with gaiters and army greatcoat,
made the starkest imaginable contrast with the dress of the desert
Arabs. He glanced imperiously to his left, towards the depression
of Al Ats, and then half right to the cluster of hills at the south-
east. He took his watch from his jacket pocket and examined it
closely. Then he strode with evident purpose towards the amir's
tent. It was 5 p.m.

Ibn Saud and Captain Shakespear had known each other for
five years now and they were the closest of friends. From the
time of their first meeting, when Shakespear was the Consul, or
Political Agent, of Kuwait, they had talked often of Arab freedom
and of the ambition of the young chief of Central Arabia to drive
the Turks from his territory and restore the kingdom of his
ancestors, the Wahhabi kingdom of the Sauds, which embraced
almost the whole of the peninsula from Yemen in the south to

Aqaba in the north. Now Great Britain was at war with Turkey and Captain Shakespear was his country's Political Officer on special duty in Arabia.

Each day since he had joined the Saudi war party early in January he had sat in his tent and written reports to his government and letters to friends in office, setting out the case for an alliance between the Arab leader and Britain which would bring the tribes and leaders of the desert people to the allied side. Then, when he had finished his official work, he would join Ibn Saud in his tent and sit with him and his brothers and sons, and the tribal chiefs, and talk of the past, for Abdul Aziz never tired of the history of his family and people. Day after day they would go over the story of the past two hundred years, the religious origins of his family's authority in the desert, the spread of its power, and the intervention of the Turks. These were for the most part simple, illiterate men, more practised with the sword than the pen. Their history was passed down from father to son by word of mouth; it was the staple food of conversation in the desert, and Shakespear had heard it all countless times before. But when the urgent matters of the moment had been dealt with he relaxed and listened and drank coffee to the ringing accompaniment of pestle and mortar.

He was an honoured guest and Abdul Aziz a courteous host. He sat at the amir's right hand with brothers, sons and other close relatives of the desert king completing a circle as they squatted cross-legged on the ground round the central platter of lamb and rice. The Englishman was accustomed to the ritual of the Arab table and he knew well the soft-voiced chivalry of his friend's welcome.

As each man took his place he said: 'Bismillah,' In the name of God.

The amir, in the way of the Arab host, tore off the tenderest parts of the lamb and laid them before Shakespear with lumps of fat from the animal's tail, and tongue and eyes, and Shakespear spoke in praise of his host's lavishness. And as each man finished his meal with dates picked from a sticky mound he belched with open satisfaction, uttering 'Allah karim', God is bountiful, and wiped his mouth with his hand. As they rose Shakespear joined the family of Al Saud in the ritual expressions of gratitude: 'Unaam allah aleyk! Allah yi kithar khairak!' The Lord be gracious unto thee! and The Lord prosper thee! And the amir made the customary responses, 'Alaikum bil afia,' God's health unto thee, and 'Mal allah wa malak,' It belongs to God and thee.

Shakespear was at home with the proud men around him, though his tastes and habits differed from theirs and he made no bones about the fact. When they had done with the long drawn out business of eating, he and his host were anxious to resume talk of matters vital to Arabia and to Britain. Abdul Aziz liked to talk of politics and history. Every now and again he turned to his kinsman Ibn Jiluwi, or to his brother Saad for confirmation or approval, and he used his hands to illustrate his words.

'My trust is first in God and then in you, O Shakespear.' The customary pleasantries were a preamble to a bitter attack on the men who had left him to his own devices not much more than a year before and had told him that he should sign a treaty with the Turks. They had forced him to enter into a bargain with the Ottoman power, to become their mutasarrif in Najd, because he could not survive without the aid of one of the great powers and his security was constantly threatened by the self-declared ally of the Turks, Ibn Rashid, whom they armed to the teeth; and by the chief of the Muntafiq tribe in Mesopotamia, Ibn Sadun, whom the Turks also armed and set against him.

'Now, O Shakespear, you ask me to promise the Great Government my support because it is at war.' Abdul Aziz rubbed his fingers together as if to conjure words from the air. 'Well, I give you my promise that I will do nothing to harm your country's cause and I will fight the enemies of Arabia who are also the enemies of the Great Government. But now I depend on the Turk for money and I have few guns and little ammunition, while every day armaments arrive at the fortress of Shammar, for the use of my enemies. And all the time the Ottoman sends soldiers and advisors to me to demand my help … ' The story was familiar both to Shakespear and to the British Government, for Shakespear had relayed it to them until they were sick of hearing it.

Shakespear had sought a treaty with Ibn Saud for five years, expressing his own views on the matter forcibly, often stridently. He was supported, though circumspectly, by the Resident in the Persian Gulf, Sir Percy Zachariah Cox. In the last months of 1914 Britain had been anxious to gain the support of the Arab leader at the heart of the peninsula and of the desert tribes who were loyal to him. Now the war seemed to be going well enough without that support. Steady progress was being made in driving the Turks from lower Mesopotamia, the Royal Navy was in command of the gulf, confident plans were afoot a thousand miles to the north to take command of Suez. Neither generals nor politicians could see any great need to pander to Ibn Saud.

As Abdul Aziz went on with his story, probing the history of his land, he was cut off in mid-sentence by a sudden disturbance. A messenger galloped into the camp and the amir's men came to tell him that the emissary was from Husain, the Sharif of Mecca, and his son Abdullah. The visitor was taken to Ibn Saud's own tent and the amir asked all but Ibn Jiluwi and Shakespear to leave.

The chief held the message in his hand and quoted from it. Abdullah, it seemed, had taken command of the tribes of Hijaz because of his father's age and infirmity, and had gone to Madina, the prophet's city, to escape the Turks, who were demanding that he declare *Jihad*, or holy war. Abdullah explained that he was biding his time, until he heard from Ibn Saud.

'What shall I say to him?' asked the amir.

Already the desert was thick with apostles of holy war. The so-called Pan-Arab movement was whipping up a fevered call to arms in Mesopotamia and the northern cities. 'Protect Islam from the infidel' became the battle-cry, and it was taken up in the mosques and on the street corners. Sir Percy Cox and Shakespear had already forestalled the Turks and their allies in Central Arabia by giving a solemn undertaking that freedom of worship would be guaranteed to the Arabs. But no such promise had yet been made by the British authorities to Arabs outside the gulf and Najd.

'Jihad, proclaimed by the sharif, by the man believed by millions to be the descendant of the Prophet, would have the most terrible consequences,' Shakespear told Ibn Saud. 'You, Abdul Aziz, must work for England's victory as the best way to secure Arab freedom. The Great Government was forced into war with Germany, and Germany has forced war between my country and Turkey. The last thing my government wishes is an extension of that war. I have already assured you of my country's wish to protect your holy places. You, O Abdul Aziz, mightiest prince of

Arabia, must tell the sharif and his son that my government has no designs on the holy places, and that he and his father should use their influence for peace, for if he desires the benevolence and countenance of the Great Government, he must turn away from the Turk. The power of Turkey is doomed, though the Sultan's rule over the holy places is a matter for you Arabs. Tell Abdullah to bide his time, to promise as little as possible, until the wishes of the Great Government are made clear.'

Ibn Saud nodded agreement. 'I have already told the Sharif', he said, 'that the Turks are not his true friends.'

Turning to the messenger, he told him to tell the Sharif Husain and his son that they should do nothing to aid the Turk and should resist the call to *Jihad*.

'The interests of all Arabs lie with the Great Government. Promise the Turk as little as possible.'

His reply should be delivered by word of mouth, he said, for a written message might be intercepted in the desert. But he handed over three written statements given him by Shakespear; the Viceroy's undertaking to protect the holy places of Islam, the Acting Resident's notice to Arab chiefs on the declaration of war with Turkey, and the official communiqué of the British Government declaring a state of war. As he handed over the documents he also told the messenger to tell Abdullah: 'Soon I shall fight a great battle with Ibn Rashid and destroy my adversary.' Then the amir left the tent and the call went out for the last prayer of the day.

Next day Shakespear wrote a long report to the Resident in the Persian Gulf, who was still nominally responsible for the affairs of 'Turkish Arabia'. He told of the visit of the sharif's messenger, and went on:

Jihad, especially if proclaimed from Mecca by one of the Sharif's standing, is a contingency of which the consequences are unforeseeable and incalculable. Such a proclamation would at least raise the whole Arab world and Bin Saud himself would be compelled by the circumstances of his faith, his prestige and position as an Arab leader to follow with all his tribes ... Fortunately through Bin Saud's commanding influence in Arabia (and if HM Government are prepared to

meet his desires generously), we are in a position so to limit
the danger as to make it *negligible*. It is with these thoughts
in mind that I proceeded to discuss the Sharif's letter with
Bin Saud.

Then a familiar plea.

It will be noted that Bin Saud is doing all in his power,
short of openly rupturing with the Turks, to further Britain's
interests. It will be said that he seeks the betterment of his
own position, and that this is true he himself frankly admits.
I venture to urge that the co-operation Bin Saud has furnished by his own attitude and influence with the Arab chiefs
has been of no less value than the active support asked for,
and he deserves a generous response from HM Government
to his wish for a close and binding understanding.

Shakespear's report went to Sir Percy Cox and from him to
Cairo, where the Arab Bureau set up by Lord Kitchener kept
their own vigil over Arabia from the Savoy Hotel. The Bureau's
intelligence handout, called the *Arab Bulletin* and edited in its
infancy by Captain T. E. Lawrence and Lieutenant Commander
David Hogarth, was later to observe:

January 1915 was a critical month. The war had well
begun, and preparations for the great attack on the Canal were
in full swing. Everybody believed it would be successful,
and that it meant the beginning of a new epoch in Islam ...
Pan-Islamic agents were swarming in Damascus and preaching in all the mosques and villages of Syria. The Sanjak was
being displayed and the Jihad growing in acceptability.
Arab eyes were all turned to the Holy Places waiting for
word from the Ashraf and Ulema of Mecca ... Mecca however kept silent and Jihad fell flat. We had not received
hitherto any precise information of what were the influences
which prevailed on the Sharif to guard his neutrality. There
are the old conversations with Lord Kitchener, but these
had contained nothing very definite, and Abdullah's ambition, so far as we know, would have been served almost as
well one way as another. This letter from Captain Shakespear,
however, throws a flood of light on another side, and puts
us most deeply in his debt, and in the debt of Ibn Saud.

By the time that note found its way into the *Arab Bulletin* (No. 25), October 1916, Captain Shakespear had been dead for nearly two years, his cause forgotten.

The pathways to obscurity are many, though none is so sure in political service as to oppose the settled and collective view of the government of the day and be proved right by subsequent events. Such was the path of Captain W. H. I. Shakespear. His memory has lain hidden in long-forgotten archives since 1914.

Occasionally his ghost has stirred; it was brought to fitful life by another Englishman who soon after him wandered among the tribes of Arabia. In *Seven Pillars of Wisdom* T. E. Lawrence recalled the time when he sat around the coffee fire of his guides in Wadi Sirhan and listened to the Najdi Arabic of the men as they began 'to tell me long stories of Captain Shakespear, who had been received by Ibn Saud at Riyadh as a personal friend, and who had crossed Arabia from the Persian Gulf to Egypt; and had been killed in battle by the Shammar in a set-back which the champions of Najd had suffered during one of their periodic wars.'

Others skirmished with the story of this virtually unknown Englishman who had come close to the chief of Central Arabia at a time when his territory was unknown to the outside world. H. St J. Philby, who followed in his footsteps across the vast and little-known deserts at the heart of Arabia, heard tales of adventure and heroism that surrounded his name. Sir John Glubb (Glubb Pasha) made frequent reference to the special place that Shakespear held in the affection of the princes and tribesmen of Arabia. H. R. P. Dickson, historian of Kuwait, told of his fame in the gulf more than a decade after his death. But such men could only repeat what they were told and conjecture as to the character and substance of a man whose brief life meant so much to people who usually held strangers at arm's length.

A conspiracy of silence grew out of Britain's pre-war policies of non-interference in Arabia, and out of its wartime decision to reverse those policies by fostering an Arab rebellion, rallying to its side the Turkish vassal Husain, Sharif of Mecca, and his sons, with injudicious promises and indiscreet bribes. When the alliance forged in that rebellion collapsed in a predictable heap of recrimination and despair, Britain did not hurry to revive the memory of a man who fought for a contrary cause.

He was a Victorian at heart, a product of the Empire and of Palmerstonian Liberalism; stiff-lipped and unbending in matters of principle, he was, paradoxically, a cavalier of the desert, a fearless explorer. He recognized the spirit of independence of the Arab of the desert and his determination to expel the Turks and their allies from his territory. He saw at first hand the loyalty of the majority of the tribes of Arabia to the amir of the central province of Najd, Ibn Saud. He argued that if Britain stood aside from the struggle for freedom in that vast and divided land, others would fill the void.

It was an unpopular view. Despite the persistent claim of historians that when the Kaiser's Germany began to look towards Arabia prior to the First World War it saw an Empire nominally ruled by the Turks but in reality controlled by Britain, the opposite was in fact the case. Britain's presence in the area was timid, faltering, and based on the negative proposition that whatever Arabs might want, the Turks were their legitimate if incompetent rulers. There is not a single official document on record to support the commonly accepted historical theory. There are plenty that prove the opposite.

The official view was put simply and unmistakably by Sir Louis Mallet, Sir Edward Grey's right-hand man, in a note to the India Office on June 7th, 1913, a note which sparked off the admission that Sir Percy Cox and Shakespear 'frightened' the Foreign Office:

> The general attitude of HM Government, which in this matter is based on considerations of European policy, is to consolidate the power of Central Government in Asiatic Turkey, and if HM Government were to approach the Ottoman Government, as suggested by Sir Percy Cox, with a view to concluding direct agreements with Ibn Saud as an autonomous ruler, it would give rise to suspicion, and might have far-reaching and regrettable effects. Sir Edward Grey is, moreover, far from convinced that the ultimate triumph of Ibn Saud over the Turkish authorities is assured.

The British Government, preoccupied with Europe and intent on keeping clear of any involvement in the affairs of other parts of the world save those traditionally within its sphere of influence, looked for malleable men to carry the flag in the East: men of no great imagination, but professional and capable of carrying out instructions to the letter. It did not expect its distant outposts to set the pace in the making of alliances or the establishment of new codes of behaviour. In Captain Shakespear, it inadvertently found a man who did both. In earlier times he might have brought valuable new provinces to the Empire. As it was, he succeeded in winning the friendship of the Arabs of the gulf and the desert with a facility that made him famous among them; and in alienating the sympathies of his political chiefs, with the single exception of Cox.

From the moment he arrived in Arabia he was caught up in the squabble between the two great powers of that country, the House of Saud at Riyadh, led by Abdul Aziz ibn Saud, and the pro-Turkish House of Ibn Rashid at Hail. His own government wanted to have nothing to do with that battle. Back in 1902, Ibn Rashid had threatened the security of Kuwait, where Britain had kept a tentative presence for some 150 years. Ibn Saud, just restored to his own kingdom, rushed to the defence of the tiny gulf state.

Two years later, when Britain had installed a Political Agent at Kuwait, Shaikh Mubarak asked his advice regarding the dispute between the two warring powers of Central Arabia. The Secretary of State told the P.A. that he 'should express no opinion as to the advice to be given to Ibn Saud by Shaikh Mubarak', but should repeat an earlier warning. 'HM Government wish it to be made clearly understood that their influence and interests are to be strictly confined to the coastline of Eastern Arabia, and that nothing is to be said or done to connect them, in even an indirect way, with the fight now going on in the interior.'

Neither immediate rights and wrongs nor the long-term consequences of desert conflict were of interest to Britain in those days; but they were of consuming interest to Shakespear, and so he became involved in conflict with his own superiors. Yet the fact remains that out of the trust and friendship which flourished between this Englishman and the Amir of Central Arabia in the first decade of this century, Britain was offered the custodianship of a poor and desolate kingdom. It was too late when that kingdom became the richest on earth to regret the patronizing scorn with which the offer was received, too painful to recollect the supine politics of the past.

Shakespear had no literary ambition, no pretension to fame in his own time or to the acclaim of posterity. He was a man of action, a patriot who made no bones about his own loyalties yet who recognized the right of his Arab friends to choose their own road to freedom. His actions must speak for themselves, alongside those of his superiors, for only in Arabia did his name and reputation survive, passed on by word of mouth from father to son until the unwritten history of the desert was washed away on a sea of oil.

2

The Man in the Making

The last quarter of the nineteenth century was a prosperous and optimistic time for the Raj.

In 1876 Lord Lytton held his great durbar at Delhi, announcing to an envious world the assent of Queen Victoria to the title 'Empress of India'. By then the Shakespears of the sub-continent were a well-established and respected family, and connections with other distinguished British clans in India underlined their own prominence. In the early years of the century John Talbot Shakespear of the Bengal civil service married Emily, the eldest daughter of Mr W. M. Thackeray, another civil servant of the Bengal administration, and in 1812 their first son, Richmond Campbell Shakespear, was born. Mary Anne Shakespear, John Talbot's niece, married Emily's younger brother, the Reverend Francis Thackeray.

Dowdeswell Shakespear, Richmond's brother, and cousin of William Makepeace Thackeray, was embodied in Colonel New-come who ended his life at Greyfriars, the novelists' portrayal of Charterhouse, the public school he attended with the young Shakespear.

Into Victoria's reign and beyond, the Shakespears extended their fortune by devoted work and by marriage, and their fame by valiant deeds in military and civil fields. For almost the entire nineteenth century, the family was represented in the Indian Army, from the general staff to the most junior ranks.

Proceeding up the family tree, as it were, they could trace a direct line as far as John Shakespear of Shadwell, rope-maker to the king. He was born in 1619 and married twice. His wives, Mary Judd and Martha Seeley, produced many children of whom eleven are recorded. Beyond John of Shadwell there is conjecture that the family lineage reached Thomas, the bard's uncle, through an illegitimate and unrecorded son. Uncle Thomas is said to have dropped the 'e' from the end of the family name because of the embarrassment caused by the theatrical goings on of his nephew, a far-fetched theory since the playwright often spelled his name without its terminal vowel. Whatever the truth of the matter, the Shakespear family used the coat of arms of their supposed forbear until the twentieth century, when, in 1918, Miss Mary Shakespear applied for a coat of arms in the name of her grandfather, John of Brookwood, the common ancestor of all the Shakespears of India, and her request was granted. The Shakespeares and the Shakespears were separated for good.

William Henry Sullivan Shakespear, unlike most male members of the family for generations before, entertained neither military nor political ambitions. He was of pacific temperament, a man for the quiet life, unassertive in appearance and purpose. He was fond of outdoor life and it was no surprise to family or friends when, on leaving Bromsgrove School close to the family home in the Midlands, he sailed for India to join the Imperial Forestry Service. He exhibited one distinct family trait, however: an inclination to marry strong women. In January 1878 he followed that inclination to the altar of St Peter's Chapel in Bishop's College, Calcutta. His wife, Anne Caroline Davidson, was a woman of considerable beauty, regal bearing, and unshakeable determination.

If the Shakespears were essentially a middle-class family, distinguished and devoted servants of the Indian administration, with good positions in life but no large fortunes to fall back on, the Davidsons were of a special brand, colonial landowners. Anne, known throughout her life as Annie, was born in Jamaica. One of her ancestors, it was said, had impersonated the Duke of Northumberland in order to escape Cromwell's men, but was found out and banished to the West Indies. He could not have suffered a kinder fate, for he was soon the owner of a thriving slave-trading business. The family grew increasingly prosperous on the proceeds of ever-expanding plantations and free labour.

Within a year of their marriage, Annie gave birth to her first child, a son.

It was only to be expected that the infant would be given the most illustrious Christian name that can be attached to a Shakespear, William. The father's second name was also entered on the birth certificate in a flurry of paternal pride. The youngster's third name came from his mother's side of the family. William Henry Irvine Shakespear was born at Multan in the Punjab, on the 29th day of October, 1878.

His father was an assistant conservator in the Forestry Department; he was now twenty-nine years old and making unspectacular progress in his job. Mild of manner, retiring, utterly overpowered by his wife, he found contentment in the forests and open spaces of India.

Annie went about the business of raising her infant son with vigour and determination, with the overweening dedication of a mother who has found the vehicle through which her own intense feelings of loyalty, duty and aim are to be realized. In less than two years from the birth of her first son, a second boy arrived. Favoured names having been consumed already, the new infant had to be content with George Albert, perhaps deriving from the royal princes of Queen Victoria's family. Another two years saw the arrival of the third and last child, another boy who was named Henry Talbot, the latter name deriving from a marital link between the Shakespears and the Fox-Talbots of photographic fame at the turn of the eighteenth century.

Annie was, after her fashion, a devoted mother to all three. But there can be little doubt that William was the hub of her world. She sowed the seeds of character at an early age. She became his infant teacher, his mentor in matters of speech, writing and manners, encouraging him in his precocious ability to wrap his tongue around the language of Punjabi servants, so that he was bi-lingual by the time he was five or six. As the time arrived for his formal education to begin she made plans to take him to England and supervise the first two years of his preparatory studies.

She left Bombay with her three sons in February 1887 and arrived in England in March. She took rooms in Portsmouth and the boys were entered into the preparatory school of the Misses Lacell. William remained there for just over a year, until 1889, when he went as a day boy to Portsmouth Grammar School. By 1890 he had progressed into the top form and was regarded as one of the brighter boys of the school. In the meantime, his brothers were following him through the same preparatory and grammar schools. But it was the eldest boy's progress that chiefly concerned their mother and when she was assured that his academic and athletic advancement was satisfactory she relaxed and returned to her husband in the Punjab. The boys waved her a fond farewell and William went back to Mr Pares' House, 'Prescote', where he was now a boarder.

He was twelve years old and responsible for his brothers. He promised his mother that he would write regularly and inform her of their progress.

At thirteen he was captain of the 4th XI football team and had won 3rd XI colours. Next year he went into the lower army class and in March 1893 was promoted to the upper army class. By then he was in the 1st football XI and the school cricket team. Academic and sporting success bolstered his natural confidence and growing self-reliance. By his fifteenth year he was strong, assured, and set on a military career. And after a separation of three years he looked forward to the return of his mother who was coming back to England to supervise the transfer of her three sons to King William's College in the Isle of Man.

The bond between Shakespear and his mother was strong and it was to remain so for the rest of his life. She was a commanding and elegant woman and her eldest son enjoyed nothing more than to be in her company and bask in the warmth of the attention and respect she attracted. She in turn was delighted to find that the schoolboy she had left behind, raw and a little bewildered, was now a grown and mature youth. She could hardly contain the pleasure of seeing him, and her other sons, again. But she never allowed emotion to disturb the outward mantle of good breeding. Their greeting was warm, but essentially dignified.

There is no knowing exactly why King William's College was chosen, though Annie doubtless had her reasons. It seemed to attract the sons of army officers and Indian civil servants and enjoyed a good reputation for its army class and for sports and recreational activities. In his first year, at the age of sixteen, William matriculated in French, Latin, mathematics, scripture and English. Towards the end of the year 1894 he transferred to the army class.

His stay at King William's was happy, and it played a vitally formative part in the development of skills which were to stand him in good stead in adult life. Swimming, diving, long jump, running and hurdling: all brought him success and acclaim. Captain of the house rugby XV, captain of school cricket, first in the batting averages; *praepositor* and member of the school sports committee. By the age of seventeen he had gained higher school certificates in chemistry, French, natural philosophy and Latin, though he was disappointed at the end of 1895 to find that in the Woolwich entrance examination he had come no higher than 72nd among the several hundred who went in for it.

He did better in the following year, gaining 11th place in the Sandhurst entrance exam, and the army class drawing prize. He registered only one disappointment at the Royal Military College – his failure to win rugby colours, though he played for the first XV. He was there for just under eighteen months from August 1896 until the end of 1897, and left as he entered, in 11th place.

He was gazetted a second lieutenant on the unattached list in January 1898, at the age of twenty. On February 6th in the same year he left for India aboard the transport ship S.S. *Nubia*. His younger brother Henry had taken his place at Sandhurst. George went into the South African police force. A shuttle service of Shakespears between the Empire and the mother country was to go on for many a year.

By March he was with his first regiment, the 11th Devonshires, at Jullunder. It did not take him long to impress the army and, indeed, the civil authority with his energy and talents. Within a year of his arrival in India he had become a practised cavalry-man, passed his equitation class with the 16th Queen's Lancers at Umballa, demonstrated his keen eye in marksmanship, joined the Bengal Lancers at cholera camp, and passed the higher and lower grades of Urdu, which examinations he took at the same time. By 1900 he had added Pushtu to his language qualifications, passed the Staff Corps retention examination and carried out a second term of cholera duty, this time as Squadron Officer of the 17th Bengal Lancers. In October he was made quartermaster of his new regiment.

In a matter of two or three years he had absorbed as much by way of variety of experience and service as the army affords most of its officers in a decade. He had marched his regiment from Mian Mir to Rawalpindi, a 21-day stint, assumed command of the senior squadron in exacting manoeuvres, passed various language tests, and finally taken up plague duty in the great 1899 epidemic.

But already army routine was beginning to pall. Though duty at cholera camp had provided a certain sense of immediacy, cholera was a well-known disease in India, and the sick camps associated with it were almost an accepted part of army duty. Plague was another matter and the terrible outbreak in India at the turn of the century provided Shakespear with his first real opportunity to get to grips with a genuine problem and to exercise his talent for improvisation.

The disease struck suddenly as was its habit. From the celebrated outbreaks in ancient Rome to the Black Death of Europe and the Great Plague of England, and more recent attacks in places as far apart as Persia and Japan, Russia and Paraguay, it had appeared without warning or explanation, and fizzled out just as mysteriously.

Nobody knew much about its origin or cause, much less about how to treat it. Some medical authorities doubted whether many of the epidemics known to history as 'the plague' were really plague at all. There was a well-known saying that the disease never struck the other side of the Indus. But it appeared in Bombay in 1896. In the following year nearly 50,000 people died from it in the Presidency of Bombay. By 1899 it had spread to the Bengal Province and 100,000 died. Panic swept the sub-continent and Bombay became the medical world's most important centre for studying the disease. Plague committees were set up and administration was left to the army as the problems of control swamped the civil authority. Little could be done to lessen the spread of the epidemic or to alleviate the suffering of victims, and the military could do no more than distribute food and clothing, allay unnecessary alarm and prevent people from moving around more than they had to. Army officers were picked carefully and put in charge of areas often with several million inhabitants, charged with the tasks of disposing of the dead, keeping essential services going and providing as much relief as was possible.

Shakespear took up his post of Assistant District Officer in A Ward, Bombay, on March 6th, 1901. Nothing much had been done to trace the outbreak to its source, but a number of officers and doctors had come to the conclusion that an assault on the city's rodent population might help; it was by now fairly certain that the rat was involved in the transmission of the disease.

As the death roll mounted, Shakespear and one or two fellow officers led a massive rat-killing campaign. As many soldiers as could be spared were mustered and armed with traps, sticks, pistols, knives and any other suitable weapons and Shakespear led them into the poorest, dirtiest and most thickly rat-populated areas of Bombay. In a week or two they killed tens of thousands of rodents. It was an unpleasant task, but the young officer was in his element. At last he had found something useful and active to do. During the year he was sent from one part of Bombay to another – A Ward, B north and B south, Central, F, G, C and D Wards – as officiating district officer. At the end of the year he wrote a long and impressive report on B Ward north, though he had been in charge of it for just one week.

At twenty-three years of age he had taken charge of several parts of the city in conditions which came close to chaos, organized one of the nastiest and most effective de-infestation operations ever, and contributed to official reports which, surprisingly, showed that the incidence of the disease was greater in rat-free areas than in infested regions. Investigation then revealed that it was fleas carried by infected rats which spread the disease, and that it was probably transmitted by the insects' excreta, perhaps through the agency of bed linen. He remained in charge of E Ward east until March 1902 and compiled the annual report on that area, a horrifying account, for the death roll was now in the region of half a million in one year. The Governor of Bombay, Lord Northcote, commended his work, and thus brought him to the notice of the Viceroy.

Ambition and a thirst for responsibility showed in his impatient and bristling manner. He already looked older than his years. His hair receded slightly and a high forehead was evident. Lightish brown colouring was made to look darker by the application of pomade and wax to head and moustache. Dark eyes, aquiline nose and jutting chin gave him an appearance at once brooding and determined.

The rigours of plague did not prevent him from continuing his language studies. While dealing with the terrible problems of death and rampant disease in Bombay, he took his higher Arabic test and passed it easily. Lieutenant Shakespear rejoined his regiment at Rawalpindi in April 1902. Not for long though. By the fourth year of his service the old queen was dead. Edward was on the throne and Balfour's Conservatives had taken over from Lord Salisbury's Conservative and Liberal Unionist alliance. The stable world of Victoria's reign was becoming restless. The Boer war, the 'khaki' election, the accelerating industrial revolution, gave rise to uneasiness among men who so recently had seen an endless vista of prosperity and peace before them. Shakespear was now twenty-four, an acting captain and set for rapid promotion. Yet he chose this promising moment to reconsider his future; it was both his strength and his weakness that he could not mark time, and his need for adventure outbid the attractions of advancement in a secure system. In the changing world, new priorities emerged to offend older men and challenge the young. With the going of the queen and her chief ministers an august age had passed into history. Curzon arrived in India in advance of the motor car and wireless telegraphy. A monarch of a different kind was on the throne. Speed and uncertainty reigned where there had been calm and measured tread for so long.

Shakespear was not given to the contemplation of such matters. His attitudes were instinctive rather than rational. He was intelligent but not intellectual; his skills and accomplishments were in the fields of travel and enterprise. He decided to apply for transfer to the Viceroy's Political Department.

3

Preparing the Way

In 1904, in his twenty-fifth year, Shakespear became the youngest consul in the Indian administration. He was posted to the Persian port of Bandar Abbas as Consul and Assistant to the Political Resident in Bushire. The Indian Foreign Secretary, Sir Henry McMahon, had heard of the exploits of this irrepressible young army officer, and he had no hesitation in recommending him to Major Percy Cox, the newly appointed Resident in Persia, as his deputy.

Seldom can two such disparate men have found so much common ground, such a ready appreciation of contrary opinion and conflicting attitudes. Cox was to become the confidant of kings and viceroys, of desert chiefs and political figures, the hub of Britain's involvement in some of the most inflammatory areas of the East. He moved among early oil barons, kings, shahs and Arab shaikhs with cool detachment. His dress was always immaculate; in later years he went to desert meetings in Homburg hat and pin-stripe suit, monocle poised. And he seldom erred in his judgment of men or matters. Though governments did not always make his task easy, he never allowed frustration to diminish his sense of duty to the administration of the day. He was the civil servant extraordinary.

The young man who came to join him was of a very different cut. Both were soldiers, as were most of the administration's Political Officers, but Shakespear remained one in dress and manner. He arrived at his first political billet in uniform, complete with topee and gaiters. His luggage was comparatively light. It included the blue-and-gold dress uniform of the Bengal Lancers for use on ceremonial occasions, the largest Union Jack he had been able to purchase, a massive plate camera with a clockwork mechanism that enabled him to take panoramic pictures, and a sextant. His ability at languages made him a useful addition to the Residency staff at Bushire. He had been made an examiner in Persian, Pushtu Urdu and Arabic and an official interpreter at courts martial within a few months of passing his final examinations. But his aims already stretched beyond the assignments of the moment and the plans of the Resident. He went to Bandar Abbas, hoisted the giant flag that was to announce his consular authority wherever he went in the East, and strode to his office. His political career had begun.

He was already well informed about events in the immense area covered by the Viceroy's Political Department, and ultimately by the India Office in London. Before leaving India for his new appointment he was sent to Calcutta to sit the High Proficiency Examination of the Political Service. He failed it dismally. His chances do not seem to have been affected, however, since he was sent on to Simla to study the correspondence and official documents relating to Persia and Arabia. Working through them with his usual haste, under the watchful eye of Sir Henry McMahon, he found evidence of disconcerting changes of emphasis and attitude on the part of the Imperial Government. Hesitancy had begun to show itself where there had so recently been conviction and self-assurance. Ever more concerned with events in Europe, Whitehall was reluctant to glance eastwards. When it did, it looked with nervous concern on the ambitions of other European powers in the area. The expansive Victorian view of the world had started to give way to introspection, and the government had already begun to doubt the wisdom of its men on the spot. Before long it was driven by its own sense of impotence to doubt their word. The Russians and the Turks were engaged in a war of nerves, and it did not take France and Germany long to sense that there were profitable spoils to be shared in an area which stretched from Egypt across Arabia and Mesopotamia to Persia, Afghanistan and Tibet. Britain had maintained a presence, and in some cases a predominance, in these areas since the early days of the East India Company.

As for Arabia, Britain had more or less washed its hands of that barren and uninviting territory when the East India Company abandoned the last of its interests there more than a century before. But it had until recent years maintained a vigil over the activities of warring princes and their Turkish masters. Now, non-interference was the watchword. It was 'Turkish Arabia' on the file dockets of the Foreign Office and the Indian Government – sacrosanct preserve of the Ottoman. The problem from Britain's point of view was admirably summed up by a man who had much to say on the subject, Sir Louis Mallet of the Foreign Office: 'We have the greatest difficulty in squaring *de facto* with *de jure*,' he wrote.

Shakespear scrutinized the files and did not like what he learned. Persia bored him. He found the climate 'pestilential' and the people 'intolerable'. He made the best of things by making frequent journeys of exploration inland and visits to the islands of the gulf. Any excuse to escape the oppressive heat and the even more oppressive people around him. He toured the islands of Hormuz, Larak and Henjam, and followed the Lar caravan route down to Khamir. But for much of the time he sat in the consulate and looked out across the sea to Arabia.

While on the way to his appointment at Bandar Abbas he had stopped off at Muscat for ten days before embarking on H.M.S. *Sphinx* which took him to Persia. And on the day of his arrival at Bushire, he reported to Percy Cox and promptly took passage back across the gulf. He was away for three days, 'on business', according to his diary. In fact, he went over to Oman and wandered around the *suq* practising his Arabic among the merchants and shoppers, and giving the inhabitants their first sight of a spectacle that was to become familiar in many parts of Arabia in years ahead – an Englishman in the dress of an Indian Army officer.

The years 1904 and 1905 dragged. In August 1905 he made another journey in Persia, following the Yezd caravan route in 'awful heat'. And he went down to the Residency at Bushire to help out with increasing office work. By now he and Cox were close friends. Their differences of temperament and attitude seemed to bring them together, though the older man was not the easiest or most approachable of administrators.

In conversation at the office and at his home, Cox was able to assess his restless charge, and soon realized that he had a far from orthodox or diplomatic servant on his hands. He was clearly not the man for run-of-the-mill assignments or for office routine. Cox knew better than anyone that success in government service demanded an ability to work patiently at policies designed elsewhere, and, as often as not, to make virtue of inaction. Shakespear could not sit in an armchair for five minutes at a time. He paced up and down a room, argued forcibly, expressed his feelings about politicians and policies without much tact or concern for his own junior position, but he talked sense. Cox privately agreed with much that his impatient and dynamic assistant had to say, but he decided early on that if Shakespear was to survive in government service he had better be found a post where vigour and energy counted for more than diplomacy.

Persia was in disarray at this time, threatened from without and torn by internal strife. On several occasions Cox sent Shakespear into the interior to deal with local squabbles and he usually succeeded in calming the easily roused tempers of local politicians and administrators.

At the end of 1905 cables were laid to Bandar Abbas and a telegraphic service established there. The Russians were pressing their claims in Persia, though rather less imperiously than hitherto, for they were currently licking wounds received in the Russo-Japanese war. The Czar, disputing Britain's right to make arbitrary arrangements with regard to the country's economy or its communications system, intensified his diplomatic offensive and decided to send consular representatives to those places in dispute, including Bandar Abbas. Russia's man arrived there in 1906. He and Shakespear took an immediate dislike to each other. Cox, however, was not going to risk a major confrontation on the strength of a local war waged by the two consuls. Shakespear was promptly sent to Muscat, a not unimportant post since its shaikh enjoyed prestige and a considerable measure of authority among the warring factions of Arabia. It was a stable and relatively peaceful part of a troubled East, and an established British protectorate.

Within a year of Shakespear's departure from Bandar Abbas, Britain and Russia signed a pact which divided Persia into spheres of economic influence. Persia was not consulted. Turkey, custodian of the Caliphate, played a meretricious role from the sidelines. The discovery of oil in 1908 was to give a new sense of urgency to British diplomacy in the area, but for the moment it had fallen into a rut of indecision. Shakespear was glad to be away from a hotbed of intrigue and distemper.

4

The Open Road

While he was away in Persia and Muscat he followed with interest and envy the activities of his friends and colleagues back in India. Newspapers came regularly, if a little late, by mail steamer and as he read the latest news and social gossip he could not avoid a twinge of regret at the thought of what he was missing.

The motor car had arrived just about as he left. For several years specially built vehicles had been entering India, usually costing thousands of pounds, playthings of a few of the richer princes. Now the horseless carriage had arrived in force. Most regarded it as the work of the devil, opposing its spread by the imposition of speed limits, banning it from certain areas and ridiculing its owners. The elephant retained its supremacy, carrying its human cargo in canopied splendour: 'My Lord Elephant', haughty and mighty symbol of traditional India. Despite the impropriety of mentioning the upstart device, however, much less of owning one, several young army officers and even a few civilians had taken the plunge in the past year or two.

Two years before, in 1905, some of them had caused a stir in official circles by organizing a competitive run from Delhi to Bombay, over nine hundred miles of barely surfaced roads with only one hotel on the entire route, no servicing facilities whatever and few amenities of any kind between start and finish. Newspapers and government officials condemned the event, just as they condemned in general what one writer called 'this noxious invasion'. But the young bloods were not to be put off. They applied to motoring clubs and manufacturers abroad for support, and to their surprise they met with an overwhelming response.

Of those who started from the old Mongol capital, seventeen retired. The rest went on to Bombay and to a triumphal reception at the Taj Mahal hotel. Newspapers reported the event grudgingly and with little detail, but Shakespear read what was printed with intense interest, reclining in a hammock at the Bushire Residency, wishing passionately that he was among the pioneering motorists of India.

His transfer to Hyderabad in 1907 gave him an opportunity to make up for lost time. He hardly paused for breath at the official residence before hurrying off to Simla to seek the advice of friends in the Foreign Department and Intelligence as to what model to buy. The choice was alarmingly wide and Shakespear could not even drive as yet.

His friend Hunter drove him to Karachi where he could see for himself. The agonizing decision was made easier by the fact that the dealer had just taken delivery of the new Indian and Colonial model of the 8 hp Rover, a beautifully upholstered tonneau. It cost a mere £250. Within a few weeks H.M. Consul was to be seen practising the handling of his shining new Rover on public roads, tinkering with its engine, examining it from under and within and generally making a lot of smoke and noise.

He had been on almost unbroken duty for nine years since he left England as a newly commissioned officer in 1898. One Christmas spent with parents in the Punjab before their retirement to England three years earlier had been his only official leave, though he had spent long periods of duty in exploring Persia and the islands of the gulf. Now he had an urge to see England again and visit his parents at their home in Brighton. Why not make the journey overland and put his car to the test?

Early in 1907 he shipped his vehicle to Bushire, where he proposed to discuss his future plans with the Resident and thence make his way north towards the Black Sea and Europe. From there he could arrange supplies of fuel and other needs, and seek the assistance of British Government representatives *en route*, for the motor car was still frowned upon in Ottoman provinces and severe restrictions were placed on it in many countries. With little experience of driving or the mechanics of the motor car and no assurance that he would find sustenance for himself or his vehicle on the way, he knew that he was setting out on a crazy and hazardous escapade. But that fact only added to the excitement of the adventure. There was another incentive too, for there were press reports of a stupendous race being planned by the Italian

Prince Borghese and several other intrepid spirits from Peking to Paris at the instigation of the French newspaper *Le Matin*. One of them was even proposing to drive a powered tricycle through China, the Gobi desert and Siberia. If they could do it, even allowing that theirs was an organized trip with petrol and spares laid on along the route, then he could see no reason why he should not make the solo journey from Persia to Britain.

With words of warning ringing in his ears, a supremely happy Englishman put his car into gear and made his way northwards in early April 1907. The sun shone and, as he surveyed the vista of hills and valleys ahead through the celluloid of his driving goggles, the world seemed rosy and harmonious. He had checked his store of fuel, spares and victuals before leaving: twenty two-gallon drums, eight tyres and two artillery-type wheels, four additional accumulator batteries, pick and shovel, several yards of rope, a coil of wire, axe, portable jack, oil for headlamps, a pile of blankets, groundsheet, and enough tinned food to satisfy the needs of a small army. He never travelled any distance without a small supply of whisky and wine to see him through the cold nights and long, lonely periods in the empty spaces of the East, and this journey was no exception. The precious cargo was wrapped in a blanket and carried at the front of the car between the legs of his 'boy', a wiry old man named Ali, whom Shakespear engaged to accompany him to the Turkish border. Other supplies were heaped into the back of the car or tied to the rear and underbody in protective sheets.

He was already a master of the open-air life. He prepared himself for journeys into obscure and often unmapped regions with determined professionalism, and he had no time for those Europeans in the East who tried to follow oriental customs. His equipment was planned to the last detail. Camp bed, primus stove, a well-stocked medicine chest (which had the added advantage of enabling him to pose as a doctor when the natives proved troublesome), and vast quantities of tinned food accompanied him. Ill health or an upset stomach could prove disastrous in the wilds, and from the earliest days of his military service he trained his servants to cook in western style. He could sustain himself, whatever the terrain or climate, for weeks or months on end, as long as he had a gun with which to claim a meal and a few garments to keep him warm at night. Army training and his earlier Persian excursions, when he had usually gone alone on horse-back to the trouble spots of the interior, had made him self-reliant and capable of enduring his own company for long periods. He was never bored. He read widely, and there was always his camera and the intricate business of developing his film with whatever water was available, or his sextant with which to survey the lands through which he travelled.

Bushire had hardly faded before there was a loud bang. Ali threw his arms in the air in the conviction that he was about to meet his Maker. A tyre had burst – and at the high pressures to which they were inflated in the early days of motoring tyres punctured with explosive force. Shakespear cursed in several languages, found his jack after an impatient search among his chattels, and set about replacing the offending part.

They were soon in cultivated territory, travelling by compass in the main and checking their bearings when they came to a habitation, for there were no signposts or detailed maps in those days. And already the hilly country was taking its toll of fuel supplies. The full tank with which he had left was emptying alarmingly, so he started to implement the advice given him by his fellow enthusiasts at Simla: to freewheel down hills while applying his foot to the brake pedal intermittently so as not to set fire to the lining. He managed well enough until he came to a particularly steep hill and found that the brakes would not hold the weight of the heavy car with its coach-built body and solid metal components. The gear lever was mounted on the steering column, giving the driver a choice of three forward speeds. He tried to crash it into low gear as he careered towards the foot of the hill, but he was going too fast. He turned full circle and hurtled backwards into a ploughed field. Fortunately they were still in cultivated country and the soft earth helped to bring the car to a halt. He drove on with no more than a nasty shock to remind him of the dangers of freewheel driving.

They climbed steadily to Shiraz with its fine gardens and buildings; the view towards Persepolis in the distance was implanted in his memory for years after. Then they turned due north towards Isfahan, the other ex-capital of Persia.

On the first night of his journey to England he slept in the open. The sky was clear and it was a pleasant evening, so he spread his groundsheet and blankets on a miserably bare patch of ground and settled to a few hours of sleep. Ali, his companion, preferred to huddle in the front of the car.

The ascent towards Isfahan and the high plateau of central Persia caused no special problems apart from the car's greedy consumption of fuel. They traversed grim pitted paths and wound their way up rock-strewn hills – every now and again glancing to left or right to take stock of the breath-taking view, or to blink at a sheer drop. The Rover was a well-behaved car. Its single-cylinder engine with a displacement of little more than one litre and its robust transmission did most things that were asked of them without fuss or commotion. But progress was sedate. He had been driving for less than two months. Still, he regarded himself as something of an expert and he was picking up mechanical knowledge as he went with the aid of the car's instruction booklet. Specified speeds in the three gear ratios were from 8 to 24 miles per hour. He found that he could improve on that, achieving 30 miles per hour with a favourable slope between elaborately measured and timed distances. He had fitted a 'spider' seat at the back and his companion was usually reclining on its upholstered bench, as often as not asleep.

Shakespear was not the first of the new, motorized elite to visit Persia or even Isfahan. A Rumanian chauffeur by the name of Keller had driven there in a Mercedes in 1905, having set out with his employer Prince Bibesco to journey from Bucharest to Tehran. The nobleman turned back before he reached Persia but his indomitable chauffeur completed the journey. First or not, the Englishman was pleased enough to reach Isfahan where fellow countrymen had held court for three centuries since the earliest days of the East India Company. He ate and slept well that night.

He had travelled nearly 300 miles so far, at an average rate of just over 100 miles a day. Slower progress was ahead.

Revolution was imminent in Persia, and foreigners were by no means welcome. Yet, to his surprise, this very conspicuous foreigner was often waved to by wayfarers or by groups of bystanders. Now and again the car was stoned by young boys, but more playfully than maliciously. The greatest dangers lay in the trackless mountains and snowdrifts and rivers ahead. The journey to Tehran by way of Kum was, in fact, less hazardous than he had been led to expect by advisers and well-wishers back at Isfahan. He kept to the edge of the Lut, the great salt desert, with the

Karan mountains rising to peaks of 13,000 feet to his left. He had to drive carefully, for the choice offered by the treacherous region through which they passed was between dry sands and gravel which threatened to tear tyres to ribbons, and immersion in the saline swamps that lay in wait if they went off course. He kept carefully to the dry land and suffered only two punctures. He dared not travel at night for his oil-lamps were liable to blow out in the wind, and even with them on the danger of landing in a swamp was too great. And so they travelled slowly through the heat of the day, refreshed by the breeze that wafted over the open car, and slept in the vehicle at night. It took them nearly 24 hours to reach Kum, less than 150 miles from Isfahan. From there it was just about 100 miles to Tehran. Petrol was low and the road steep and winding and strewn with rocks and obstacles of one kind or another. They made the journey in eight hours, and when they arrived the last canister of fuel was empty.

Tehran, like the rest of Persia, was a hotbed of intrigue. There was a threat of war with Turkey and the shah was in open conflict with the *majlis* (parliament). Revolutionary factions, both Right and Left, roamed the streets. The Englishman had no wish to delay there and his Persian companion had seen enough of the motor car. He was paid off and returned to the quiet of the south while Shakespear replenished his larder. The automobile had arrived in the capital by now, and fuel and spare parts were available to supplement the articles he had taken on at Isfahan. He found a younger companion for the last and most difficult part of his journey and set off after a day of discussion with British officials, a good night's sleep and a hearty breakfast. The Political Agent's function was expected to embrace Intelligence activities, and though his reports were usually channelled through the Resident, Shakespear was supposed to keep his eyes and ears open on his journey and to inform the Political and Secret Department of the India Office of his findings when he reached London. Since the turn of the century the division of British interest in the East between the Foreign and India Offices meant that each went its own way, and neither took much trouble to help the other. The Viceroy's man was now in the 'ambassadorial' territory of the Foreign Office. Photography and note-taking would be too dangerous in the troubled zone he was about to enter; there were no real roads between Tehran and the Turkish border. Shakespear and his new companion, Taki, set off with every expectation of a rough passage.

Snow from the high mountain ranges melted into the rivers below; the hillsides were flowing with water, and rivers swelled and burst their banks. The car struggled up a steep hill and came down the other side with a gnashing of gear teeth and a protesting engine. It hit a pool of water as it dived to the bottom of the decline and suddenly the protest was over. Shakespear surveyed the silent and deserted scene, removed his goggles, and twirled his moustache – a habit of his in moments of emergency – before taking a closer look at his first major mishap.

The car was half submerged, much of its engine and vital parts wallowing in water. The only course open to him was to push it. He and Taki took off their boots and socks, rolled up their trousers and heaved. The monster was stuck irretrievably. Fortunately the day was still young and they went off in search of some human or animal agency of relief. They clambered over rocks and along winding paths, the Englishman holding on to his compass as he went in the hope of remembering the way they had come and of being able to retrace their steps. In a search that lasted for two frantic hours they saw no sign of human habitation. Neither, for that matter, did they see an animal, though the region was a veritable reserve of wolves, hyenas, tigers and other wild creatures. They found their way back along craggy, waterlogged paths. They would have to wait until someone came their way.

As he caught sight of the Rover it looked at him accusingly as though he had deserted it; the water had receded and the radiator dripped with the last few drops of the flood. He held his breath and turned the handle. The engine spluttered and died. He had to wait several minutes for the electrics to dry. Then it purred into action. Half the day had been wasted but they were on the road again.

Taki was a pleasant change from the taciturn old man who had accompanied him on the first stage. He smiled constantly and was keen to help with the chores of the journey. His smile was broader than ever as they made their way along a gully at the foot of an almost perpendicular cliff.

Shakespear was able to practise his Persian on the lad and they talked amiably as they made steady progress towards Tabriz. The

Shia Muslim of Persia were hot-headed about their religion – as they were about most things – but Taki was a pleasant exception; he talked intelligently of his country, of his faith and of his own plans to be 'an important man in Persia', and the Englishman listened sympathetically.

Water poured down the rocks from the melting snow and streams became torrential rivers. They slept for a few hours in the cover of a rock projection and woke to the cries of animals that sounded uncomfortably close and hungry. Somehow they negotiated the twisting rivers of the region, often fording them with self-made bridges. They drove straight through floods in the fervent hope that they were not deep enough to drench the engine. A passing peasant and his horse helped tow them from a bog. But despite wet and dangerous tracks and every conceivable obstacle, they kept going and arrived at Tabriz in under twenty-four hours from the time they left Tehran.

He had to part with his companion at this stage, for the youngster could not be taken into Turkey due to enmity between the two countries at that time. Shakespear went on alone, buoyed up by the thought that he was approaching Europe for the first time since his schooldays.

Idle thoughts of pleasures to come were soon dashed by the realities of the climate of north-west Persia. All went well until he reached the flooded lands surrounding Lake Urmia. The daring Keller must have come this way two years before. How he or Shakespear managed the journey, and how those heavy vehicles of solid metal and wood ploughed their way through swamp and marsh, must remain a matter of conjecture. Neither man sought recognition for his pains; neither made much of it. When he was stuck – and he was stuck time and time again – Shakespear would trudge shoeless through the water and put a pole under the rear wheels to provide traction, and then slither and slide on his way. The journey seemed never ending. At last he found himself in Turkey, heart of the Ottoman Empire, and, more importantly to him, gateway to Europe.

If the motor car was still the bane of officialdom – frowned upon in Turkey more than in most other places – it had a natural attraction for the young. Everywhere he went from now on, local people gathered to look, and to argue as to the likely origin and destination of this mechanical invader. In much of the East there was as yet no name for it. Most people called it the 'iron horse'. To young boys it had a marvellous appeal. They tried to clamber on as it went by and debated fiercely the secrets of its propulsion. Shakespear had no difficulty in finding another companion to help with the never-ending problems of survival on roads that were intended for the bullock and the horse and cart. The boy Abdul, resplendent in fez and his best suit of clothes, smiled broadly and waved enthusiastically to onlookers as they made their way from Sivas to the coast and along the Black Sea towards Constantinople. Since he had made good time, Shakespear ambled along by the sea.

The route from now on contained many an obstacle, but compared with the previous journey it was easy. The driver changed his leather helmet and coat for the more elegant rig of the Edwardian motorist, Norfolk jacket and peaked cap; the latter was exchanged for a straw boater when they stopped in a town. He settled to the enjoyment of a sunny drive made all the more invigorating by the breeze that rushed past his now cleaned and polished vehicle. Despite several punctures and the constant fear of running out of fuel, he travelled in the best of humours. Still the route passed through mountains and dipped steeply into valleys. Rocks and fallen trees lay on the roads and precipices reminded him of the finality of false judgement. A platform of tree trunks roped together saw them across the river Sakarya. A ferry took them over the Bosporus to Constantinople.

The British Embassy at the heart of the Ottoman Empire was a splendid place, presided over at the time by Sir Nicholas O'Conor, a man of dry wit and imposing presence who received the youthful visitor from the Indian administration with warmth and hospitality. Shakespear had shaved off the untidy stubble around his chin before reaching the capital, but the ravages of the journey showed. He had washed mostly in cold streams on the way and had not seen a bath since leaving Tehran. A warm luxuriant bath and the application of razor and pomade soon restored precision to his features and toned their light colour to a more familiar dark brown. He hardly recognized himself in the mirror.

Sir Nicholas talked warily of the politics of the East. He was more concerned, in any case, with the story of his guest's journey through Asia Minor and his intended route through Europe. The ambassador had his own car and a chauffeur who, it appeared, was little short of a mechanical genius. After a sumptuous and friendly lunch, the chauffeur was summoned and the three men inspected the Rover and decided that it had behaved handsomely so far.

Next day Shakespear toured the Ottoman capital while the ambassador's driver went enthusiastically about the task of preparing his car for the next stage of its journey, changing wheels and fitting new tyres, deftly playing with engine and electrical connections, examining springs, transmission shafts and brakes, and polishing until coachwork shone with the virginal glow that had greeted its owner in a Karachi showroom only a month or two earlier.

Shakespear was glad of the opportunity to walk around the city and to see the glories of Byzantine and Islamic building about which he had read: St Sophia, of course, and St Irene, Constantine's own monument, the glorious façade of St Theodore Tyrone – almost all now converted to Muslim worship. To his own surprise, he enjoyed Constantinople and found his fellow countrymen there among the most hospitable of people. There was a long journey ahead, however, through yet more mountains and on roads as rough as any he had yet encountered. Rested and well fed, he took his leave of the ambassador – who was sadly to die at his post a year later – and left Constantinople after an enjoyable respite.

His journey grew into a notable marathon of early motoring history. With messages sent on ahead to embassies and consulates asking for supplies to await his arrival, he continued his journey more or less alone, though he took on a helping passenger whenever he could find an able-bodied man willing to travel 'steerage'. But from Greece onwards he was alone for most of the time. He travelled through Macedonia and Thessaly down to Athens, where he spent more time examining the surviving monuments of the ancient world; then along the Adriatic coast, through Montenegro and Dalmatia to Italy. He could, in fact, have taken ship across the Adriatic to Italy, but he had set out to drive to Europe, and drive he would. Punctures were his recurrent problem. Otherwise the journey was almost casual. Many people even in Europe had yet to see a motor car, and his fame went before him as he progressed northwards. Somehow the word seemed to reach towns and villages before him, and large crowds would gather to watch his triumphal entry. From Trieste he turned south-west to Venice, Padua, Ferrara, Bologna, Pesaro, and then across country to Rome.

By the time he had visited the ruins of Rome and made his mark in the eating houses and night spots of the ancient city, he began to feel mentally and physically exhausted. The long drive – he had now covered about 2,000 miles – combined with an intense round of sightseeing and a spirited assault on some of Europe's main centres of entertainment, left him with a feeling of having attempted too much too quickly. He had intended to drive up the west coast of Italy and then across France to the Channel. On the spur of the moment he changed his plan and continued north. Switzerland, with its snow-clad peaks and warm sun, and its comparative sobriety, seemed a better idea altogether than the sensuous and gastronomic temptations of France.

It was a strange coincidence that, among the many well-to-do holidaymakers at Adelboden in the Bernese Oberland, there should have been a gathering of the Baird family. They too had won respect and distinction in India, and had been on nodding terms with several of the Shakespears. The father, Lieutenant-Colonel Andrew Wilson Baird, was a man of many parts: soldier, linguist, brilliant scientist and outstanding administrator. While a serving soldier he had plotted the tidal currents of the Indian Ocean and carried out much original work in oceanography, for which he was made a Fellow of the Royal Society. When he retired from the army he became Master of the Mint at Calcutta.

His wife was, in her own way, as remarkable. Margaret Elizabeth Davidson was one of the outstanding musicians of her day, taught by Wieck, Schumann's son-in-law. She and Clara Schumann became close friends and they often played together. She was sought after by some of the most gifted men of her time, Rossetti in particular, but she eventually married the soldier-scientist from Scotland and after spending many years with him in India, settled with her family at 'Palmer's Cross' in Elgin, Morayshire.

The Bairds had seven children, five girls and two boys. Between them they inherited a fair share of their parents' talents, and the household was filled with musical entertainment of the highest quality and with informed debàte. The girls also inherited their share of Mrs Baird's singular beauty. They were enjoying a happy and relaxed holiday at Adelboden in the spring of 1907, as had been their habit for the past two or three years, Colonel Baird remaining in Scotland where he had more important things to do.

The small resort was awakened rudely from its quiet pursuits. The Rover's hardy and resourceful engine had behaved with great good manners and fortitude. Now it protested vehemently, coming to a halt outside the Victoria-Eden Hotel with much spluttering and exhaust emission. The consul from the East disembarked and made his way unconcernedly through a batch of onlookers. The thought of a rest in that comfortable resort revived his flagging spirit, for by now he had driven himself and his car almost to a state of collapse. He lazed gratefully. A drink on the verandah, an occasional stroll and sleep, undisturbed by the need to journey on to some self-appointed destination; he sought no more of life.

Shakespear had an appreciative eye for a pretty woman, though that was not exactly an apt description of the young woman who caught his attention soon after his arrival at Adelboden. Helen Dorothea Baird was a rare creature. Soft chestnut hair and deep-blue eyes were the outward complements of a gay and lively personality which, to the unobservant, belied a serious mind and sensitive disposition. She, like Shakespear, had spent her childhood in India and they might well have met through the proximity of their families in Bengal. An introduction cannot have been difficult to arrange, for Mrs Baird was a pleasant, friendly woman and Shakespear was not lacking in confidence; neither was there a shortage of common ground. They had many mutual acquaintances and Mrs Baird and her husband had been on terms of friendship with his uncle Alex. However their meeting may have been effected, he and Dorothea were instantly and profoundly attracted to each other. She was twenty-six and he a year older, but neither had yet met anyone of the opposite sex who was of more than passing interest, though she had many suitors.

She called him 'The Consul', partly, no doubt because she thought it suited him, but perhaps too because William, attached to so distinguished a surname, is slightly absurd. At any rate, Shakespear never used his Christian name, even in letters to his own family, though some relatives knew him as 'Consul Willie'. To everyone but Dorothea he used his initials, W.H.I.S. She was always known by her second name, though he soon invented an extension of it, 'Dorotheaye', by way of endearment.

She was a widely read and amusing conversationalist, devoutly interested in Arabia, to which she had been introduced by the works of Sir Richard Burton and Charles Doughty. If she had been asked to describe an ideal suitor she could hardly have improved on the imposing and very informed young man who had descended so unexpectedly and so noisily upon her holiday residence. For his part he had not met nor imagined so extravagant a combination of beauty and wit as he found in her.

The rest of the holiday was idyllic. He spent as much time as need be under the bonnet of his car, restoring its exhaust pipe to gas-tight performance and renewing some vastly over-worked parts; and when it was in health again they motored together through the Oberland, Dorothea's bonnet tied down by a scarf, fur muff and stole completing her fashionable and serviceable costume. Motoring trips alternated with meals with the family and with long walks during which they talked endlessly and with shared fascination of the East and Arabia. Their unexpected meeting came all too soon to its close. The Bairds had to return to Scotland. He continued his journey alone to England and his family in the South, though gratefully accepting an invitation to Elgin before they parted.

He drove straight to the South Coast and to Brighton, where his parents had been in retirement for three years. They had bought a fine house in Regency Square just off the sea front where they lived in quiet seclusion under the protective wing of Annie. He had never seen much of his father, for even when he was at home in Bengal the old man had usually been out in the forests and open spaces. But he had kept up a close companionship with his mother, writing to her frequently and seeking her advice on most things. Perhaps it was her dominant personality that found an answering voice in his own determined make-up. Perhaps the absence of a strong relationship with his father helped to tighten the maternal bond. Whatever the reason, he enjoyed a rapport with his mother that he had not so far found with another human being. And with a mother's subtlety she fostered those qualities that she had vested in him, imbuing him with an ever-present sense of duty, patriotism and ambition. She was proud of him and expansive in praise of him. She spoke fondly of her other sons but she channelled all the intensity of her pride, her aims and hopes in the direction of her eldest. The impartial observer may have concluded that there was something of frustration in her devotion to William for she rarely addressed a question to her mild-mannered and gentle husband, leaving him to potter amiably with the plants or to read quietly, surrounded by the brass elephants and water-colours of India, while she talked incessantly to William of his future in the Political Department. Already he was the youngest appointee in the ranks of the Indian administration, and had attracted the attention of the Viceroy and his Foreign Secretary for his dynamic if impatient approach to the politics of the East. Friends in the administration had told his parents as much, and neither Cox nor McMahon had been meagre in their recognition of his talent and resourcefulness. But, while his future in the service was much on his mind, another and more powerful aim had taken shape, a major journey of exploration. A journey by car across Asia Minor and Europe was one thing, but even in 1907 it was by no means an historic achievement. A journey across the great central deserts of Arabia would represent a challenge of a different and more significant kind. Annie approved of the idea.

Thus a number of matters occupied him as he motored the length of Britain in the direction of Aberdeenshire and Elgin. Foremost among them, though, was the desire to see Dorothea again. He stopped off at Whitehall to deliver a report on the journey through Asia Minor, which now seemed to have receded so far into the past that he had the greatest difficulty in remembering his impressions, and then made haste to Scotland.

Colonel Baird was not easily impressed. Even he, though, was intrigued to meet the young man from India who, by the time he reached England, had motored virtually without assistance for nearly four thousand miles. It was one of the most remarkable journeys of the early years of motorized transport and, if it went unnoticed by the world at large, the patriarch of 'Palmer's Cross' was keen to hear about it.

Shakespear and the colonel found a good deal of common ground, and the older man was amiably tolerant of his visitor's talkative manner and his emphatic views on the politics of the East and the policies of the Liberal administration of Campbell-Bannerman. The visitor, anyway, was intent on impressing the colonel's daughter; he and Dorothea spent their days walking together and resting on the banks of the River Lossie which flowed past 'Palmer's Cross', chatting, laughing, oblivious of all around them, except for Colonel Baird, who appeared every now and again to demand 'What are those Gipes up to now?' Nobody ever discovered the meaning of the word 'Gipe'. Evenings were spent in wide-ranging and often intense discussion, with intervals of music when Mrs Baird or Dorothea could be induced to play. Shakespear melted into the scheme of things at Elgin and regretted that he must leave it and return to the East.

He took his leave reluctantly and wondered if and when he would see Dorothea again.

5

History Lesson

His leave came to an end in the late summer of 1907. He took ship from Southampton in September, along with his inseparable companion, the Rover. He left with a glow of satisfaction. He could now claim some familiarity with Europe, a continent which had existed for him only as a textbook recollection before his motor journey. Few men of his time could boast a more difficult or lengthy drive. He returned to India with but one real regret, the parting from Dorothea. They wrote frequently, but that was small compensation for the distance that separated them.

By November he was back at his post at Hyderabad as second assistant to the Resident, C. S. Bayley, though not for long. In 1908 he returned to the gulf as first assistant to Cox.

The time was approaching for a change of Political Agent in Kuwait, a strategically and politically vital part of the gulf coast, and both McMahon and Cox regarded him as the obvious candidate for a job that required the physical strength to make long and often dangerous trips into the desert and the moral courage to stand up to the toughest and most implacable ruler in Arabia.

He spent a year at Bushire familiarizing himself with the history and politics of Arabia, with the characters and family histories of the desert princes, the rivalries and alliances of the tribes, and most importantly with the policies of his own country.

By the end of that year he was itching to get back to Britain. As he worked in the heat of the Persian summer, taking charge of the Residency for a time while Cox took a well-earned rest, he wrote to Dorothea more and more frequently, telling her of his plans, of his expected appointment to Kuwait, of his anxiety to meet the young Amir of Najd, Ibn Saud, and his intention to explore the depths of Arabia; and of his wish to see her again. He planned to slip home at Christmas and wondered if he could visit her family again at Elgin. Though their letters to each other have not survived, a great deal can be surmised from his notes and remarks to friends, and from what she confided to her daughter in later life. It was her deep interest in Arabia that fired his own ambition and, inadvertently perhaps, diverted his passion.

She had read far more of the literature of Arabia than he, and Doughty's *Arabia Deserta* had proved for her an almost religious experience. That simple, honest tale, so hard to come to terms with in its biblical language, yet immeasurably rewarding to those who make the effort, had become her textbook and her guide, for she, like many in late Victorian England, learned more of Arabia from reading it than had others from travelling there. In their correspondence during the year that divided their first meeting from their second, he talked of his growing desire to explore the lands over which the great tribes roamed and the desert armies battled, and she responded with wit and the insight which came from extensive reading and from her own ability to tell a colourful story. She told Shakespear many vivid tales from travellers in Arabia – including Byron's grand-daughter, Lady Anne Blunt, who had been to Hail with her husband, Wilfrid Scawen Blunt. She also sent him books on the subject, one of which was a pocket edition of Palgrave's *Central and Eastern Arabia*, which he read and re-read, and carried with him whenever he went on a journey. Shakespear was fascinated by the mercurial politics of the area, and before he set foot there he had studied its history in detail.

Since the earliest pioneers of the East India Company came in the reign of James I, Britons in Isfahan and Shiraz, Basra and Kuwait, Aleppo, Muscat, Bandar Abbas, Abu Shahr (or Bushire as it became), in India itself, had recorded the happenings and folklore of the East. When the Government of India took over the responsibility for these regions of Asia and Asia Minor, it inherited an incomparable record of the past. It was, all the same, a skeletal story as far as Central Arabia was concerned, for in the course of two hundred years only a handful of European men, and one woman, had penetrated to the depths of Najd, mostly unofficial travellers whose accounts appeared in books and treatises that were often voluminous and almost always difficult for anyone but a student of Arabia to follow.

The story begins in the mid-eighteenth century, when long-festering religious feuds gradually infected the whole country. Traditional tribal discipline and the observance of religious law broke down, and the greatest horrors were perpetrated in the arid reaches of Najd and Nafud, the central provinces. At this time the Ottoman power had been in nominal control of Arabia for more than two centuries, but it had not so far tried to extend its authority to the inhospitable depths of Central Arabia. And it was an Arab of Najd, educated in the cosmopolitan climate of Damascus, who showed his countrymen the way of salvation. His name was Muhammad ibn Abdul Wahhab al Suleiman. He came home to Najd with a new, ascetic version of the faith of Islam, and he preached it for all he was worth. And the first man of influence to fall under his spell was the chief of the poor but important region of Aridh, a leading shaikh of the Wuld 'Ali division of the great Anaiza tribal confederation, Muhammad ibn Saud. His conversion dated from 1745, and he became the first Wahhabi Amir of Najd, the founder of a disciplined and cohesive state. His son, Abdul Aziz, and his grandson Saud, created a vast, unified empire, Wahhabi Arabia. By 1770 a massive and zealous army was on the move. By 1800 the Ottoman Army had been routed and virtually the whole of the peninsula was in Saudi hands, ruled from Dariyah, the capital of Najd.

Muhammad Ali the Egyptian Viceroy of the Ottoman failed to conquer the Sauds, but his son, Ibrahim Pasha, took the Wahhabi Amir prisoner and sent him to Constantinople, where he was beheaded. Dariyah was destroyed, and so began the long resentment of the Ottomans by the House of Saud, which reasserted its authority the moment the Egyptians and Turks left, at a new and more convenient capital, Riyadh. In the wake of the Turco-Egyptian destruction of the Arabian heartland Britain had entered the scene, sending a special emissary, Captain George Sadlier of the 47th Infantry Regiment, to talk to the Sauds and the retreating Egyptians. A brave and resourceful man, Sadlier was no politician; he returned to India a bewildered man, for the Arabs gave him a short answer and the Egyptians were too keen to get home to stop to speak to him.

Faisal ibn Turki (Faisal the Great) ruled in Riyadh from 1843 to 1865, and during his reign the Wahhabi empire was restored and the major part of Arabia proclaimed allegiance to the Sauds.

Hail, the capital of Jabal Shammar, was governed from the earliest days of Saudi dominion by a viceroy who was originally chosen from the Ali branch of the Abda, the premier clan of the Shammar tribe. Then a dispute broke out between the chiefs of the Ali and a rival branch of their tribe, the Rashid. The senior shaikh of the latter, Abdullah, acknowledged the authority of the Sauds and he was made ruler of Hail in the early part of the nineteenth century. But, as often happened in the desert, loyalty was worn on the sleeve and Abdullah promptly declared the Royal House of Jabal Shammar. At the end of his reign he left enough sons to ensure the continuity of his rule and a brother, Ubaid, whose descendants contributed their own share of spite and dishonour to a story of a homicidal rule which has few historical precedents. Of nine sovereigns of Hail up to the end of the nineteenth century, eight died at the hands of family assassins.

While Faisal reigned, Central Arabia was orderly, but when he died his sons Abdullah and Saud fought for the throne, though Abdullah was his nominal successor. Soon Riyadh and the lands it governed were divided by the strife of these brothers and between them they brought the Saudi kingdom to ruin and gave the Ottoman power an excuse to intervene once again.

Abdullah, in his anxiety to overcome his ambitious brother, sought assistance from Muhammad ibn Rashid, ruler of Hail, who by then enjoyed the support of the Turks. Abdullah went to Hail to meet Ibn Rashid and Saud saw his chance and grabbed the throne. Najd became a battlefield, with Saud's badawin army on one side and the fierce, disciplined Shammar army of Rashid on the other. They met head on at the town of Judi in 1885. The Shammar made short shrift of Saud's men. The usurper was killed. Abdullah, who went to Hail with outstretched hand, was kept a prisoner and he died in exile. Ibn Rashid took over the whole of Central Arabia and now it was his turn to appoint a viceroy at Riyadh. The rest of the family fled to safety, the sons of Saud to the Hijaz where they sought refuge with the Sharif of Mecca, the remaining sons of Faisal including the heir presumptive, Abdur Rahman, to Hasa and then to Kuwait. He took with him his own eldest son Abdul Aziz.

By the end of the nineteenth century, Muhammad ibn Rashid was dead but Hail remained effectively the capital of central Arabia, supported by its Shammar army.

The titular Amir of Riyadh, Abdur Rahman ibn Faisal, girded his loins in Kuwait, encouraged by its determined ruler, Shaikh Mubarak, who was by now the father figure to this branch of the Saud family. In 1900 they launched a full-scale assault on the Shammar. Abdur Rahman and Mubarak led a large detachment into the interior towards Qasim. Abdul Aziz, son of Abdur Rahman, just eighteen years old, led a smaller diversionary force towards Riyadh. These desert armies, travelling at speed over dry and forbidding country, often in intense heat by day, in utter darkness by night, might cover fifty or sixty miles in a full march with their fastest *dhaluls* or racing camels. Mostly, they travelled by night, for news was fleet of foot in its passage across the wilderness and detection was all too easy by light of day.

Eventually, the main force came to a place called Tarafiyya, a salt basin, virginal in the white of its gently sloping surface. It was a fierce and bloody battle. Both sides were cut to pieces, but the Shammar were numerically stronger and its survivors could be called the victors, though there was little cause for celebration. Those who got away on the Saudi side made their bedraggled way back to Kuwait, Abdur Rahman and Mubarak at their head.

Abdul Aziz, when he heard of his father's defeat, turned back before reaching Riyadh. Abdur Rahman, humiliated on the field of battle, renounced his claim to the throne in favour of his son. The young pretender lost no time; less than a year after the resounding defeat of his father's army he raised a small, well-trained band of men and, with Mubarak's encouragement and support, made a quick and silent trek to the Wahhabi capital. In the concealment of night, fifteen of his most trustworthy men made their way to the palace of the Rashidi governor, known as Ajlan, while the rest of the party remained under cover. The governor slept in a nearby fortress, knowing the danger of exposing himself to the assassin's knife, for Abdur Rahman had tried to kill his predecessor years before, an act which contributed to the Saudi ruler's exile. Abdul Aziz and his men were able to make their way into the palace without causing alarm, herding the women of the harim into a guarded room so that they would not make a noise, and themselves remaining under cover till daybreak. When the governor and his men arrived in the morning they were set upon at the main gate. The struggle was over in a few seconds. The unsuspecting Ajlan was murdered

along with his guards. Abdul Aziz, son of Abdur Rahman, son of
Faisal, was king at Riyadh. Ibn Saud had come home to face the
task of uniting a bitterly divided land, his nearest relatives now
allied to other princes, his purse empty and only Shaikh Mubarak
of Kuwait to be counted on with certainty.

In 1904, at the time Shakespear joined the Political Department,
Lord Kitchener, then Commander-in-Chief in India, joined with
the retiring Viceroy Lord Curzon in compiling an appeal to the
Secretary of State for India. The Indian Government and its army
chiefs had never entirely reconciled themselves to the idea that the
Arabian peninsula, larger in area than the sub-continent of India
and strategically vital if Britain should ever find itself at war with
one of the great powers, was best left to its own devices in dealing
with the Turk. Despite the insistence of successive governments
that the Ottoman Empire was a *fait accompli*, its authority
inviolate however incompetent or unpopular it might be, they
decided to stress the need for a more positive approach by Britain.
On March 26th, 1904, they despatched a letter from Fort William
to Whitehall. It said:

> HM Government are aware that throughout the greater part
> of the nineteenth century, the Government of India had
> frequent intercourse with the Wahhabi amirs and that in 1866
> Muhammad ibn Abdullah entered into treaty engagement
> with our Resident in the Persian Gulf, whereby he bound
> himself not to oppose or injure British subjects residing in his
> territory, and not to interfere with the Arab tribes in alliance
> with the British Government. Since the Turkish occupation
> of Al Hasa and the rise of the amirs of Najd, however, our
> relations with the Wahhabi house have ceased, and we now
> have no intercourse with either of the great factions of this
> part of the Arabian Peninsula.

After citing the various political and military reasons for the
desirability of a British presence in the area, the statement went
on:

> When the political situation in Najd has developed, and
> above all if the present representative of the Wahhabi family,
> Abdur Rahman ibn Saud, succeeds in establishing and

extending his ascendancy, which from late accounts received
seems not improbable, we think it may be desirable to enter
into relations with our old ally.

The appeal fell on stony ground. But the facts of history and the
realities of the present were on the side of Kitchener and Curzon.
Conflict between the rival centres of Riyadh and Hail went on
unabated. In 1906, the Saudi amir met his namesake Abdul Aziz
ibn Rashid at Raudhat al Muhanna, close by the ill-omened
battlefield of Tarafiyya. Revenge for his father's defeat at the
hands of the Shammar was swift and sure. The Amir of Hail was
slain and his force vanquished. The leading families of Hail, the
Rashid and the Ubaid, were divided in their loyalties, the former
under the protection of the Turks, the latter sympathetic to the
Wahhabi faith preserved by the Sauds and willing to accept the
authority of the rulers of Riyadh.

Now, with the death of Abdul Aziz ibn Rashid, power at Hail
was in the hands of a regent of the Subhan family, since the
hereditary amir, Saud ibn Rashid, was a minor in the care of the
Sharif of Mecca. The relationship between the two great ruling
houses of Central Arabia entered a state of flux. War continued,
mostly at the behest of the Turks who were determined to keep
them at each other's throats, but to the accompaniment of cloak-
and-dagger negotiations which worried not only the Ottoman
power but Britain too.

Britain's embassy in Constantinople was following the struggle
with considerable interest when Shakespear arrived in the gulf.
For nearly ten years, the ambassadors there had been aware that a
special relationship existed between the Rashid and the Sultan.
Whenever the ambassador was instructed to ask the Grand Vizier
what was going on, he found that the head of the government was
genuinely in the dark and informants of some reliability had told
Britain's officials that there was a direct link between Hail and the
Sultan, that payments to the Rashid were made from the privy-
purse and instructions relayed direct without the knowledge or
approval of the Prime Minister. When Sir Nicholas O'Conor was
asked by Lord Lansdowne in December 1902 to interview the
Grand Vizier at the time when Kuwait was threatened by the army
of Hail, he told the Foreign Secretary: 'I did not enter into a discussion as to how Ibn Rashid's movements had been encouraged or

abetted by the Ottoman Government, as I felt sure this was a question which had been secretly handled by the Palace, and of which subsequent proof would be very difficult, but I tried to convince his Highness that it was a grave business . . .'

The fires of hatred would be stoked for many a year to come, for the boy king in the care of the Sharif of Mecca was under the influence of exiled and discontented members of the Saud family who were also in the sharif's care. Meanwhile, however, Ibn Saud was gaining in strength and influence among the tribes.

Shakespear went to Elgin for Christmas in 1908. Dorothea exerted a powerful pull at this time, but there was another reason for his desire to join the Bairds. Douglas Baird, now a lieutenant in the Indian army, had met his younger brother Henry Talbot in the Bengal Cavalry. They had struck up a friendship, with the result that they too were bound for Scotland.

It was a cold winter and sad time at 'Palmer's Cross', for Colonel Baird had died in the summer of that year and the family was still in mourning. The River Lossie was covered with a layer of ice and the snow was hard under foot. It seemed strange to be talking of Arabia while their breath hung in the air and froze before their eyes, but Dorothea wanted to hear about his plans to explore the desert and about his new duties which would take him into the midst of the conflicts they had discussed in their letters for the past year. They were joined on their walks by Douglas Baird and by Henry, who teamed up with Dorothea's younger sister Winifred. She was pretty, but solemn, very different from the lively, talkative Dorothea. Withdrawn and even at the age of twenty conscious of a social superiority, she did not take to the elder brother, finding him too ebullient and overpowering and suspecting him of a wandering eye. But she and young 'Shako' hit it off well in a quiet way. There were now two romances involving the Bairds and the Shakespears, and Elgin became the focal point of the men's lives and the substance of their correspondence with each other. It was a memorable holiday for Shakespear. Daytime walks, Dorothea muffled in a fetching black fur which covered her from head to foot, he in his army greatcoat and a thick woollen scarf wound round his neck several times and hanging down his back, were punctuated by chatter that veered wildly from the frivolous to the serious. Dorothea followed the events of the day as closely as she involved herself in the exploits of the great Victorian explorers and travellers. She was politically minded but without obvious bias, he with the preconceptions of an Indian upbringing. His delight in the company of the poorest and meagrest mortals of the East went together with the belief that they responded better to a sound thrashing than to reasoning; Dorothea called him 'a Burtonesque imperialist'. She had taken to heart the radical view of an affair which began in June 1906 when a party of British officers at the town of Dinshawai in Egypt was surrounded by curious villagers. One of the officers accidentally shot and wounded the wife of the local Imam. The villagers retaliated and some of the British were injured, with the result that the 'offenders' were put into prison and flogged. Since then, the government of Campbell-Bannerman which made the first moves had given way to the Asquith administration but the call for the release of the Egyptians mounted, with George Bernard Shaw and Wilfrid Scawen Blunt in the forefront of fierce and at times comic Fabian onslaught. In 1907, Shaw wrote to a Cabinet minister, John Burns: 'Can you not take Grey by the scruff of the neck at the next Cabinet meeting, and hold him out of the window over the railings until he lets out Abdul Nabi and the rest of the surviving victims of that infernal business at Dinshawai?' The prisoners were eventually released but not until many bitter, and amusing, words had been exchanged. Dorothea had a remarkable memory and she could relate the wordy battle that had taken place in Shakespear's absence almost verbatim as they wandered in the snow together. They jumped from this subject to that, from theatre to politics to music hall and back again, while he amused her with stories of his boating antics in the Persian Gulf in his tiny, single-masted yacht and with music-hall ditties which he sang vigorously if a little tunelessly.

It did not occur to Shakespear as they discussed the fracas over the Egyptian prisoners that he would shortly become the centre of a storm in the life of Sir Edward Grey and Britain's Foreign Office.

Dorothea could sing and mimic well, and evenings around the piano were inventive and enjoyable, though Shakespear's solo turns – he specialized in the bawdier Edwardian music-hall turns – were toned down on family occasions.

There was coincidence in the popularity of an actress of the time who was Dorothea's namesake. As a young subaltern Douglas Baird saw the other Dorothea, who was married to actor-manager H. B. (Trilby) Irving, on the stage and thereafter nursed a passionate devotion for her. Her stage nickname was 'Dolly' and his fellow officers knew him from then on as 'Dolly Baird'.

The Shakespear brothers were reluctant to leave 'Palmer's Cross', white and brittle in the Scottish winter, yet warm and friendly in its welcome. But they had to return to India and the gulf soon after the festivities were over.

6

At the Court of
Shaikh Mubarak

The need for a strong, resourceful Political Agent in Kuwait had been evident to the Government of India for some time. That tiny state was of obvious strategic importance to Britain and it was one of the few places on the Arabian side of the gulf to which the government could send a representative without too great a danger of upsetting the volatile Turks.

The beauty of it was plain to see. A hundred years before, Samuel Manesty of the East India Company had moved his factory there from Basra, when the Turks took the Mesopotamian town from the Persians and started to make life difficult for the English colony. The fact that he could escape Turkish interference by so doing argues that Kuwait enjoyed a fair measure of independence even then. Ever since it had been looked on by the great powers as the finest vantage point in Arabia from which to test the temperature of the desert, to observe the conflicts and everchanging loyalties of the tribes. In the 1860s, Colonel Lewis Pelly, then Britain's Resident at Bushire, spoke of Kuwait as a clean and active town with a population of twenty thousand inhabitants, which attracted merchants from all quarters by the equity of its rule. Admittedly, Kuwait was nominally a part of the Ottoman Empire, and its shaikh, in British eyes, merely the *kaimakam*, or governor, of that province. But the shaikh of Shakespear's time, Mubarak al Sabah, had other ideas.

When he had come to power – by murdering his half-brother Muhammad in his bed – Kuwait was in a state of lawless confusion. Muhammad had been a weak ruler, more than willing to accept Turkish protection and hopelessly unable to control the badu who plundered and terrorized the neighbourhood, as was their habit when political authority was absent. They extorted *khawa* or protection money from travellers in or out of Kuwait, and the Turks looked on with glee, hoping that in the confusion order would collapse completely, the ruling family be ousted from power and their own nominee put in control. But they reckoned without Mubarak.

Having despatched his brother in 1896, he proceeded to imprison or expel anyone suspected of sympathy with the Turks, and to rule with a rod of iron. He even imposed a levy on Turkish goods entering Kuwait. But he fought a lone battle. Britain was unwilling to intervene between Turkey and Kuwait, or any other part of the Ottoman Empire except where its own interests were directly threatened. In the end Russian attempts to find a 'warm water' port in the gulf and the prospect of a Berlin-to-Baghdad railway forced Whitehall into action. In January 1899, Britain reluctantly signed a treaty with Kuwait guaranteeing its security. The way was clear for an official representative of the Indian Government to be installed. The Turks showed their resentment early on by sending a sloop with an ultimatum for the shaikh demanding his abdication. Their men were received less than politely and they withdrew in haste. Within a month of this visit, Britain sent three cruisers to Kuwait and a small detachment of troops to show the flag. The threat of Turkish intervention seemed at an end and Mubarak settled to rule the country with autocratic severity, to restore its prosperity in commercial alliance with Britain and wage a war of nerves on the weak and indolent Turkish Wali at Basra.

When a Political Agency was set up there in 1904, following a visit by the retiring Viceroy, Lord Curzon, Colonel S. G. Knox was chosen as its first incumbent. His instructions were precise. Since the Shaikh of Kuwait was a man of great strength of character and implacable determination, he could not easily be influenced in day-to-day matters. He should be watched closely, and persuaded only as a last resort. Knox's major task, for which a proven ability as an explorer fitted him admirably, was to make as many journeys into the hinterland as possible in order to keep in touch with tribal conflict, and in particular with the young Amir of Central Arabia, or Najd as it was then called, Ibn Saud. Knox did his job well. He was a punctilious man, a fine Arabist and a reliable informant and observer; he saw the two great powers of Central Arabia, the families of Saud and Rashid, fight an endless and cruel war of attrition while the Turks encouraged them.

In 1901, within two years of its treaty with Shaikh Mubarak, the British Government had entered into a secret agreement with Turkey undertaking to remain strictly neutral in the affairs of Arabia and to restrain Shaikh Mubarak from taking offensive action against the pro-Turkish desert force of Ibn Rashid; Turkey for its part undertook to restrain Rashid from attacking Kuwait. They called it the Anglo-Turkish Accord. Shaikh Mubarak, naturally enough, was not informed of its content. Six years later Britain made another secret accord, this time with Mubarak. Having accepted the arrangement between Turkey and Germany whereby the latter would be permitted to build the Baghdad railway with an outlet in the gulf, Britain gained control over the most suitable debouchure for the railway by signing the so-called 'Bandar-Shuwaikh' lease with the Shaikh and making further promises of protection and assistance in return. But Britain's concern remained peripheral. In 1906, Percy Cox exclaimed in a letter to Knox: 'I very much fear that the present Cabinet will have nothing whatever to do with the affairs of Central Arabia.'

In fact, the Campbell-Bannerman administration, like Balfour's Conservatives before and its own Liberal successors, exhibited the symptoms of imperial powers in decline – uncertainty and indecision. Britain responded to Turkish aggression with the unsure touch of those accustomed to command who find themselves on the defensive. When, in 1908, Asquith took over the government, the problems grew for those men of the Indian administration whose job it was to maintain the prestige and authority of Britain at its distant outposts. Positive fear set in. The affairs of Europe preoccupied the Prime Minister and his Foreign Secretary, Sir Edward Grey, to a point where open conflict broke out between the Foreign and India Offices.

Knox was constantly told to assure Shaikh Mubarak that if he offended the Ottoman authority he could expect no help from Britain. The same warning was given time and again to Ibn Saud in his battle with Ibn Rashid. To one plea from the warrior king of Central Arabia, Knox replied:

You say that you are under the protection of the British Government .. But it is as well for me to remind you, O my friend, that the Great Government does not accord its protection rashly or without much forethought. It is not – praise

be to God! – of those who promise much and do not per-
form. Hitherto no reply has been vouchsafed by the Great
Government to your petition. May that reply be soon received and may it be propitious and you be preserved.

Fine words, but small comfort.

Shakespear came like a whirlwind. The quietly efficient Colonel
Knox had gained the confidence of Shaikh Mubarak and was
respected by him, though generally each went about his tasks
without bothering the other, until Knox was compelled by one of
the shaikh's frequent desert forays to protest on behalf of his
Government. The new Political Agent was not at all like Knox,
and the wily old Mubarak saw from the beginning that things
were going to be different. The two men engaged in a series of
angry disagreements almost from the moment they met, and out
of them grew a firm and unshakeable friendship. And out of their
understanding came the close comradeship of the Englishman and
the hereditary King of Central Arabia, Ibn Saud.

When he arrived to take over from Knox, he wore his customary
khaki dress and carried the inevitable Union Jack which he raised
in front of the mud-brick agency building on the seafront while
minor bunting was draped from flagpole to ground. A little
later his car arrived, to the fascination of both populace and ruler.

The agency was close by an imposing array of buildings occupied by the shaikh and his family on the hill which ran back from
the seafront towards the centre of the town. Dull grey, and a
mixture of just about every Islamic style, it had windowless outer
walls and a random, box-like construction giving it a look at once
inhospitable and unlovely. Each morning Mubarak would advance
from his living quarters high on the hill to the *serai*, or administrative part of the building, on the seafront, a more formal and pleas-
ing structure. He was always accompanied by a bodyguard of
badawin and fearsome-looking Negroes and by his closest retainer,
Muhammed. In good weather he sat on a verandah facing the
sea while his secretary read his correspondence to him and he
dictated his replies. When he had finished with official business
he would take a cigarette from the diamond-studded case by his
side and look out through binoculars at the dhows in the bay
bobbing lazily on the water.

Later, he would go in procession to the bazaar where he held his *majlis*, or council, and dispensed advice and justice. While he was away the badawin guards who were left behind amused themselves with their guns, firing from rooftops and ground level at marks on the walls. The buildings on the hill were divided by a narrow lane with a wooden bridge over it joining the two upper-most blocks of the palace. Gigantic Negroes would reach over the iron railings of the bridge and empty their rifles and revolvers in a noisy display of the poorest marksmanship. As soon as the shaikh's carriage showed up the firing ceased and order was restored, but wise members of the community kept out of the way while Mubarak's soldiers and slaves were at play.

The old man – he was now seventy years of age – had few wives in his harim, for his needs had diminished in recent years. But every now and again he felt a desire for change and so a steamer was despatched to Basra to bring musicians and dancing girls to amuse him.

Muhammad introduced him: 'Captain Shakespear'. Or, more accurately, 'Captain Skaishpeer'. The Arabs could never pro-nounce his name. He felt slightly uncomfortable as he was ushered into Mubarak's presence. He had put on a dark suit, stiff collar and regimental tie for the occasion and he was never entirely at home in formal clothes.

Mubarak glared ferociously at the newcomer. His spotted kaffiya framed his face and shoulders and Shakespear observed the furrowed brow, large semitic nose which twitched ever so slightly, cultured moustache, well-trimmed and hennaed beard, tight-drawn lips and strong, assertive chin: it was the face of a decisive and cunning man, clever perhaps and cruel. In turn the shaikh directed his fierce and distrustful gaze at the tall, inscrutable Englishman who stood before him, the waxed military moustache rivalling his own in its shaping, the high forehead, straight nose and jutting chin portraying quick intelligence and seriousness of purpose. Like all men brought up in the desert tradition, Mubarak seldom permitted himself or those around him the undignified assurance of a smile, but the stern face softened, the arrogant, piercing stare relented, when he was pleased. He rose to greet the new Political Agent and offered him a seat at his side.

The customary salutations and polite chatter out of the way, coffee served, the two men talked of politics and the relations between Kuwait and the princes of the desert, between Britain and Mubarak.

He was the strongest and most influential Arab leader of his day, and his voice was heard with deference far and wide; he was astute and, unlike most other Arab chiefs, worldly. Even the Turks, with a strong garrison on his doorstep at Basra, were afraid of him, and the governor of that *vilayet*, or administrative district, showered him with gifts to keep him sweet. Shakespear began by listening intently. Among the piles of documents he had studied before coming to Kuwait, several had been concerned with the Mubarak family background, with his youthful banishment at the hand of his brother, his homicidal assumption of power, his protection of the Saudi Amir Abdur Rahman ibn Faisal and his eldest son Abdul Aziz. Now he heard these things again from the lips of the man to whom the future King of Arabia had become an adopted son. The audience was long. At their first meeting they had established a friendly and easy relationship, and when the time arrived for the shaikh's daily *majlis*, Shakespear was invited to go with him. Flanked by his ever-present bodyguard, the shaikh led the way to his carriage, the Englishman at his side. Two black horses pulled them to the *mahkama*, the administrative building in the bazaar. In front walked the badawin guard, behind them the ruler's Negro slave, mounted on his white steed, dressed in blue robes, his rifle loaded at the ready.

'Mubarak the Great', they called him.

It was with some surprise that Shakespear had read, on his arrival in Kuwait, a memorandum circulated by the ambassador at Constantinople. According to the ambassador, fortune favoured the northern family, the Rashids, and the Sauds were 'in danger of becoming perhaps merely notable as hereditary amirs of the Wahhabis'. Shakespear had not gained this impression from reading the documents available at the Residency or from talking to Percy Cox. Sir Edward Grey, the Foreign Secretary, in passing the information to the India Office, included with it a genealogy of the two chief families of Central Arabia. Shakespear knew that his own country's policy in the Near East had to be viewed in a world context: England's anxiety to placate the Turk was determined by the turn of events in Europe, where Germany was beginning to take up aggressive postures, and Czarist Russia, contemptuous of the Ottoman power, was forcing Whitehall's hand in Persia and the gulf. Nevertheless, Shakespear saw no reason to allow his government the luxury of self-deception. He went to Shaikh Mubarak with the document to test it 'with sources which may be assumed to be as partial to the Wahhabi chief as the original is to the Rashids'. Mubarak dismissed it as nonsense. 'Ibn Saud has the support of the majority of the tribes and he is the more powerful leader,' he told the Political Agent. But he added that he lacked money, provisions and animals. 'The power of the Arab is in his camels and mares,' he remarked, and he saw danger in allowing the Turks to go on arming the Rashids while Ibn Saud was left to fend for himself.

Shakespear reported back to the Resident in September 1909, emphasizing the folly of aiding the allies of the Turks and praising the work of Mubarak in striving to maintain a *status quo* in Central Arabia. ' .. all Shaikh Mubarak's dealings with the Badawin tribes have as their ultimate objective this balance, together with his own aggrandisement, whereby his support becomes and remains the most desired end of each of the rival chiefs,' he told the government. And he made the first of many pleas to his superiors not to allow Arabia to fall into the hands of the Rashids. His observations were greeted with little enthusiasm. It was not long before Sir Henry McMahon and the Secretary of State for India were warning Cox that his man in Kuwait must stand firm by Britain's policy of non-interference in the affairs of 'Turkish Arabia'.

7

First Steps in the Desert

Nearly a year was to elapse before there was an opportunity to meet Ibn Saud. In the meantime Shakespear was busy with other matters: sailing in the gulf became his hobby; preparing for desert exploration his obsession. Army training and early travels in Persia and India had taught him the importance of thorough preparation. Shakespear approached his exploratory work with professional attention to detail. He became a master of surveying and map projection. He built a bathroom section on to his tent so that he could enjoy the luxury of a soak in a hip bath after a hard day's work, when water was available. Most importantly, he set out to demonstrate to the Arabs of sea and desert that he was worthy of a place in their midst. Some people who have read in passing of Shakespear's antics or who have learned about him from Arab witnesses believe that his modes of dress and conduct were flamboyant and unnecessarily risky. His determination to go out in the roughest seas in a boat which local sailors thought just about suitable for a rainpool; his journeys in the Rover, which had seen little service since he returned from Britain in 1907 but which now took him into the sandy hinterland of Kuwait where a sudden wind might submerge car and driver; his open use of camera and sextant; his western army dress which singled him out for attention: all might indicate an extrovert more concerned with effect than achievement. But that judgment would be shallow. He realized something which seems to have escaped even the most able explorers who preceded him: that the Arab of the desert is a proud and arrogant man who is better persuaded by example than by affectations of disguise and speech. A man who could challenge them at their own most cherished pursuits, who could ride and hunt with them, who could vie with the instinctive seamanship of the gulf sailor, who could sit in their simple homes and talk of the things that mattered to them – such a man was different. In Shakespear they found not an intruder but a friend and ally.

In his day the boundaries of the shaikhdoms and amirates of eastern Arabia were ill defined. Nothing would stop the badawin in their migrations from winter to summer quarters, from pasture lands to hunting grounds. Town and desert merged at the point where the badawin pitched their black tents. It did not take Shakespear long to find his way among the people of the Ajman and Mutair, the great sharif tribes whose wealth was vast camel herds and whose leaders' allegiance was sought by the most powerful princes of Arabia. They often camped in and around Kuwait and he came to know their men and leaders well.

Others approached these wandering people with diffidence. Most, in fact, preferred to avoid them, hiding under their disguise and making themselves scarce when they spotted an encampment or desert scouts. Shakespear approached them from the start without disguise, but he learnt and observed the strict etiquette of the desert, never imposing himself on them unless invited, and speaking to them about the things that were of importance to them – the weather, their flocks and herds, the *ghazu*, or desert raid, their sport and their proof of manliness.

His badawin friends usually pitched their tents in folds of the landscape to make sure that unwelcome visitors did not easily find them. Like a practised traveller, he would circle them to announce his presence and advance deliberately from the front so that he could be observed. He was almost always sure of a warm welcome. His host would spread out the *mattrah*, the guest's mattress, highest luxury of badawin furniture, offer Shakespear his sheepskin-covered camel saddle as an arm rest, and serve coffee from the fire hearth, a hole scooped from the sand in which camel dung and sprigs of *arfaj* provided the fuel. The ritual of conversation, the deliberate avoidance of the direct question, polite and indirect enquiries as to health and the beneficence of Allah, the aroma of coffee and the sweet smell from the hearth – these were the simple pleasures of the desert which captivated the Englishman and drew him ever farther away in spirit and activity from the mundane routine of work at the Political Agency.

'Trust to their honour and you are safe ... to their honesty and they will steal the hair from your head.' Burton's view of the badawin in his *A Pilgrimage to Al Medinah and Mecca* was not far from the truth, and Shakespear read the observations of his Victorian predecessor on the 'wild men' of Arabia with amusement and approval. Shakespear himself could not write of the badawin as did Gibbon, in *Decline and Fall of the Roman Empire*, who did not even have a personal knowledge of the Arabs, but used the Danish explorer Carsten Niebuhr as his source:

> Their spirit is free, their steps are unconfined ... The nation is free because each of her sons disdains a base submission to the will of a master ... the fear of dishonour guards him from the meaner apprehension of pain, of danger, and of death ... his speech is slow, weighty and concise; he is seldom provoked to laughter ... and the sense of his own importance teaches him to accost his equals without levity and his superiors without awe.

Nor did he look on these perverse people as did Charles Doughty, with Christian charity and forbearance. He liked the badu, he said, 'because they were men.'

He acquired a well-trained hawk, which he called 'Shalwa', and a pack of salukis, stout-hearted and tireless desert greyhounds. Whenever he had the chance, he would ride into the hinterland with his retinue of servants and his salukis, his topee shielding head and neck from the sun, armed with camera, survey equipment and a disguised store of liquor piled on to baggage camels, Shalwa perched on his wrist, chained to the *dasma al tair*, the falconer's leather glove. Sometimes he would visit a tribal shaikh, in the hope of plucking information from the desert grapevine. On such occasions he was usually entertained in the *majlis* tent, where rich men fed their guests in opulent style and slaves poured coffee. He would have to sit patiently through the long ritual of conversation until the moment came to turn the talk to political matters. Those moments had to be divined carefully, for the host could be deeply offended by a sudden or ill-chosen approach.

If he passed in the early morning he would greet the badu as they took their sheep and camels to pasture, often several miles from their tents, while in spring time the young children would wander among the lambs in their keeping, nearer to the tents. In the evening the same people would return with their animals and the women would emerge from the harims – divided portions of the family tents – to milk the camels and goats and prepare the *leben* or buttermilk, shaking the skin containers on tripod stands to thicken the milk. Other women would carry water from often distant wells in skins on their backs, or heaps of *arfaj* to keep the fires burning. Others worked at their spindles or looms, weaving the wool of the sheep into tent cloth, saddle bags, halters and other necessary items. Sometimes they worked at the patterned *gata*, the dividing curtains of their tents.

One did not stare at the badawiyat, the women of the desert, who were in purdah, eyes peering from the slits of their *burgas*, black-garbed mostly but now and then in coloured dresses. Women never entered the living quarters when a guest was present, and Shakespear and his companions would see them only when they were at work. If his host wanted a fresh supply of dates or coffee beans to offer his guests he would call out and one of the women of the harim – often there was only one – would hand the required article over the dividing curtain.

Justice was handed out by the shaikhs with arbitary finality. On one occasion Shakespear came upon an execution scene. The young offender kneeled in the sand, the massive figure of his Negro executioner looming over him, his curved, polished sword shimmering in the sun. The victim held a ritual bowl in front of him to catch the unclean blood as his neck was severed. It was as if the intruders had stumbled on some nightmarish Oriental drama. As the young man's prayers and confessions of guilt died away, the sword was raised, and the victim looked up and smiled. Shakespear clicked his camera, then looked away. It was the kind of thing Shakespear constantly complained about to the shaikhs during his years in the desert. In the course of many long journeys and innumerable meetings with tribal chiefs in *majlis* he lectured them on their 'barbaric' and 'medieval' practices. But he might as well have saved his breath. The tribesmen and their chiefs would listen to him with Sphinx-like expressions and await an opportunity to turn the conversation to matters of deeper interest. Many of the badawin still knew nothing of lands outside the territory of the *Aarab*, and they would ask Shakespear time and again 'How many camel marches is it, O Gonsul, to the land of the Eglys?' and Shakespear would explain that it was a long way and that it was necessary to cross the water. Then he would tell them of England's heavy rainfall and the greenness of its vegetation, and they would look with wide-eyed astonishment at the storyteller and contemplate fat sheep and rich pastures and observe that the badu must be happy in that distant country. The shaikhs, for their part, were keenly interested in modern arms and methods of warfare, a subject on which Shakespear was prone to lecture them at great length, to the accompaniment of illustrations drawn with a stick in the sand.

When he was received as a guest, he enjoyed a position of privilege, protected by the time-honoured custom of *dakhala*, or sanctuary. Without that protection a visitor would be liable to robbery without hesitation or even to murder.

He did not wear Arab clothes, but he demonstrated that he could outdo the best of them at the hunt and in the sport of desert princes – falconry. He was as good a shot with rifle or revolver as they had ever seen, and could ride as they rode, without saddle and with no bridle or bit to control their nervous war mares, the blue-blooded horses of Najd which they called 'drinkers of the wind' – just a rope stirrup and a sense of balance.

Mostly, though, Shakespear preferred to keep his own company for, if he understood the badawin way of life and revelled in the courage, the simplicity and hospitality of these people, his own tastes were not always compatible. There were times when he went to considerable lengths to avoid them, so that he could sit undisturbed in his own tent working at his maps or photography and enjoy a meal cooked by his servant to the accompaniment of a glass of wine. Whenever he went into the desert one of his baggage camels was loaded with a crate of wine, and usually with several bottles of whisky. Ibn Saud was zealously opposed to the consumption of alcohol, and Shakespear was careful to keep his habits from the prying eyes of desert men.

At first his camera caused some excitement. Few men of the desert, even in the first decade of the twentieth century, had seen or heard of such things. Many spoke of the 'evil eye'. When he set up his massive wooden box with its black cloth and tripod, and prepared to photograph the scenery and people, they would often run for cover. He photographed everything in sight, so long as his precious plates lasted, but he was restricted by the number he could carry. When the servants and guides had gone to bed, usually after the last coffee in early evening, he would set to work developing the day's pictures. Then he would finish a bottle of wine, read for a while, and sleep in serene quiet.

By November 1909 he was ready for his first desert journey. Only Knox before him had travelled to any extent in the hinterland of this region, from the Al Hasa coast in the south and Basra in the north towards the interior of Arabia. Others had passed by, but not to explore. Even close to the gulf shore there were gaps to be filled on the map of Arabia.

Few outsiders had braved these inhospitable lands. Sadlier had gone this way in pursuit of Ibrahim Pasha; Colonel Lewis Pelly, Resident in the gulf at a time when Victorian Britain played a dominant role in the East, had visited Najd and its southern capital in 1865. Of other aliens who went to the heart of the land many died on the way, and few of their tales were told. There was barbarism and cruelty in the desert and much bigotry and zealotry. Few had the stomach or the will for the journey. Two of the finest of all Arabian explorers set out to reach the Wahhabi capital of Riyadh but turned back before they reached it. The Swede George Augustus Wallin was sent by the Ottoman Viceroy in Egypt in 1845 to find out how the Amir Faisal was governing in his second term of office. He was the most thorough of Arabists and travellers but he did not reach Riyadh, though he went deep into Najd. He died soon after returning to Scandinavia. The greatest explorer of them all, Charles Huber from Alsace, covered seven thousand miles of Arabia in two remarkable journeys in 1883-4, but he too found the rigours of southern Najd with its fanatical Wahhabi inhabitants too severe. He turned towards Hijaz and was killed by his own guides on the way to Jidda. There was, of course, Doughty, the mighty Khalil, but he, gentle Christian, was almost trodden under foot by the badu, and did not reach Riyadh either. The Blunts made an easy passage to Hail and Lady Anne became the first known woman of the West to penetrate the interior of Arabia. But they stopped short at the territory of Jabal Shammar. The German Baron Nolde went from Damascus to Hail in 1895 and killed himself in London almost immediately on his return. Palgrave, from whom Shakespear learnt a good deal, found his way to the Wahhabi capital and left by far the most graphic description of the place and people available to the early twentieth-century traveller, though Shakespear was later to discover that many of the geographical observations of that Indian Army officer who became a Jesuit priest were not strictly accurate. Much of eastern and central Arabia was unknown and unmapped in Shakespear's time, its water-courses indefinite in origin and termination, its rises and depressions vaguely recorded, most of its habitations known only to the badu. Shakespear set out to make amends on Monday, November 22nd, 1909.

His baggage had been sent on in the care of his trusty *rafiq*, Khalaq, and his personal servant from India, Wali Muhammad. He left the Kuwait agency at 10 a.m. with Abdul Aziz, his camel *jemader*. The first diary entry set the pattern for five years of extensive and thorough exploration:

> SSE after clearing Kuwait town. Over bare, rolling downs until the crest of Adan little S.E. of Sirra . . . Adan slopes gently to sea. Numerous dry water courses. Ground bare as far as Sirra. Onwards a little chedall and arfaj grazing. Stopped for coffee 11.00. Noon observation 116° 6' 30". Forward bearings ... 12.30 prayer. 1.00 stop to adjust baggage ... 4.15 Camp 1, Fantas. 15 miles, 6¼ hours. Going fair.

Exact measurement, detailed description of terrain, the correct badawin name for every place, every hill, depression and encampment; every day of every march annotated, every bearing calculated and checked, and entered in his diaries. The first journey merely took the caravan down to the coast of Kuwait to Fantas and then inland to the high ground of Burgan, and thence in a series of triangles and rectangles over ground covered by Knox in 1906 and 1908.

They camped at Wara Hill and Subaihiyah wells and filled their water skins, stopping for photographs and sightings and, of course, prayer as they went. It was, as Shakespear noted in his diary, 'a lazy march', though as they made their way to the Shaq depression which runs from north to south behind Kuwait they struck some hard going and dry country. When they found grazing among the *arfaj* patches on the way to Thamaniyah the camels ate furiously and their pace slackened. Just before leaving on the journey, Shakespear had taken delivery of a she camel called 'Dhabia'; a beautiful creature with a mind of her own, fast and brave when the need arose, immovable when she suspected that she was being harassed unnecessarily. He had dressed her in all the finery appropriate to her elegant form and his own status, for a man was judged in the desert not so much by his own appearance as by that of his camel. She had silver chains and braided girths and beads shone like jewels from her coloured halters. The saddle, made from acacia wood, was silver trimmed. Dhabia and her owner, khaki-clad and pipe smoking, Shalwa chained to his leather-gloved wrist and apparently asleep, the salukis yelping at the heels of the caravan, made a colourful if unusual sight.

They reached As Shaq by the end of the month, then went due north along the depression, then east back to the wells of Subai-hiyah, then north again across rolling, sandy downs to a hill called Saada where they pitched their twelfth camp.

Next day Shakespear met a party of shaikhs of the Mutair, headed by the powerful and imposing Faisal ibn Dawish, on a hawking expedition. He had already met Ibn Dawish at camp and the two men were on good terms. Shakespear was asked to join them and the hooded Shalwa was taken from the captivity of the stand, the *wakar al tair*, which it occupied impatiently, and conveyed by its master to join the other birds of prey as they soared into the cloudless sky and hovered, before diving like projectiles on to any creature that moved. These birds were trained to kill even gazelle, seeking out their unsuspecting, camouflaged victims the moment they stirred and worrying them into an open space where they pecked at their eyes until the unfortunate creatures lay down and died from exhaustion. Evil, majestic birds. Shalwa's victim that day was a *hubara*, a lesser bustard. Shakespear's men had moved on to Thamilat-al-Kaa on the road to Jahra, Kuwait's fortified outpost, and he raced Dhabia across the desert to join them. They arrived back in Kuwait after journeying 236 miles in 82 hours.

Shakespear was visited on his return by *The Times'* man in India, Lovat Fraser, a journalist who roamed the eastern world armed with excessive charm and wit, to the delight of everyone from the Viceroy to the lift boy at the Taj Mahal hotel. Government officials in Whitehall were especially appreciative of his dry, urbane observations and India and Foreign Office documents of the period bear witness to the impression his asides made on them. On this occasion the Political Agent took him to see Shaikh Mubarak and he afterwards wrote a crisp portrait of the old man, 'sitting in his high chamber, gazing seaward with inscrutable eyes, with the face of Richelieu and something of Richelieu's ambition as yet unquenched within him'.

8

Arrival of the Warrior King

While he waited patiently during the first year in Kuwait Shakespear prepared for a meeting with Ibn Saud, sounding out Shaikh
Mubarak and the tribal leaders who came to see the old ruler and
following the movements of the young amir at a distance.

The months from October to April were the only time when
travel into the interior was possible. Otherwise the days were
unbearably hot and the nights bitterly cold in contrast. The rain
and wind would come to create hazards and uncomfortable travelling conditions, but they were preferable to the fierce, unfiltered
sunlight which at its height made movement of any kind painful
and often fatal.

Shakespear left on his second desert journey in late January
1910, heading for As Safa across the featureless and waterless
wilderness of Dibdibba and thence to the water wells of Al Hafar
and back along the Batin, the long dry course which stretches
from the south-west of Basra down into the depths of Najd. This
time the caravan did not include Shalwa and the salukis for Shakespear was bent on a serious exploration of remote and, by repute,
unfriendly regions.

By February 1st they were at Thamilat al Turki, at the east of
the valley of As Shaq, the region they had traversed earlier. Then
they struck south-west on a march of about 100 miles, across
the Shaq depression and through the uncharted desert that led to
As Safa. The desert was cool and the men and animals succumbed
to its docility. They made their way steadily while Shakespear
fixed his position by the sun and took sightings of hillocks and
knolls, valleys and depressions, and made endless notes, which
his companions found amusing and incomprehensible. But the
desert was deceptive. Soon a *shimal*, a north wind, began to blow,
and sand eddied around them. It was as difficult to camp as to

move on, for the soft sand would not hold the tent pegs and they had to hang on to the canvas to stop it blowing away. They veered to their right, towards a depression, where they hoped to find shelter. They pitched their tents at the bottom of a slope and hoped the wind would subside. But as darkness fell it worsened. Rain came to add to their misery. Some of the tents were blown down and they took turns in holding down Wali Muhammad's cooking tent while the rest of the party drank coffee inside to warm themselves for a journey in the wet. There was no point in staying where they were. They moved on through the night to the waste of Al Gara.

By the fifth day out they were in unnamed desert and they began the descent to the Safa basin. They went through a valley called Shaib al Faisal on to a ridge with a cliff-like edge at the west of the Abu al Kaa basin, where they camped, exhausted by wind and rain, after marching night and day for nearly sixty hours without rest or fodder for the animals. They were approaching good grazing, however, and they moved on next day to Taleh al Fasqah where a valley ran almost at right-angles to their path. There was open grazing in front of them and they decided to rest there. Hadi and Ali the Ajmani *rafiqs* lit the coffee fire and the men gathered round to chat. The *rafiqs* had been scouting in the desert and met up with fellow tribesmen earlier in the day who told them the latest news of Ibn Saud and other desert chiefs. They told a tale that could have come from the pages of the *Arabian Nights*.

It seemed that two nephews of Abdul Aziz had recently plotted to poison their uncle by putting something in the coffee which awaited the amir after morning prayer. But the wives of the two young men, Abdul Aziz's own sisters, being unaware of their husbands' intentions, went as usual to taste the coffee to make sure that it had been properly prepared. Both fell dead within seconds of taking the poison. The nephews, alarmed by the news and knowing full well what would be the result if they tarried, hastened to Al Rigaia, near Al Hasa, where they could claim protection from the Turkish garrison.

The men listened intently to the tale, for gossip concerning the Amir of Najd was the staple diet of desert conversation, and so they did not hear the noise that came from the high ground above the valley. Shakespear was wondering when he would receive news of Ibn Saud's journey to Kuwait; if the story he had just heard was true, Abdul Aziz was probably pursuing his nephews in the direction of Al Hasa. While he was deep in thought, little Khalaq, his chief guide, was more profitably occupied. The guide's long experience of the desert never allowed him to become complacent. Even when he was asleep he was somehow alert to danger, and as he snoozed he thought he heard a click in the distance. They were camped in a shallow depression so that they could not be seen from any distance, but anyone coming close could easily discern Shakespear's white tent which stuck out from its black companions like a bishop among its opposing pawns. Hadi and Ali had been joined by Abdul Aziz, the camel-minder, and they were talking loudly. Khalaq told them to shut up and everything went quiet. Sure enough there was another clicking noise from above and no great distance away. Then they heard whispers and the men round the coffee fire let out the familiar badawin cries, part plea, part imprecation, *wellah! billah! wellahi-billahi!* They leapt for their guns. Shakespear had already grabbed his. The Englishman thought he could see a shadowy figure edge along the ground, the moon picking out his squat form against the grey-yellow sand. He aimed and waited for the other side to shoot first. A shot rang out and he pulled his own trigger, but the shape had moved. His tent presented a nice target and he moved away from it to the right of the encampment, while the others slithered to the left. There were more shots, both sides aiming blind, and then a groan and Shakespear realized that Khalaq had been hit. He threw down his rifle and crawled across to his guide. Blood oozed from a wound on the right of his chest. Shakespear leaned over him and put a handkerchief to the wound to soak up the blood while the others went on firing at the darkness. But now there was more shouting than gunfire, the guides and their assailants hurling abuse at each other and then announcing their names and tribal allegiances. *Wa hyat Ullah!* On God's life! *Mel'aunin!* O cursed ones! *Ana Mutairi. Ana Ajmani.* I am a Mutairi. I am an Ajmani. And then, *bess! bess!* Enough. Somebody above shouted to his companions to stop shooting. A dozen or more Arab voices engaged in a volley of recognition and two of the intruders jumped down the slope to the camp. They were acquaintances of Hadi and Ali from the Mutair, Ibn Dawish's men, dirty, evil-smelling rogues with greasy, plaited locks hanging like twisted rope from beneath their kaffiyas, bullet-filled bandoliers across their bodies. Shakespear was not the best-tempered of men. Now his blood was up. Khalaq was not only his chief *rafiq*; the little man was his most reliable and faithful companion. He hurled himself at one of the visitors, dragged him to the ground and beat him mercilessly. The assailant's fellow-attackers tried to go to his assistance but Hadi and Ali pulled them away, screaming at them to keep out of the fight and telling them that they had injured the *rafiq*. Shakespear left the Mutairi on the ground, battered and bruised, and picked up Khalaq and carried him to his tent. The blood still flowed and he tried to stop it, but his medicine chest was woefully inadequate for an emergency of this kind, and so were his medical skills. He bandaged the wound but Khalaq looked white and limp. There was still a lot of talking among the badawin and he put his head out of his tent to discover that the invaders and his own men were in deep conversation round the coffee fire. *His* coffee fire. He told the uninvited visitors to go to hell, and angrily assured them that he would see that their chief punished them. Then he went to Khalaq. The bullet must have penetrated his lung for blood seeped up through his mouth. He was hardly breathing now, but there was nothing his leader could do but watch and mop up the blood. To keep himself awake he sat in his chair and read FitzGerald's *Rubaiyat*. When he next looked at the patient, Khalaq lay still and calm. The wrinkles had gone from his serious, worried young face. He was dead. *Ullah yussulat aleyhim*. 'May God bring evil upon them,' said Hadi. Shakespear cursed in his own tongue.

They were at the furthermost point of their journey. It would be easier to go on along their planned route by way of the Batin than to turn back. But they were still a long way from their destination. He woke his guides and Abdul Aziz, and told them to dig a pit in the sand. They buried Khalaq as decently as they could, his head pointing due west to Mecca, and then they went on their way, tired and disconsolate. Shakespear wished that he had exacted restitution there and then, but there was no way of knowing who had fired the fatal shot.

They went from As Safa to Hafar across the Subhan desert, some sixty miles, in just over two days, with only one inhabited place on the route, Masjid ar-Rashid. They filled their water skins at Hafar, after fourteen weary days in the desert. Saddened by the unnecessary death of Khalaq they made their way relentlessly along the Batin. They bivouacked in a crevice at 10.15 p.m. on the night of February 11th and resumed their march at 2 a.m. The men were tired but Shakespear was a hard task-master. He seemed able to endure any amount of physical hardship and, though his men cursed him for his implacable determination to go on when their own legs were too heavy to carry them, they admired his courage and tenacity. He pushed them along the Batin, past a mound which the badawin called Kasr Ballal and the Khardja hills to a ridge which led down to the water wells of Rigai. Their seventeenth camp was at the remains of some old reservoirs at Qulban. The Batin became shallow and they climbed on to the west bank and went on to Halaibah. Shakespear stopped to examine some more dried wells and, surprisingly, stunted plum trees, sign of an ancient and perhaps prosperous habitation. He was half a mile east of Knox's 1906 camp. And in the direction of that camp he spotted a group of shaikhs at lunch, among them Jabir, the son of Mubarak. They had come out to meet him and tell him that Abdul Aziz had arrived in Kuwait and was anxious to see him.

He did not hurry. There was vital map work to be done on the way. He reached Kuwait on the last day of the month.

He was invited to dinner at the shaikh's palace on the night of his arrival. He was tired, bearded and dirty, having been short of water for a large part of the return journey. And he was still angry and distressed at Khalaq's death. A few hours in bed, a shave and a stiff whisky soon put him in the mood to meet the amir, however. He had waited for the best part of a year for this opportunity.

The first encounter was encouraging. He reported after the event: 'Shaikh Mubarak was even more lavish in his entertainment than is his usual very generous wont, and at a very rough guess entertainment and presents for these princes cannot have cost less than £20,000.' He went on to describe the young amir: 'Abdul Aziz, now in his 31st year, is fair, handsome and considerably above average Arab height ... He has a frank, open face, and after initial reserve, is of genial and courteous manner.' His brothers he found to have similar features but were of 'dour and taciturn manner'.

Next day the Political Agent entertained Mubarak and his Najdi guests at his own residence, rivalling the shaikh in the generosity of his welcome. At first the brothers looked on Shakespear with some suspicion, but Abdul Aziz and the Englishman struck an immediate accord. Shakespear, true to form, had provided an English menu: roast lamb with mint sauce, roast potatoes, tinned asparagus. It seems the Arabs enjoyed the experience once their first doubts were expelled. They talked freely and soon came to terms with the strangely sympathetic Englishman who appeared to understand their hopes. Even the brothers dropped their reserve eventually and joined in the conversation. The amir was surprised by the Englishman's command of Najdi Arabic and by his knowledge of the desert, gained in just one year. As they left, Abdul Aziz turned to Shakespear and said: 'As a true friend of Mubarak you are my friend.' The Political Agent's parting shot was to ask the amir if he could take photographs of him and his party the next day. Ibn Saud readily agreed.

'Abdul Aziz in particular, is a broad-minded and straight man ... His reputation is that of a noble and generous man who does not descend to mean actions,' Shakespear told his superiors. He concluded his observations with the sentence: 'Abdul Aziz did not discuss politics with me beyond remarking that he thanked God there were not Turks nearer his capital than Al Hasa, and that the English, as friends and brothers of Mubarak, were themselves his brothers and friends.' It must have had a mixed reception from men who had recently told Shakespear, as they had told Knox before him, that 'British protection for Mubarak's friend is out of the question'.

The amir invited Shakespear to visit him at Riyadh, such was the instant bond of friendship forged by these two men. Abdul Aziz was somewhat the taller of the two, but otherwise they were remarkably alike in manner and build, strong as bulls, serious and impetuous. Ibn Saud said that he had never seen a white man at his capital, though he had heard tell of Colonel Lewis Pelly's visit when he was the Resident in the gulf.

The Wahhabi princes left Kuwait on March 4th, 1910, not for Riyadh but for another battle which they had planned with Mubarak during the visit.

9

Conflict and Competition

In March 1910 there was much activity at the oasis of Jahra, with badawin arriving from all directions and sitting around in groups while they were sorted by the bustling shaikh into raiding parties and issued with ammunition and camels. Shakespear rode over to the scene and watched with interest. Soon the Saudi princes with whom he had so recently enjoyed a friendly meeting arrived in martial mood. Mubarak and Ibn Saud had gathered men from practically every friendly tribe in Arabia, and a good many from those whose allegiances could never be placed with certainty but who contrived to start out on the side of the likely victor.

The Ajman, a tribe who had made a number of raids on the shaikh's subjects and property of late, were not in the old man's favour. But they made their submission to him just in time and he accepted the apologies of their leader, Ibn Hithlain, on condition that he put his men at his disposal for the coming battle. Shakespear estimated that from six to eight thousand men were gathered at Jahra, while Ibn Saud had rounded up as many in the desert. While they awaited the instruction to move off, they spent their time working themselves up to a high pitch of excitement with the assistance of much unmusical drumming and haphazard gunfire. An area of several hundred miles between Al Hasa and Basra had been denuded of men. The shaikh insisted that this wild-looking army was assembled to repay the Dhaffir and Muntafiq chiefs and their tribes for some recent raids on Kuwait. The Political Agent gave him a knowing glance and rode off to inspect the troops. He was convinced that the real objective was Ibn Rashid's Shammari army, now rampaging in the desert under its leader Hamud ibn Subhan.

But it was, in fact, the powerful Muntafiq tribe, led by Dhaidan ibn Sadun, who met the oncoming force at a place called Ar Rakhaiya, near the celebrated battlefields of Sarif and Tarafiyya. Ibn Saud had talked Mubarak out of leading the Kuwaiti force on account of his age and ill health. The old man agreed reluctantly, protesting that he had no great confidence in his son Jabir, who, it was proposed, should take charge of the contingent. Muhammad, Ibn Saud's younger brother, stayed behind with Mubarak while Saad went with Abdul Aziz to the front. The battle was short-lived. Ibn Sadun had nearly 4,000 horsemen, while the Saudi-Kuwaiti force had only 1,000 men on war mares. The rest were on camels. The Kuwait army took flight almost before the battle began, losing its war flag and almost all its camels and mares. The Ajman fought bravely with Ibn Saud and for once remained constant in battle, but seeing the Kuwait army in disarray they gave up what had become a pointless struggle. To add insult to injury, Shaikh Sadun instructed his men to disarm the enemy and take possession of their animals but not to harm them. Thus the bedraggled and defeated army of Ibn Saud and Mubarak made a shamefaced return to Kuwait, most of them clinging to camels in groups of five or six to a beast.

Naturally, Shakespear had to report the affair to the Resident, who passed on the news to the Foreign Department at Simla. On March 22nd, 1910, Sir Henry McMahon told Cox to pass on a warning to Shaikh Mubarak by way of the Political Agent: 'You will see that the Government of India direct that a warning be conveyed to Shaikh Mubarak, in terms of previous warning, not to enter into any operations calculated to involve him in difficulties in Najd or with the Turks.' The previous warning referred to was that of 1901, when Lieutenant-Colonel Kemball had been Resident and the shaikh was preparing an expedition against Ibn Rashid.

When he went to deliver the reprimand he discovered that the shaikh was out at Jahra, preparing another raiding force. The Political Agent found a far from subdued Mubarak once more sorting out his fighting men and allocating their animals. After passing on the strictures of H.M. Government, to which the shaikh listened with polite attention, Shakespear asked him what had gone wrong when his army ran into the Muntafiq.

'O my friend, that was nothing,' replied the shaikh. 'A dust cloud blew up at the critical moment and my men could not see.'

The Political Agent conveyed the unlikely explanation to the government. His note was dated March 30th: 'The following description of this regrettable incident as furnished to me by Shaikh Mubarak himself is interesting, if fallacious ...'

The words 'regrettable incident' had been used by the Resident in his condemnation of Mubarak's skirmish. Shakespear's repetition of them showed where his sympathies lay. He concluded by telling the Resident that he had no evidence of Mubarak's intention to attack Ibn Rashid and that any effort to prevent the shaikh from attacking his tribal enemies would be an unwarranted intrusion into his personal affairs.

He could not help wondering, though, what the Indian Government would say when they got wind of the encounter now being planned at Jahra.

By the beginning of April, Ibn Saud and his brother Saad were back at the oasis, lending a hand with more feverish preparations there. The Shaikh of Kuwait seemed to be leaving nothing to chance in his determination to raise an effective and properly provisioned force. Everyone was made to contribute to this new war effort. Those petty shaikhs who had given one *khabra* (a tent, seven men and five camels) for the previous offensive were now asked to increase their contribution by three men and two camels. Even Kuwait's prostitutes were forced to help. Shakespear was vastly amused to learn that whereas last time they had been asked to give coffee pots, Mubarak now demanded bedding.

Men from Fao and Dora in Mesopotamia were enlisted under the nose of the Turkish Wali. Clearly Mubarak and the Amir of Najd meant business. The shaikh announced that he would give the force final instructions on April 1st.

Meanwhile, the Foreign Office showed increasing alarm at the turn of events in Arabia. It had, until a year previously, circulated a monthly journal of Eastern affairs, but on the advice of the ambassador in Constantinople, Sir Gerard Lowther, it was withdrawn from circulation. Major J. G. Lorimer, the Resident in Baghdad at this time, suggested that in the absence of any guidance from Whitehall and in view of the feud between the Foreign and India Offices, he and Shakespear should institute an informal news service together with the consul at Basra, F. E. Crowe. Shakespear took up the suggestion with alacrity, sending his first instalment to the other men. It consisted mainly of notes on the progress of the desert war now being conducted under the aegis of Shaikh Mubarak. 'Like the curate's egg', he said, 'good in part.' Lorimer, a patient man and remarkably well informed, had already started to compile a *Gazetteer of the Persian Gulf*, which was to be at once the most thorough, detailed and neglected account of the history of Central and Eastern Arabia ever written. He and Shakespear became close allies in a long and, in the end, hopeless battle with authority. Mubarak's campaign was unaccountably delayed. The Political Agent went out into the desert to consult his badawin friends and questioned the shaikh himself, but he could find no acceptable reason for the sudden drop in temperature. Perhaps it had all been an elaborate attempt by the shaikh to mislead both the British and the Turks. At any rate, by the end of the month the badawin conscripts had been released so that, according to Mubarak, they could carry out some urgent raids on their own account, and the pearl-divers of Kuwait were allowed to return to their livelihoods. An eerie quiet reigned.

But another more serious battle had broken out in the north. Shakespear heard about it from a surprising source, and the more he heard the clearer it became that the events at Jahra had in fact been an ingenious exercise in pulling the wool over his and other interested eyes.

While preparations had been going on for the ill-fated clash with Sadun's men, Shakespear had received an unexpected communication from a young lieutenant in the Royal Sussex Regiment serving in India. His name was Gerald Leachman.

Dated February 23rd, 1910, the letter bore the address 'Camp of Ibn Rashid, three days' march from Hail'.

Dear Shakespear,

   I know you by name from Gibbon in the Intelligence at Simla. I am here at camp with Ibn Rashid near Hail. Three days ago I was with a very large mass of the Anaiza on their way to attack Ibn Rashid. In the evening Rashid appeared and utterly defeated the Anaiza who got away with their camels only. Rashid's men looted thousands of tents. I took refuge with some Shammar who were prisoners with the Anaiza and with whom I had been for a few days before they were captured.

He went on to say that he would spare Shakespear the details of the squabble between the Anaiza and the Shammar, now led by Ibn Subhan as regent for the infant Saud ibn Rashid, since he supposed Shakespear had the subject at his fingertips. The regent, he said, wanted 'news of his victory to resound as much as possible'. After asking the Political Agent to take delivery of his mail in Kuwait, Lieutenant Leachman concluded:

They say civil war has broken out in Ibn Saud's kingdom, between his two brothers. I believe this is true. You know who the rival factions are so I won't bother you with details.

Sincerely,

G. LEACHMAN

The paths of Leachman and Shakespear were to weave an adventurous pattern across Arabia in the next few years.

Shakespear did indeed know of the battle raging between the Anaiza confederation of Ibn Shaalan and the Shammar. The northern town of Jauf, Shaalan's headquarters, had become a dependency of Hail. But a few months before, the Anaiza chief had re-taken it with much bloodshed, killing the Rashid governor and other officials. While Mubarak and Ibn Saud conducted their comparatively minor skirmish in eastern Najd, Ibn Rashid sought revenge in the Nafud to the north. According to Crowe at Basra, who received his information from the Turks, the ruler of Hail had taught the Anaiza a salutary lesson. But it was Leachman who, to Shakespear's annoyance, flirted with fortune in the desert and bombarded Britain's officials with eye-witness accounts of the proceedings.

In April a letter arrived in Baghdad addressed to Lorimer:

I write from the camp of the Amir Ibn Rashid, near Al Shahiyah on the Zubaidah road to Baghdad, three days' march from Hail. After I left Karbala I travelled with the Shammar Badu under Majid ibn Ajal in a south-westerly direction. We left Karbala on 26 January. I was with the Shammar till 12 February. On that day we ran into a big ghazu of Anaiza on their way to fight Ibn Rashid. They attacked the Shammar but left before they actually closed and I and my party slipped out and crossed over to the tents of the Anaiza Shaikh, Fahad Beg, who took us in. The Shammar had every single animal and possession taken.

His description of the seizure of Jauf by the Anaiza contradicted Crowe's Turkish-inspired account. He continued:

> ... they [the Anaiza] moved on across the Nafud, having left a garrison at Jauf. A ghazu of Rashid's men halted their progress temporarily, but they joined up with the Amarat and when I met them they were an enormous mass of men. However, on February 17, at about three in the afternoon, the Shammar attacked the Anaiza camp, which extended for several miles, and after a good fight drove right through the camp. I took refuge with some Shammar prisoners and rescued some of my kit. The Anaiza ran fast, pressed by the Shammar. But night stopped the pursuit by Rashid's men and they returned to loot the camp. Not a stick remained in the vast, derelict encampment by morning. Fahad Beg sued for peace ... This movement of the Anaiza was concerted with Ibn Saud with the idea of utterly finishing the Rashid power. I came with the Shammar back to this place where Ibn Rashid is camped.

It was a remarkable account by a European new to Arabia of a battle between the two powerful and bitterly opposed tribes. It is doubtful whether an outsider had ever before been as close to so fierce a desert conflict and survived to tell the tale. Leachman was obviously a young man of immense determination and courage. He had circumvented all official attempts to prevent him from leaving his regiment in India and entered Arabia as a private citizen without a vestige of official support or protection. Shakespear was not often given to envy. Usually he had neither time nor patience for rivalry, yet he was intensely jealous of Leachman's position, in the thick of the real action while he toyed in Kuwait with the diversionary tactics of Shaikh Mubarak. Perhaps Leachman also threatened a plan he had in his mind – to make a journey that would finally put the obscure regions of Central Arabia on the maps of the West, and would rank alongside earlier feats of desert exploration.

Worse was to follow. The day after he sent a messenger to Baghdad with his letter to Lorimer, Leachman gained an audience with the boy king of Hail, now returned from Mecca, and his regent, and was thus able to present the British Government with an inside view of Ibn Saud's rival. He was the first Englishman to gain access to the royal palace of Hail since the Blunts were there some thirty years before.

Leachman was impressed by the regent, Zamil ibn Subhan, who had recently assumed power from his cousin Hamud, as the result of yet another murder in the Rashid household. The king was then twelve years of age and his regent thirty-five. The latter was keen that the visitor should hear details of their recent victory, doubtless hoping that through him the world would hear of it too.

Shortly after his last communication arrived in Baghdad, Leachman's presence among the Shammar was reported to the Wali of Basra. He asked Britain's man Crowe what should be done with him. It was recommended that he be 'treated civilly and sent on his way'. When the Wali asked Crowe what Leachman was doing in the desert, Crowe replied: 'He's an English dervish studying botany.'

Another Englishman arrived in Kuwait at about the same time as Shakespear and by now the two men saw a good deal of each other, though they had little in common. He was a west countryman named William Richard Williamson, but he had adopted the Arab title of Abdullah Fadhil Zobair. He assumed Arab dress, manner and speech, embraced the Muslim faith, went on the pilgrimage to Mecca, took a number of wives and became a successful merchant. The Political Agent was aware that the Turks were after him as the result of certain commercial activities in and around Basra, and that Britain had forbidden his entry into Arabia. But though Shakespear had no special liking for Williamson or for his pretence, he was seldom on the side of authority in such matters. He allowed his fellow countryman to maintain his elaborate disguise and they would often pass in the *suq* and along the seafront, exchanging a polite and formal *Salaam alaikom. Alaikom as-salaam.*

A more troublesome invader of the year 1910 took the shape of a motorcar which Shakespear purchased for Mubarak. The old man had had a ride in the Political Agent's vehicle and had become a speed fanatic. He was driven through the town daily by his irrepressible Persian chauffeur to the terror of the inhabitants and the hazard of property. From then on Shakespear devoted much of his time to towing the Shaikh from scenes of near disaster and mending some much abused parts of the car. By this time he had spent a period of leave going through the Government workshops at Bushire so that he could take on almost any mechanical task. On one occasion a rather severe crash resulted in a broken back axle, but he was able to mend it.

10

Diversion and Invasion

Lethargy settled over the warring tribes in the latter part of 1910. Reports reaching the British Government suggested that though Ibn Shaalan brooded ominously over his recent defeat no immediate reprisal was threatened. The Anaiza were in control of Jauf again; other scores could be settled at leisure. As for Ibn Saud and the Regent of Ibn Rashid, there had been a suspicious silence for some months.

Shakespear reported to the Resident that peace prevailed, and wondered to himself if something was afoot. The intervention of the Turks was not hard to detect and Shakespear and Lorimer kept closely in touch, gauging the temperature as they talked to Shaikh Mubarak and the Turks in Baghdad, comparing notes on reported meetings and pay-offs in the desert. A number of gifts from the Turks to the Arab chiefs had come to the notice of the British representatives in the area. Mubarak had received several thousands of pounds in cash in recent months.

At the same time the Wali of Aleppo arranged to pay Ibn Rashid and his sister Jauzah a joint allowance of £250 per month while Turkish emissaries were sent to speak words of comfort to the pro-British Shaikh Khazal of Muhammerah, a tiny dependency at the head of the gulf situated precariously between Persia and Mesopotamia.

Since the exile of the Sultan Abdul Hamid a year before, the 'sick man of Europe', as the Czar described the Ottoman power, had been in a state of near panic, compounding its problems in Europe by jumping from one horse to another in Arabia in a desperate bid to find a strong leader who would return favour for favour and demonstrate allegiance to the sultanate. .

The lull in tribal warfare was ominous. They awaited the inevitable breaking of the storm. In the interval, Shakespear was able to get on with some pressing personal business. In terms of routine efficiency and devotion to the minutiae of the diplomatic tasks assigned to him, he was probably the least efficient Political Agent in the East. He was the despair of officialdom, and was saved from disciplinary action only by the generous intervention of Cox at Bushire. Often when he was wanted most urgently he was in some inaccessible part of the desert, or at sea in his yacht. Now he had found another diversion.

In the autumn of 1910 he left for a boating expedition in the gulf. His seamanship had become as much of a by-word among the sailors of Kuwait as had his hunting and exploratory work among the badu. He often sailed his tiny, single-masted boat across to the shaikh's island resort of Failaka, in rough seas and fair. He seemed to court danger in everything he did; he would never take a sure footpath if he could find a ravine or precipice, and calm waters held no attraction for him. Now he decided to abandon his own craft for the Residency steam launch, the *Lewis Pelly*, without the slightest experience of ocean navigation. That vessel was supposed to supplement the slender resources of the mail boats and other craft of the British India Steam Navigation Company in transporting government personnel in the area, but since nobody but Shakespear had the slightest wish to take it to sea, he commandeered it with Cox's blessing. Access to the steam launch had several advantages for Shakespear. Cruising up the coast to the Shatt-al-Arab, to the principality of Muhammerah and the date plantations of Fao made a pleasant change from the hard and wearying exertions of exploration in the desert. Navigation, often in rough seas and strong currents, presented another challenge to his restless nature; he had hardly learned the basic elements of ocean navigation before he was sitting at a drawing board designing a new and advanced launch for the use of future Political Agents. But most importantly, it gave him an opportunity to escape the pressures of the Agency where he was often at loggerheads with Shaikh Mubarak and was at the mercy of any prominent visitors who happened to stop off at Kuwait. His involvement with Intelligence at Simla was another reason for his urgent desire to escape prying eyes and casual visitors. His ability to come to terms with Arab leaders and his expertness in survey-ing the gulf hinterland and in mapping the eastern regions of Arabia had already caused Army Intelligence to take a close

interest in his comings and goings, and McMahon sent a number
of senior officers to talk to him and obtain detailed reports
which were not filed through the ordinary Residency channels.
Every government servant was, of course, expected to fulfil
an Intelligence function, but in Shakespear's case the liaison was
direct and often embraced activities and the use of funds that were
outside Residency control. In any case he was a man of generous,
even spendthrift, habit and he used government funds ex-
travagantly to enhance his cause and his popularity with the Arabs.
His most regular contact was Captain George Standish Gage
Craufurd who arrived in India in 1894 with the Gordon High-
landers and who joined McMahon's staff in 1910 as Intelligence
Officer (GSO2) at Jask. In the meantime he had served with
distinction in South Africa and had been awarded the D.S.O. for
his gallantry in fighting the Boers. He and Shakespear spent
many enjoyable hours together at the Agency, but the *Lewis
Pelly* gave them an opportunity to combine business with pleasure
and they were so often at sea together that the Royal Navy had to
mount an almost permanent search operation in order to find them
when events demanded the Political Agent's return to base.

Shakespear took off on his first voyage with no proper instruction in navigation and with only a few servants and Kuwaiti
seamen aboard, teaching himself the finer points of chart reading
and fixing his position as he went. A steam launch proved a very
different proposition from his small, single-masted yacht. There
was not much time in which to achieve mastery of the vessel,
however. After only a few days, as he cruised off the Arabian
coast, a message came over the loud hailer of a naval sloop re-
questing him to return immediately to the agency. His clerk, a
fussy, meticulous little Indian by the name of D'Mello, was waiting anxiously to apprise him of latest developments.

Another vital piece in the jigsaw of current Arabian politics
was about to fall into place. In early September the shaikh had
received an alarming letter from Husain ibn Ali, Sharif of Mecca,
a prince who owed his position and fortune to the Turks and for
whom both Mubarak and Ibn Saud entertained the utmost con-
tempt. Nevertheless, the Sharif of the Holy City was a power to
reckon with and was often spoken of in the British as well as the
Turkish press as the 'Amir of Arabia'. He told the shaikh that he
had decided to take an army into Najd to 'Put down the Wahhabi

1 Shakespear in the dress uniform of the Indian Political Service

2 Dorothea Baird, later Mrs Lakin, photographed in 1908

3 Shakespear in the single-cylinder Rover in which he made the overland journey from the Arabian Gulf, across Asia Minor and Europe, to England in 1907

4 The British Political Agency at Kuwait in 1909 after
Shakespear had taken up residence. The Political Agent's
massive Union Jack flies from the flagpole, and his yacht is
moored in front of the Agency

5 The Shaikh of Kuwait's palace with negro guard on the roof
and members of the family and staff in the courtyard

6 and 7   From the moment of his arrival in Kuwait Shakespear
began to build up a unique photographic record of gulf
and desert and of the ruling families. *Above,* a picture
taken in the desert of the future king of Saudi Arabia.
Below, Shaikh Mubarak of Kuwait (centre) with his guest,
the young amir of Najd, Ibn Saud, and members of the
Saud family

8 Ibn Saud with brothers and sons near Thaj, when the amir camped with Shakespear

9 A desert execution photographed by Shakespear in 1911

10 The main street of Riyadh in 1914

11 Ibn Saud distributes camels to his fighting men

12 Ibn Saud's army on the march, photographed by Shakespear
near Thaj in 1911

13 Breakfast with Ibn Shaalan and the ruling family of the
Ruwala at Jauf

14 Halt for coffee on the Labba road along the north-east edge of the Nafud desert

15 Shakespear's escort in the Kuwait hinterland in 1909

abuses of the House of Ibn Saud,' and that he would be accompanied on the expedition by his sons Ali, Faisal and Zeid.

Back in 1907, Colonel Knox had told the government: 'We shall never stop Mubarak from interfering in the affairs of Central Arabia.' It would have been closer to the truth to say that Mubarak's strength and influence among the Arabian princes was such that it was impossible to stop them from confiding in him and seeking his advice and support for their schemes. The sharif asked Mubarak to arrange for supplies to be sent to him at Shaqra in Washm, a strange request since it would have been necessary for the shaikh to make any such arrangement through Ibn Saud. Mubarak told Shakespear that he had no immediate intention of replying to the Turkish vassal and that he would let events take their course.

Then news arrived of a battle that was sure to arouse great interest in Constantinople and London, between the armies of Husain and Ibn Saud. A short, sharp battle had, it seemed, resulted in the rout of the sharif's army. But the sharif's men had captured Saad, the amir's favourite brother, and had retreated with him towards their own territory. Abdul Aziz had said that he valued the life of his brother more dearly than his own. To save that life on this occasion he was compelled to make the sharif a promise of an annual payment of £6,000 and to hand over money and horses, including some of Riyadh's finest war mares, immediately. There was some doubt at the time about the exact terms of the agreement forced on Ibn Saud. But, whatever they were, the world press was presented with a story of the Saudi king's abject surrender to the sharif. Both Turkey and Britain were handed a dramatic and unexpected propaganda weapon in their combined effort to restore order to the desert.

The Egyptian newspaper *Al Ahram* reported during October 1910 the course of a battle which began to look larger than Mubarak had been led to believe. According to the Egyptian newspaper a force of 20,000 men was gathered by the sharif, mostly tribesmen traditionally loyal to Ibn Saud, who had been collected on the road from Taif to Kurma. They had joined up with 5,000 of Ibn Rashid's Shammar horsemen to form an imposing army.

'It was', said *Al Ahram*, 'part of the Turkish effort to pacify Arabia.' By early November, the Sharif of Mecca was back in the Holy City, having surrendered the captured Saad to Ibn Saud and taken the booty of the forced exchange with him. He sent a message to the Sultan in Constantinople announcing that Ibn Saud had 'surrendered'.

The Times of London reported the news on October 6th: 'Following the capture of Saad, all the tribes of Najd have submitted to the Government,' it observed, demonstrating the naivety with which the world viewed Arabian politics at that time. It was still not known exactly where or when the battle had taken place. All that Shaikh Mubarak could tell Shakespear was that Ibn Saud's kingdom was intact, Husain of Mecca had withdrawn from Najd, and the forces of Ibn Rashid were on the defensive and keeping out of harm's way.

His third desert journey was the shortest of all Shakespear's excursions. It was uncomfortable but light-hearted, and it took him a stone's throw away to Zubair and Basra to the north of Kuwait.

'Beastly cold', said the first day's diary entry on January 7th, 1911. They camped south of Jahra and huddled round the coffee fire in mid-afternoon. Wind and rain made it seem like an arctic expedition. Next day was no better and they pitched their tents on the road to Raudhatain in north Kuwait. The men could hardly feel their hands and even Wali Muhammad's cooking suffered from the weather. Instead of some such delicacy as hare cooked in red wine, Shakespear on this occasion had to be content with an 'evil-looking concoction' of rice and fatty mutton, half-cooked and practically inedible. Camp III was in an exposed position on the Hamar ridge, from which they could look out to the waterway at the head of the gulf surrounding Kuwait's pancake island of Bubiyan. Their water skins froze in the night. They altered their course on the fourth day to find grazing for camels that were nearly as weary as the men they carried. After refreshing their animals they moved on to a point two miles from Zubair in Mesopotamia, and the men hurried off into the town while Shakespear stayed behind to bring his notes up to date and develop his film, for even in the freezing cold his camera was constantly in use and he never failed to take the bearing of a habitation or landmark.

The men did not return that night; next morning he mounted Dhabia and went to Zubair to find them. When he sighted them they were having an angry dispute with a crowd of locals, all of whom appeared to be taking the greatest offence at the loudly voiced accusations of Shakespear's men that they were thieves and sons of dogs. If any sense could be made of the frenzied argument it was that the men's entire belongings, including their camels, had been stolen while they were enjoying themselves in the bazaar the night before. Shakespear dragged them away from the shouting mob, sat Abdul Aziz, Ali and Wali Muhammad on Dhabia and sent them back to pack up the tents, and went off himself to find the Mayor of Zubair in order to lodge a protest. After a good deal of table thumping, the official insisted that he could not replace the stolen camels but he would punish the culprits when they were found and the animals would be returned to Kuwait. Meanwhile he made amends by placing a horse and carriage at the disposal of the Englishman. Thus Shakespear and his men made a dignified entry into Basra. The Residency steam launch was tied up in the harbour. They rounded up the crew and made themselves at home on the ship, complete with Dhabia, who resented the efforts of the men to shove her aboard but finally made a grudging way along the gang plank. She lay down and looked sick all the way back along the Shatt-al-Arab and Kuwait coast.

This was a period of some administrative pressure. The agency clerk did his best while his master was away in the desert or at sea, but there were matters which only the Political Agent could deal with. One of them was an application from the Anglo-Persian Oil Company for exploratory rights in Kuwait. Shakespear was not greatly interested; he had no wish to see his beloved desert turned into an oilfield. He discussed the request with Shaikh Mubarak and with the latter's approval informed his superiors that conditions in and around Kuwait were far too unsettled to permit of any kind of investigation at that time. None the less, several important and curious visitors came in the wake of that request, their eyes cast on the pale ground with its occasional tell-tale hint of black.

11

Among Friends

There was a second and more important journey in 1911. The British Government was anxious to hear Ibn Saud's account of the conflict with the Sharif of Mecca. The time seemed ripe for another expedition to the desert. Shakespear had already discussed with Ibn Saud the possibility of meeting at camp, where they could talk without disturbance. The amir agreed. Ibn Saud was on his way to confer with the shaikhs of the Khalifa from Al Hasa, a family with close ties with the amir and with the Shaikh of Kuwait. But another vital objective for Shakespear was to explore an intriguing and as yet little-known region bounded by the Hasa coast to the east and by the great Dahana sandbelt at the rear. It was an area known to the Greeks and Romans, for Strabo, who gained his information from Artemidorus, mentions the people of a place called 'Gerrha' situated thereabouts. The ancient historian's account gave routes which, though difficult to follow, showed the way to the 'richest of all tribes', who apparently possessed great quantities of silver.

The weather was good in late February as the caravan made its way south on Knox's 1908 route to the wells of Dhajal. The Englishman had come prepared for sport as well as exploration and politics, and the salukis were given plenty of exercise as the party made speedy progress over difficult terrain. On the sixth day out, however, rain and wind came to slow their passage. On March 2nd they made their eighth camp south-west of a salt lake which the badawin called Umm al Khawaisa and near the sweet-water well of Ghar al kahafa. Shakespear took the bearings of these landmarks and checked them on his maps. He found Knox's earlier estimates more or less correct. Next day they descended into the valley of Abu Thahir where they found Shaikh Ali ibn Khalifa at camp. The shaikh and the Englishman had already met in Kuwait and promised to meet on a hunting expedition. Now was their opportunity, and they spent a day together in the wilds with their hawks and Shakespear's salukis, and came back with a heavy load of gazelle and hares to add to the evening meal. After that pleasant interlude they marched together out of the valley and on to the wells of Hinna. They were now in remote and largely uncharted territory, and Shakespear decided to send the salukis back to Kuwait in the care of Ali and two of his badawin companions. The going was 'poor' according to his diary entry of March 6th. They were trudging through wet, muddy land when they met up with a party of Bani Khalid shaikhs who had also come to greet the Amir of Najd. Their new companions directed them to an isolated spot in the desert called Ellaimiya, as nearly as Shakespear could transliterate the badawin name, where Ibn Saud was at camp. They met up with the amir in pouring rain on March 7th. Shakespear found the handsome Arab leader as friendly, as confident and assured, as ever. His brothers and elder sons were with him, and their white tents contrasted with the distant black dots of the badawin homesteads around them.

Next morning an immense caravan moved off northwards, the war flag of Riyadh at the fore, the Saudi, Khalifa, Bani Khalid and Shakespear contingents following. They camped several miles beyond the ruins of Thaj in a dell called Musaiba, where there was grazing for the animals. But Shakespear had seen enough as he passed through Thaj to justify a return. He spent part of the first day at the amir's camp skirmishing around some of the vital political issues he was anxious to discuss with Ibn Saud, and when the time came for his host's afternoon siesta he mounted Dhabia and set off to investigate the desert township to the east, accompanied by his guides and one or two of his baggage men.

He was not disappointed. There were ruins and loose stones everywhere. He saw that one of them bore an inscription in a language that was foreign to him; nearby he found stones with similar inscriptions. He gathered them with great excitement and cleaned them. Then he sat on a large rock and copied the inscriptions into his notebook. The Arabs looked on with merriment when they found him sketching stones.

Shakespear had heard of the Greek and Roman legends of rich traders who had passed this way, and a wealthy community that was supposed to have settled in the region. There was a place not far to the north which the badu called Al Gherra, similar to the name Strabo had given to the settlement, and here at Thaj there had obviously been a township. Since no known outsider had trodden this path for several hundred years, he thought it worth recording his discovery. He supposed the inscriptions to

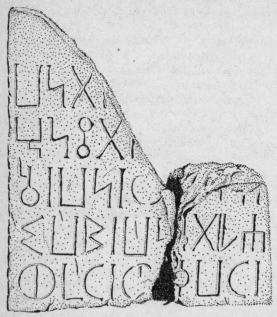

One of the stones of Thaj, found by Shakespear on his 1911 journey and recorded on film and in his notebooks

be in Himyaritic, the southern Arabian language which spread through much of the peninsula in pre-Islamic times. In fact, the inscriptions of Thaj were epitaphs, gravestone memorials in Sabaean, a closely allied semitic language used from about 800 B.C. to A.D. 450. The first such inscriptions were discovered in the Yemen in the 1830s, and similar epitaphs have since been found at Ur, Babylon and several parts of Arabia, evidence of the trade routes followed by richly laden caravans from the south before the dawn of Islam, and probably before the Christian era.

Despite their importance, the finds of Thaj (and of the nearby wells of Hinna where Shakespear stumbled on more of them) took more than ten years to come to the notice even of experts in early Arabian epigraphy. In the 1920s, the explorer Douglas Carruthers found the photographs and notes which Shakespear had left in the archives of the Royal Geographical Society.

The noted Sabaeist Margoliouth observed: 'I am not aware of any Sabaean inscription or the like having been found in the neighbourhood of Kuwait. The forms of the letters would be classed as ancient by the experts. The three which are taken as characteristic of the highest antiquity all occur. I think the epitaph is at least earlier than our era ...' It remained for later scholars and explorers to show that Thaj, though a prosperous city, was not the site of the fabled Gerrha. Neither, for that matter, was Al Gherra.

The stones and their mysterious messages were soon pushed to the back of Shakespear's mind. He had come to Thaj not for archaeological purposes but to parley with Ibn Saud, and he quickly turned his mind to the demands of duty.

The two men spent the best part of a day chatting idly over coffee, sometimes alone, at others with the family of Abdul Aziz. Then they went on a hunting expedition and exercised the amir's war mares. Ibn Saud had many sons by this time, many of badawin mothers and unknown to Shakespear, but the amir's favourites, Turki, Saud and Faisal, were usually with him and the Englishman found them lively company in the desert.

It was early evening on the second day before they began to talk in earnest. They sat in the amir's *majlis* tent, alone at first except for the slave who kept them supplied with coffee. The brothers and boys of Ibn Saud went to bed, except for Saad, who joined them, and the three men talked late into the night.

For hours on end, Abdul Aziz unfolded the repetitive story of his family and of his struggle to restore the fortunes of Al Saud. Though he knew it all by heart, Shakespear listened patiently, for it was not often that outsiders heard such things from the mouth of the king.

He told the Englishman of his relations with the Turks and his hopes for an Anglo-Arab alliance. 'We Wahhabis', said Ibn Saud, 'hate the Turks only less than we hate the Persians for the infidel practices which they have imported into the true and pure faith revealed to us in the Koran.'

As for the recent encounter with Husain's force, Ibn Saud insisted that he had not made promises apart from that of money forced by the capture of his brother, which, said the king, was the consequence of treachery by tribesmen who handed him over to the enemy to save their own skins. As soon as Saad returned to his camp in Washm he retracted his promise of an annual pension to the sharif. But his brother's presence in the enemy camp had made it difficult for him to strike as he would have wished. He was sure the Turks had put Husain up to his ridiculous excursion, and he would have liked to teach the sharif a lesson, but Saad's imprisonment had led him to make the ill-advised confession that his people were poor and ignorant and willing to accept the sultan's sovereignty. He insisted, though, that he had not himself admitted to being a vassal of the Turks: and since his Wahhabi faith forbade it he certainly did not confess to an acceptance of the Ottoman Caliphate. Saad nodded agreement as Abdul Aziz told his story.

Shakespear told his host of the allegations being made by Husain and the Turks. Ironically, he knew that his own government would be delighted to believe that Ibn Saud had finally come to his senses and accepted the authority of the Turks. He would be just as delighted to disabuse it.

They talked for three days. There was mention of meetings that had been going on for some months between Arab leaders with the idea of concerting their efforts to rid the land of the Turks. It was the first real hint of a planned rebellion in Arabia, and in the present mood of his government Shakespear knew that it was an unmentionable subject. Yet clearly the Arab leaders were seriously contemplating an uprising. Already there had been meetings between Ibn Saud and the chiefs of Muscat, Asir and Yemen. It was an interesting portent for the future, but Shakespear had no doubt as to the reaction of his own government to any such proposal. He warned the amir to tread softly, for Ibn Rashid was still strong, Husain almost sure to join the Turks, and Britain was committed to the recognition of the Ottoman authority. The response of the Turks would be swift and unmerciful.

Between talks round the coffee fire, the two men demonstrated the qualities that brought them together so powerfully. Both were quick-tempered, assured, impatient of interference, incapable of resisting a challenge. They were sympathetic companions in the desert as in politics. They took their hawks into the wilds and pitted them against each other in pursuit of the great bustard; they vied with each other in horsemanship and marksmanship; they revelled in each other's company. But over official business they were always serious and formal, each addressing the other as 'Your Excellency', though every now and again lapsing into the familiar.

As Abdul Aziz went on with his story, he underlined time and again the agreements that his forbears had made with Britain (most of them, he said, verbal agreements) in the hope of nullifying or mitigating the rule of the Turks. Now he wanted to bring those pledges and hopes to fruition; and he seemed to Shakespear to be making not so much an historical appraisal as a plea. 'I would welcome British protection,' the amir told him. And he added that he would like there to be a Political Agent in Riyadh.

It was an intensely personal exchange. Ibn Saud was utterly frank, even telling Shakespear the details of payments made to him by Ottoman authorities who made one offer after another to him and other leaders in an effort to buy their loyalty. And the Political Agent told him in turn that though they had spoken as friends it was his duty to tell his government everything that had passed between them.

'I expected that, my friend,' replied the amir.

They parted, knowing that there would be much intrigue and bloodshed before they could realize their joint hope of an alliance. They had spoken of 'revolt': though it had little meaning then, the word would have considerable currency in the not very distant future.

Before they went their separate ways, Ibn Saud west to Riyadh, Shakespear northward to Kuwait, the Arab leader repeated an earlier request to his friend to wear Arab dress in the desert.

'You are in great danger, and I shall not always be there to protect you,' he said.

'Why,' replied Shakespear, 'am I not among friends?'

His fourth desert journey covered 597 miles and took 205 hours. So far Shakespear had covered 1,397 miles, mostly over unknown territory, in his two years in the gulf.

12

Lord Morley Regrets

Shakespear's sense of personal responsibility for bringing his government round to a positive sense of involvement in Arabia was intense by now. But political ends could be achieved by example as well as by debate, and he began to view his exploratory work as a necessary and desirable part of his strategy. The journey he planned to make across Arabia occupied his mind with growing insistence. Already he had started to mark out his route; already he was talking to Cox and to Intelligence at Simla about his plans. But it looked as if others beside Leachman might beat him to it.

For the time being however there was the pressing task of writing a convincing account of his meeting with the Amir of Najd. His report, dated April 4th, 1911, was effusive, as were most of his accounts of meetings with the Amir.

'Abdul Aziz ibn Abdur Rahman al-Saud has a frank and generous nature, an impression confirmed by all the shaikhs and Badawin tribes with which I am in contact in my travels,' he wrote. He went on to outline the 'full and deep' discussion that had taken place between himself and the amir on matters of doctrine, religion and custom, and on the faith and policies of the Wahhabis. 'His reasoning was always calm and intelligent,' said the Political Agent. He reassured his chiefs of his awareness of official attitudes: 'I told the Amir that I was certain HM Government would do nothing to challenge Turkish authority in Central Arabia. I reiterated that opinion several times.'

Then he went over the events of recent months with particular reference to the Sharif of Mecca's expedition:

It was probably made at the instigation of the Turks but finding Abdul Aziz too strong for them they withdrew after an exchange of presents. But Saad, the brother of Abdul

Aziz, was treacheroulsy handed over to the enemy by the Atayba, thus hampering his ability to strike. He made no profession of being a vassal of the Sultan and being Wahhabi does not admit to the Sultan's Khalifate in Islam.

Then came the less reassuring conclusion to his report:

I would like to remark that serious consideration of the Central Arabian problem seems to be called for in the light of recent events ... All reports point to increasing unrest and hatred of Turkish pretensions. If a combination were to take place between the principal leaders in Arabia – and the fact of a serious discussion of a simultaneous revolt between men of such divergent religious tenets as the Imam Yahya and the Wahhabi ruler make such a union at least possible – I am inclined to the opinion that a revolt is not only probable but would be welcome by every tribe throughout the peninsula – From all I can learn hatred of the Turk seems to be the one idea common to all the tribes and the only one for which they would sink their differences. The strength of the Turk has always been his ability to play off one tribe against another. Now this cardinal fact has begun to penetrate the unsophisticated brain of the Arab.

It was an alarming report, for which Simla and Whitehall were by no means prepared. It was the first overt mention of the idea of Arab rebellion. The government recoiled in horror.

Shakespear's final words to his superiors were small comfort: 'I held out no hope of Government assistance for the Wahhabi power. Ibn Saud told me that he would rather have the truth from the English than the equivocation experience had taught him to expect from the Turks.'

His report deliberately played down its political substance, and was set in a low key to suit the sombre reception he knew it would receive. References to a policy of non-interference were followed by soft-pedalled appeals to reconsider attitudes in the light of possible Arab alliances embracing such divergent bedfellows as Ibn Saud and the imams of Muscat, Asir and Yemen – he dared not even suggest that things could reach the stage of an understanding between Ibn Saud and the Sharif of Mecca, though he had reason to believe that to be another possibility. So sensitive was the government to any suggestion of involvement in Turkish affairs that it reacted with anger even towards its own representatives when they tried to tell it the facts. Whitehall openly regarded the Indian Government men on the spot as meddling nuisances. The cause was not hard to detect. The Ottoman Empire was already under severe attack in Europe and North Africa, it was increasingly provoked by the Czar of Russia and King Humbert of Italy, and the British public, insofar as it had a view on the matter, was in sympathy with the Turks. The Sultanate itself had recently suffered a palace revolution. Abdul Hamid, the old sultan, had been exiled two years before and was now a familiar figure in the gambling casinos of Europe. Muhammad V was trying to infuse new life into the empire, and Britain's Ambassador at Constantinople was doing everything in his power to show the new sultan that he had the support of Britain. Anything that tended to give an opposite impression brought the wrath of the ambassador and Sir Edward Grey on the head of the offender, and on the heads of his superiors.

The twelve months following Shakespear's meeting with Ibn Saud were punctuated by the loss of all Turkey's European possessions, the Italian invasion of Ottoman Tripoli and the Dodecanese islands, and by a confrontation of British, French and German interests in Mesopotamia. He had not chosen a good moment to propound the cause of Arab freedom.

As usual, it was Mubarak who had the last word in the sharif affair. He was by no means satisfied with Ibn Saud's explanation. The old man wrote to his 'son' telling him that he must make no more foolish observations, especially to the Turkish authorities. 'At present the door to Central Arabia is shut,' he said, 'but if once it is opened, no matter how little, God knows when it may again be closed.'

He told Shakespear: 'Abdul Aziz is powerful among the badu, but he loses his temper too easily. He is unsophisticated and has no tact.'

Politically, Shakespear was the prototype man of Empire, convinced that his country ruled much of the world by a conspiracy of natural aptitude and divine ordinance. But, unlike others who saw merely that the growth of the Empire was at an end and its influence waning, he believed that its protective wing should be spread generously, and he could see no reason why Arabia, cruelly divided by the rule of Constantinople, should be denied its shelter. He set out at this stage to promote the idea of a pact between the Amir of Najd and Britain which would recognize the overall sovereignty of the Turks – for he could see no hope of ending that sovereignty altogether – but would give the Indian Government the right to intervene politically on Ibn Saud's behalf. The most important immediate aim was to prevent Turkey from setting the leaders of Riyadh and Hail at each other's throats. Hail was now under the control of a regent who was willing to talk to the Saudi chief, indeed there was evidence that Ibn Subhan was willing to accept Ibn Saud's leadership in an alliance. Shakespear saw an opportunity to bring permanent peace to the desert regions, especially if the ambitious Sharif of Mecca could be contained.

He was supported in these aims by the Resident. Percy Cox was equally convinced that if Britain left Arabia at the mercy of a weak and desperate Ottoman power, and Ibn Saud was kept short of arms while the Turks armed the sharif and Ibn Rashid, the delicate balance between the existing desert alliances could shift dramatically. Britain had to choose between preserving its own long-term interests in the gulf and elsewhere and accepting the stewardship of Turkey, which rested on the principle of divide and rule. In Cox's view neither Ibn Rashid nor the sharif was to be trusted. He and Shakespear were rapidly becoming the bane of Whitehall, and the Foreign Office, remote from the facts and dependent on its embassy at Constantinople for guidance, began to make it clear to the Government of India that its wings had to be clipped.

Social as well as political attitudes were changing fast in the early years of the twentieth century. Victorian Britain's imperial power was not so credible; communications were spreading through the world; the motor car was competing with the horse.

Shakespear and a few other officers of the Indian administration saw mechanized transport as offering a golden opportunity to carry forward the spirit of discovery and exploration that had to their way of thinking given vigour and point to the idea of Empire. In fact several officers in India were already talking of flying and one had become the proud owner of an aeroplane. But most had to be content with cars. Such men sought ways of using their vehicles to traverse territories like Arabia where the camel and horse had reigned for thousands of years. While Shakespear planned his future journey by camel across the Arabian steppes, his friend Captain Fraser Hunter of the Indian Survey Department applied to make a motorized crossing of Arabia from Madina to the gulf, thus anticipating much of Shakespear's proposed route, though in reverse. He intended, in addition, to carry on across the Rub al-Khali, the Empty Quarter, which no westerner had so far crossed even by camel. It was an impossible venture, for there were no roads in Central Arabia, and a car was sure to sink into soft sands to be buried in the wilds when a desert gale blew. But the application was serious. In March 1910 the Viceroy had sought permission for Captain Hunter to make the trip. The Secretary of State for India, Lord Morley, approved. But when the Foreign Secretary found out and asked the opinion of his man in Constantinople, Sir Gerard Lowther, the conflict of interest between the India and Foreign Offices, seldom far from the surface in matters affecting Arabia, broke out into a battle royal. After several appeals by the Viceroy and a compromise on the part of Captain Hunter, who revised his route so as to avoid all sensitive areas, offered to pay his own costs and merely sought the 'moral support' of the government, his application was turned down flat. A telegram was sent to the Viceroy: 'Lord Morley regrets.'

While all this was going on, however, a remarkable and unsuspecting young Dane was giving rise to a volley of communication between Copenhagen, London, Constantinople, Bushire, Simla and Kuwait. Shakespear was caught in the crossfire.

It had begun back in 1909, the year of Shakespear's arrival in Kuwait, with an application by the Danish Royal Geographical Society to Britain's ambassador in Copenhagen for permission for an expedition to visit the Persian Gulf 'and lands adjoining' sometime in 1910, with the objective of carrying on the scientific studies of the great Danish explorer Carsten Niebuhr in the eighteenth century. The ambassador was instructed by Sir Edward Grey to call on the Danish Geographical Society and make vigorous enquiries as to its exact intentions. The Danes were polite and patient. They gave the British Government as much information as they could, insisting that the aims of the expedition were entirely scientific. Such was the uncertainty of foreign policy in London at that time, however, it was clearly impossible for them to believe that the Danes merely wished to make botanical and geological surveys. The debate between a highly respectable Danish Royal Geographical Society and a highly suspicious British Government went on for nearly two years. In the end – after receiving a memorandum on July 13th, 1911, informing them that H.M. Government could afford no protection or safeguards – the Danes gave up the unequal struggle. But neither they nor Britain had bargained for the enterprise of a youthful member of the proposed party by the name of Barclay Raunkiaer. He decided to make the journey alone, knowing nothing of Arabia, unable to speak the language and with not so much as a letter of introduction.

He was just the kind of man to appeal to Shakespear. On February 1st, 1912, the Residency diary noted:

A traveller arrived on 29 January overland from Basra. He carried a letter of recommendation to Shaikh Mubarak from the Wali of Basra describing him merely as a traveller of Danish nationality wishing to go to Hofuf. His name is Barclay Raunkiaer and he is a naturalist explorer under the auspices of the RDGS. He speaks English well but knows very little Arabic and is accompanied by one servant interpreter only, a Baghdad Christian. He wears Arabic costume and is at present lodged with the Shaikh.

When he told the Resident of Raunkiaer's unexpected appearance Shakespear received the reply: 'Please give Shaikh of Kuwait a hint that Government of India do not desire that Danish explorer should be given any facilities.' The Political Agent was speechless at the timid, petty reaction of his chief. He knew, though, that Cox spoke not for himself but for his superiors.

While the government looked on with trepidation – especially when it heard that Raunkiaer had met the Wali of Basra in the International Hotel and that they spoke together in German – Shakespear remained calm, recording in the diary: 'He is still here but hopes to start for Buraida, Anaiza and Riyadh, and thence to Hofuf and Bahrain ... He is ill-equipped for his task. Will travel with the next large caravan to Buraida. He carries a letter to Ibn Saud so should achieve his objective without too much difficulty.'

The Political Agent and the shaikh bade the Dane a fond farewell. They admired his courage and resolution, though Shakespear could not help feeling a twinge of envy as others evaded the British Government net and passed into Central Arabia while he, confidant and friend of the King of Najd, was compelled to wait, in the ever-diminishing hope that he would be allowed to follow them.

He never saw Barclay Raunkiaer again. But in July 1912 the Royal Danish Geographical Society expressed its thanks to Britain through the ambassador for the help given its unofficial explorer especially by Captain Shakespear in Kuwait and Captain D. L. R. Lorimer, one of two brothers in the Indian Political Service, who was in Bahrain. The Foreign Secretary sent the message on to the Secretary of State for India with a rider of his own: 'In view of the declared policy of HM Government to discourage Herr Raunkiaer's expedition, I should be glad to learn the precise nature of the assistance rendered by Captain Shakespear and Captain Lorimer.'

It fell to Percy Cox to haul the two men over the coals.

'Oh dear, I have fallen from grace again,' said Shakespear.

13

Dorothea and the King Emperor

When he was not contemplating the problems of Ibn Saud and Arabia, Shakespear turned to consider his own affairs. He was in his thirty-third year. Dorothea was past her thirtieth birthday. They had known each other for four years, had met on two occasions and had corresponded regularly and with mutual warmth. Yet there had been no mention of engagement and, though their meetings had been lively and affectionate, she was usually chaperoned. Their devotion – for devotion there certainly was – found itself from the start at the mercy of distance and his growing obsession with the challenge of the Arabian desert. A woman of Dorothea's qualities of looks and wit was unlikely to wait for ever on his tasks and ambitions.

Now he was anxious to see her again, and a golden opportunity to do so presented itself.

King Edward had died the year before, and the new monarch, George V, was to be crowned in June at Westminster Abbey. It had been announced also that the king would visit India later in the year so that for the first time in history a British sovereign would accede to the title Emperor of India in the presence of millions of his subjects in the sub-continent. Shakespear decided to go to England for the coronation and then proceed to India with his car so that he could motor from Bombay to Delhi for the second leg of the event. Whereas many British officials in the East stayed at their posts and planned local celebrations and durbars, he would attend both coronation events even though his finances were in bad repair at this time. He was still dependent on an allowance from his parents. But he would see Dorothea again and that was justification enough for the cost of the journey.

He arrived in good time for the celebrations. By May 1911 the streets of Britain were gay with bunting and loyal slogans, and a belligerent world, if it did not entirely forget its differences and antagonisms, compromised by sending its monarchs and chief ministers to London.

Since the death of Colonel Baird in 1908, Dorothea's family had been in the habit of spending the summer in London, where they rented a house in Upper Berkeley Street. Thus Shakespear was able to spend a good deal of time with them and to see Dorothea almost daily during his stay. He went to Brighton, of course, to see his parents, but he spent most of his time in London. Again he was joined by his young brother, who was now engaged to Winifred, and the Bairds and Shakespears were united once more. Dorothea took her 'Consul' off to Aldershot where Douglas Baird was temporarily stationed and where a friend ran a flying school. Shakespear had wanted to try his hand at piloting an aeroplane for some time. Now the opportunity came his way and he took to the air with as much enthusiasm as to water and desert. After a few hours' instruction he went 'solo' and in a matter of days was flying competently. Here was another outlet for his energy and his urge to flirt with danger. He began to toy with the idea of using a flying machine to get around the gulf.

The Shakespear parents came up to London for the big event and they and the Baird family joined the millions who crowded the streets of the capital on June 22nd to see the royal procession wend its way to Westminster Abbey. But if it was a happy occasion for the world at large, it marked a sad moment in the lives of Dorothea and Shakespear.

When the celebrations were over and he and Dorothea were together in the calm of a London restored to its daily routine, some of the fire and gaiety of their relationship seems to have seeped away. There is no reliable evidence that their affection had cooled by this time; indeed, the only evidence available suggests the opposite, that they retained a deep and lasting affection for each other. But the carefree enjoyment, the laughter and shared sense of fun which characterized earlier meetings was absent. He was certainly a changed man, subdued, captive perhaps of another passion.

He had to make a choice between a woman and duty, and when it came to the moment of decision his attitude seems to have been desultory and perhaps selfish. She, certainly, had not lost interest, though she had several suitors. Whatever the cause, 1911 was the year of the parting of the ways. The position could not have been made easier for Dorothea by the fact of her younger sister's engagement to his brother. Whether she forced the issue is not known, and her own testimony in later life was contradictory.

It is tempting to try to explain Shakespear's attitude to the single love affair of his life in Freudian terms. Emotional deprivation in youth? An Oedipus complex perhaps? He was certainly greatly influenced by his mother and his attachment to her was strong. But if psychological excursions are a pleasant biographical indulgence they seldom throw any more light on the dead than the living.

If Browning was right, and 'Love likes stratagem and subterfuge,' then love found a poor pupil in Shakespear. His singlemindedness was his strength as an explorer, as a leader of men in the depths of the desert; but it was his weakness in politics and personal relationships. Even among his colleagues in the Indian Political Service he was unable to come to terms with the notion of flexibility. He simply could not understand the man who would temporize as a political stratagem; who would bend a personal belief to the convolutions of governmental policy. He crossed swords with many of his contemporaries who saw more than one useful road to an objective. He was incapable of deviousness or subtlety.

His singleness of purpose, his belief in the cause he had adopted in Arabia, were qualities that Dorothea understood well and encouraged. Had he been content to finish his term of duty in Kuwait and then take up an appointment in India or Persia, she could have gone with him, and would almost certainly have done so gladly. There was no way in which she could join his Arabian ventures or contribute to his ambition to explore the interior. But she understood.

It was the singular irony of Shakespear's life that he met, by so slight a chance, a woman who could appreciate his ambition and who even fostered his devotion to Arabia. Perhaps, when she came to realize the strength of his involvement in Arabia, she gave way to the mysterious pull of that 'haggard land' as Burton called it. Perhaps she recognized, with Burton, the 'real pain' of the traveller 'returning to the turmoil of civilisation'. There is no doubt that Shakespear looked with diminished enthusiasm on the outside world once he had started to explore the desert. She was not the person to stand in his way, however much she may have suffered. She never forgot. In later life she made different assertions to her daughter Joan. On one occasion she said, 'I gave him up in the end,' on another, 'I lost him to the desert.'

He left Southampton in September, accompanied by the Rover. Duty and romance had become uneasy partners, and now that he had abdicated one he would pursue the other with vigour, if with some misgivings. The Delhi Durbar promised to be the greatest show the Empire had ever staged, or so the newspapers said, and he believed them. There was also the prospect of the long drive from Bombay, 900 miles of road which nobody had attempted since the motor club run of 1905. But even now he began to think affectionately of the desert and of his well-trained team waiting for him back in Kuwait.

The vast site of Old Delhi was divided into lots suitable to house hundreds of thousands of visitors of every complexion and priority. Princes and nobles of India, maharajahs and maharanees, nawabs and begums; visiting royalty and the officers and administrators of the Viceroy; political figures of Britain and the Empire; every serving regiment of the army; all had to be accommodated and provided for.

The military camps, even a press camp, were loaded high with supplies. Mountains of grain, tea, coffee, vegetables and butter rose from every section of the Bawari Plain at the foot of the Delhi ridge. A contemporary record estimated 170,000 lbs of *ghi*, or clarified butter, for the Indian troops alone, along with 728,000 lbs of onions and 18,000 lbs of jam. Hotels were booked to capacity as the day approached. 'The streets', said the newspaper, the *Englishman*, 'are swarming with Americans.' And there were reports that the durbar was likely to be besieged by motor cars. Even the Viceroy, Lord Hardinge, had been seen in one of the 'wretched things', as another newspaper put it.

On December 2nd, 1911, the *Times of India* observed: 'Nine years have elapsed since Lord Curzon announced the Coronation of King Edward. Lord Curzon's was an elephant Durbar ... now the regal beast is to be replaced by the motor car.' And went on: 'The Durbar has swallowed up every other topic with the promptitude and completeness of Aaron's rod.' The press waxed eloquent and the crowds descended on Delhi.

Shakespear was making his contribution to the change of scene at that very time. He was on his way from Bombay in the Rover, a car that appeared capable of the roughest and most testing journeys – journeys of almost inconceivable length in those pioneering days – with no more demand on its owner than an occasional tyre change or the renewal of a sparking plug. He drove all day and usually slept for a few hours in the open by night, for there were no resting places on the route. He completed the journey in just under six weeks, overcoming the same problems and hazards as had confronted the competitive drivers of the Delhi–Bombay run six years before. But he was alone for the entire 900 miles.

Shakespear found a berth with his old colleagues of the Bengal Lancers and from the moment of arrival photographed everything in sight.

The king and queen left England in November, and while they were at sea the entire army and civil service were at work putting the finishing touches to a mighty pageant of welcome and homage. It was an immense task of organization and timing, marred only by a fire on the durbar site itself caused by fireworks catching alight in one of the storage tents.

December 7th was the day set for the royal arrival. Every space in Delhi and for miles around the city was occupied. Every building and vantage point was taken up. The fortunate were seated in comfort. The great mass of onlookers jostled for standing room. The red battlements of Shah Jehan's great fortress dominated the scene and made the best lookout of all for the many hundreds who occupied it, for they could see out across the vast tented plain and the River Jumna beyond. All eyes turned to the bridge that spanned the river. At last it came into sight: slowly the white-painted imperial train pulled into the newly constructed station. Cannon and musket boomed and crackled in salute. First to greet the king and queen were veterans of the Indian Mutiny, native soldiers wearing the red-and-white ribbons which proclaimed their part in that salutary rebellion. Then the royal party went into the red fort where the ruling chiefs of India were lined up to receive them. The introductions completed, the king mounted his white horse and began the processional march through Delhi, escorted by troops of all the regiments, British and native, and none more splendid than the Imperial Cadet Corps, princes and sons of princes, in uniforms of white and gold with light-blue waistcoats, mounted on black horses. Behind the escort came the Lords of India, nearly 600 of them, princes of Hyderabad and Baroda, Gwalior and Jaipur and countless other states and principalities, each with his own escort. As they arrived at the fort the king and queen were received in respectful silence. Then, as they went through the Delhi Gate at the head of the procession to the durbar camp, cheering started from the thousands of children seated along the route, their colourful turbans swaying so that from a distance they looked like tulips blowing in the breeze. And as the children's shrill cheers were heard they were joined by a million voices and Delhi exploded in a tumult of noise and a riot of colour. The royal procession wound its way along Chandni Chauk, 'Moonlight Street', the richest thoroughfare in India, and ornamented nobles rose from their seats and bowed and chanted loyal greetings. A crowd of natives gathered at the great Golden Mosque from the steps of which Nadir Shah had watched his Persian troops butcher the citizens of Delhi, and they cheered loudly and tried to rush forward to touch the king. And so the procession, several miles long, wound its way to the Ridge of Delhi and the *pandal* at its head, where the British of India, senior officers and administrators and their families, gathered to pay their respects. They presented their loyal address: 'We welcome Your Imperial Majesty as the first Sovereign of all India who has appeared on Indian soil. In this ancient city, full of historic memories, many famous Kings and Emperors have kept regal state; and the noble monuments of past glories which survive attest their greatness ... Loyalty to the Sovereign is pre-eminently an Indian virtue, inculcated by sages and preceptors from times immemorial; and in Your Imperial Majesty's wide dominions, your Imperial Majesty has no subjects more loyal and faithful than the inhabitants of British India ...' And so on ...

The king made a brief reply and then the procession moved on to the vast tented encampment. As the royal party and its escort approached, the princes of India who had remained on the ridge unfurled their personal ensigns to form a silken backdrop of gold and silver, each flag emblazoned with the arms of its household, shimmering in the sun. And as the emperor's contingent moved on to the main durbar site, the chiefs of India moved slowly along the skyline beyond the flagstaff of the great fort until they disappeared from sight at the furthermost spur of the ridge. On the Bawari Plain below, the royal standard of England unfurled from the highest flagstaff of all, and a great chant was set up: 'God save the King. God save the King.'

The *Times of India* delivered what for the moment was the final aside: 'What curious questions people ask nowadays! The Raj is Raja, what else could we be thinking of him? We do not think of making and unmaking the sun or the moon, the Ganges of the Godawary, God made them, and He made the Raja.'

Men were not to know then, in the excitement and pride of the Coronation Durbar, that this was to be the last great fling of the Raj, that from then on it was to be a downhill journey.

Shakespear called on Douglas Baird, now aide-de-camp to Lord Haig, the Inspector General of Cavalry, while he was in Delhi. Baird would have welcomed his adventurous friend as a brother-in-law. As it was, 'Shako', Henry Shakespear, was preparing to marry his other sister. 'The Consul' went back to Arabia, the splendour of Empire fresh in his mind's eye and captured graphically on his photographic plates.

14

Time of Trial

Quiet was usually the prelude to a storm in Arabia. When he arrived back in Kuwait at the end of January 1912 Shakespear was able to attend to the minor administrative tasks that had piled up in his absence and to concentrate on map projections for future journeys without the customary interruptions. The Resident seemed to be occupied with matters outside his parish and even the badu and Shaikh Mubarak were quiescent.

He was able to carry out some urgent repairs to his yacht, which had laid aground unattended for some months since he had taken command of the *Lewis Pelly*. The Kuwaiti boat-builders and fishermen brought him into a world far removed from the rigours of desert exploration and the hothouse of Arab politics. These men were at peace with themselves and they sang cheerfully as they went about their work under temporary straw roofs that protected them and their craft from the sun. He liked to work alongside them. They did not use drawings in the making of their beautiful craft, for each man's skill was learnt from his father and he knew exactly what to do. Wood brought from Africa by the dhows of the Kuwaiti merchants was cut with great care and expertness so that each plank fitted exactly to its partners and vessels took shape as though their forms were works of nature rather than of man. Shakespear watched attentively as carpenters and riggers went about their tasks, and he listened to their talk, learning much of the arts of seamanship and boat-building from them. He worked with an elaborate tool kit, brace-and-bit, ratchet screw-drivers and gleaming saws and spanners; they with ancient weapons such as the bow-drill. But he could not get on as fast or achieve as fine a finish as the men around him. He was increasingly drawn by the sea, but the desert still beckoned, as did Shaikh Mubarak.

Shaikh Mubarak was active again by February. He had announced a plan to build a *madrasah* – a modern school with facilities for teaching languages and other subjects as well as the Koran. The *ulema* of Egypt and Mecca were approached and asked to supply teachers and the shaikh was personally conducting fund-raising activities which could only be described as extortionate. Some of the merchants who were being squeezed the most protested loudly, but in the end Mubarak raised the money and building work began. A year before, another enterprising scheme, an American mission establishment, had brought an advance in medical care to the shaikh's medieval land, and the old ruler began to see himself as a social reformer. He talked to Shakespear at great length, outlining his schemes and seeking advice on matters of finance, education and health. The Political Agent was not vitally interested in such things but he listened politely. In any case he soon found useful allies in dealing with the shaikh's reforms. Two of the senior medical officers at the American Mission, Dr Paul Harrison and Dr C. S. G. Mylrea, an Englishman who had become involved with the Dutch Reformed Church of America, were only too keen to encourage Mubarak's sudden concern with advancement in education and health and they took on themselves many of the day-to-day problems of the shaikh's schemes. There were, however, other administrative matters that he could not shrug off. The shaikh was ruthless in dealing with opposition and every now and again his actions caused a storm. Over the years he had sensed many a real or imaginary plot to take his life and had sent numerous relatives into exile, including his own son and heir, Salim, who had adopted what his father regarded as an heretical version of the faith; he was summarily despatched to Basra where he joined several other exiled members of Kuwait's ruling family, the Sabah. Towards the end of 1911, the shaikh uncovered another supposed plot, this time involving one of the richest of Kuwait's merchants, Saqar al Ghanim, and several of his own nephews. The latter were sent to join Salim at Basra but Al Ghanim was put in prison.

The shaikh turned a deaf ear to every representation made on their behalf, and gradually the protestors turned to Shakespear for help because of his influence with Mubarak. Salim al-Badr, brother of the shaikh's secretary, came over from Basra to plead for the nephews, who insisted that they were innocent of any

attempt on his life. He was sent away by Mubarak and so he asked
the Political Agent to help. Shakespear learned for himself the
fate of the unfortunate Saqar al Ghanim. He was, it seemed, being
tortured mercilessly. The victim and his family, among the most
respected merchants and boat-owners in the gulf, were close
friends of Shakespear's and had shown him a good deal of
hospitality. He told the shaikh that he had gone far enough with
his ridiculous and unfounded suspicions and that he should
release the prisoner. To inflame Shakespear's anger, it was
announced that a delegation of Turks was on the way from Basra
to present Mubarak with the Order of Medjidie for his efforts in
raising money to help repair the damage to Constantinople
caused by fire the previous year. The Political Agent had been
away when the subscription was opened, but now he was able to
protest vigorously. It was the last straw in a series of disputes
between the two men. Shakespear's angry response to the ruler's
implacable determination to go his own way, was to tell him that
if he wanted to discuss matters affecting his own interests or those
of H.M. Government he could call at the agency in future.
Shakespear would not be visiting the shaikh's palace. It was not
the first squabble of the kind between these two uncompromising
men. Nor was it to be the last. On another occasion they were
reconciled by a tragi-comic drama at sea. Shakespear spent much
of the time he devoted to the Political Agency complaining
bitterly of the lateness of the British India mail steamers. This time
the ship was later than usual and he went out in his own yacht to
give the captain a piece of his mind. As he drew alongside the
'mail' an Arab vessel cut across his bow and tried to take up a
berth between him and the ship. Shakespear grabbed the offending
Arab, lifted him high over his head and threw him towards the
water. But the unfortunate man fell short and was impaled on the
Englishman's boat hook. There was nothing for it but to go to the
shaikh and tell him the sad story. Mubarak's response was not
unexpected; he even allowed himself the rare luxury of a smile.
'If impaling my men brings you and me together, my friend, you
can impale one every day,' he said.

Shakespear decided to go off to the desert rather than sacrifice
other Kuwaitis to the old man's whim. Just as he was about to
leave, however, Lord Lamington, an important figure in the
British administration, decided to visit Kuwait from Bushire. It

was an unpropitious moment. The hot season had come early, tempers were frayed, the shaikh had gone off to his island resort of Failaka in high dudgeon, and the Political Agent was about to depart in the direction of the Shaq depression. Shakespear, with his customary and cavalier disregard of protocol, pointed his caravan towards As Shaq and left the ruler's son Jabir and Dr Harrison of the American Mission to receive the visitor.

On March 24th they made their way south-west via the familiar signpost of Sirra to Wara Hill, on to Khabra Dawish and then down into the valley of the depression that they had come to know well. His personal and political anxieties of the past few months were washed away, magically, as Shakespear surveyed his devoted team. Abdul Aziz his camel man had greeted him as though he was his own father when he returned from India. So had Mathi, his new head *rafiq* who replaced poor Khalaq. And his other servants, Ghanim and Hadi and Wali Muhammad and his general factotum, little Awayd – all were delighted to see him back. They had forged a close camaraderie over the 1,400 miles they had covered together, mapping and charting as they went.

If Dhabia had been overjoyed at seeing her master back she had not shown it. She got up off her haunches as if to greet him and then lay down again and refused to budge. Now she was back in the desert, though, she behaved like the brave lady of earlier travels, frisky and as capricious as ever, but willing to go on without water or food for days on end and to find a burst of speed when it was needed. Shalwa, as ever, surveyed the scene from his master's wrist, impatient to take to the sky. The salukis followed Abdul Aziz on a short hunting expedition while Shakespear and the others made their way along the Shaq towards Khabra Dalayil and then on to the wells of Al Kaa at the northern end of the depression. From there they made their way to Kuwait's northern escarpment, As Zor, where they camped and made the best of hot weather tempered by a cool sea breeze. They climbed down from the escarpment to the sea and bathed. Shakespear had asked one of his seafaring friends in Kuwait to meet him along the coast but the boat failed to turn up and they made their way along the beach to Khawaisat. There he sighted the boat that had come to pick him up and he swam across a mud bank to get to it.

Tempers were still on the boil when Shakespear returned in the first week of April but he and the shaikh were forced to come to a truce. Admiral Sir Alexander Bethell, Commander-in-Chief of the Royal Navy in eastern waters, was to visit Kuwait shortly to invest the shaikh with a K.C.I.E., Britain's reply to the Turkish award. Shakespear and Shaikh Jabir received the admiral as he came ashore and took him to the palace, where the Political Agent relayed his remarks in Arabic and the old man was made a Knight Commander of the Most Eminent Order of the Indian Empire, entitled to a fifteen-gun salute.

Perhaps the knighthood softened Mubarak, or perhaps the temporary adjustment of his relations with Shakespear had an effect; at any rate, he released Al Ghanim a few days later, but the merchant was in poor health and his eyesight was destroyed.

When the time came for the annual celebration of the king's birthday on June 3rd, the shaikh and the Political Agent were still not well disposed towards each other. In the past Shakespear had turned the celebration of the royal birthday into the social event of the year, to which the European community came from far and wide along the gulf and the principalities and towns of southern Mesopotamia, and they were joined by the few Europeans of Kuwait. But the 1912 party was a subdued affair. It was at this time that he was being hauled over the coals for his complicity in helping Raunkiaer across the desert. The shaikh had returned to Failaka Island where he waited to receive his son and heir, Salim, who had been forgiven his religious unorthodoxy and was returning from exile in Basra. The agency flagstaff was dressed, the men of Kuwait were invited and alms distributed as was the custom; but Shakespear gave what he regarded as the worst party of his life.

By the time of Admiral Sir Alexander Bethell's visit in June, the desert had stirred from its lethargy. News came of tribal conflict between the Muntafiq, the Dhaffir and Shammar. More significantly, rumour had it that some old established tribal loyalties were changing. Ibn Dawish's Mutair had sided with the Shammar, bitter enemies till now, and Ibn Dawish and Ibn Rashid were said to be in league. Dhaidan ibn Hithlain, chief of the Ajman, whose loyalty was often in doubt, was in conference with Ibn Khalifa, the mutasarrif of Ibn Saud's territory of Al Hasa at present occupied by the Turks. There were ominous signs, too, that the Turks were active. Their garrison at Basra had been reinforced of late, and the most ubiquitous figure in Arabian politics, Sayid Talib, a wealthy merchant and deputy of Basra, was in Constantinople and by all accounts receiving a warm welcome there. The Resident was worried. Perhaps he did not know that Britain and Turkey were at that time hammering out a new Accord, designed to force Ibn Saud to recognize once and for all the suzerainty of the Ottoman. If he did know he had not told Shakespear.

Meanwhile Ibn Saud was not allowing the schemes of other men to overtake him. Soon after their meeting, the Mutasarrif of Hasa's and Ibn Hithlain's men attacked a Saudi encampment. Reprisal was swift and vicious. The camp of Ibn Khalifa was burned to the ground. Hundreds of tents were destroyed and many of their occupants killed. And three thousand camels were taken in lieu of payment for damage inflicted on Ibn Saud's camp.

There was a considerable need for Shakespear and Mubarak to repair their quarrel, for only the old Shaikh of Kuwait could untangle the web that was being woven in the desert. In July, the shaikh's hand was forced by the discovery that his yacht was rotting because nobody had thought to clean out the bilges. He came to Shakespear very nearly in tears, for his yacht was his proudest possession. In the end it had to be sent to India for overhaul, but it brought the intransigent pair together again. Mubarak claimed to be ignorant about the recent events in Al Hasa and the alleged alliance between the Mutair and Ibn Rashid. But he and the Shaikh of Muhammerah would be meeting Sayid Talib on his return from Constantinople and the shaikh hoped to find out from him if the Turks were behind the strange happenings of recent weeks. That would not be until late August, however.

Craufurd was over from India and the Kuwaiti fleet was away at sea. Shakespear and his friend decided to take the *Lewis Pelly* and follow the fishermen to the pearl banks.

Kuwait itself was quiet and lifeless. The thermometer registered 110° or more by day. Here and there a donkey or camel trudged through the town with its burden of *arfaj* or water skins. At night the men who remained slept on rooftops, for it was too hot to stay indoors. But most of the men were away with the fleet, for in the pearling season nearly everyone became a sailor or a diver.

The *Lewis Pelly* steamed into the gulf on July 31st. They were in no hurry. Pearling would go on for two months yet. The fleet's return would be the signal for a great festival of welcome and the shaikh would go out to meet the men and their haul, the life-blood of the town. Shakespear and Craufurd proposed to cruise lazily around the islands and across to Bahrain, and then to join up with the returning fleet in September. Coffee and sweet tea were served through the long hot days. Meals were washed down with plenty of wine. His desert companions did not care for the sea and so the crew was made up of townsmen and a sea-dog by the name of Ali ibn Nasir, who took the helm. Shakespear consulted his navigational charts every now and again and shouted instructions to the bridge, but they were studiously ignored for Ali knew where he was going and did not trust men who steered by charts. A blue sky and gentle breeze accompanied them.

Standish Craufurd, later to become the 5th Baronet of Kilbirney and a brigadier-general, was a short, stocky, peppery man, very different in make-up from his host. A brave and resourceful soldier, related through his mother to the Gorts of military renown, he had no time for mechanization or new-fangled ideas. He never learned to drive a car properly, despite Shakespear's attempts to prod him, and to the end of his days he urged on a vehicle as though he was riding a charger into battle. He was, however, vastly interested in Shakespear's desert journeys and much admired his friend's matter-of-fact accounts of intrepid excursions and encounters with the desert tribes. As an Intelligence officer Craufurd's main concern was with gun-running in the gulf, but the army command in India was also anxious to make full use of the Political Agent's knowledge of the topography and dispositions of the tribes in eastern Arabia and to bring up to date its sketchy maps, mostly compiled by Captain Hunter on the strength of information derived from Knox's routes and from two significant journeys made by Percy Cox into the interior of Oman in 1901 and 1906. The frequent meetings and leisurely sea journeys were occasioned by more than a desire to share the cool breezes and the relaxation of ocean voyages. Doubtless, Shakespear received Intelligence briefings during these lengthy get-togethers as well as passing on useful information.

They had been at sea for two days. A vista of peace and leisure stretched before them. They relaxed on deck, looking across to the island of Kubbar on their port side and out into a hazy, motionless distance. The water was calm and the troubled affairs of men in London and India and Arabia seemed far off and trivial. Shakespear looked idly to stern, and saw a puff of smoke on the horizon. His heart sank, for he had seen distant puffs of smoke before when he had been minding his own business at sea. Usually they came from H.M.S. *Sphinx*, a naval vessel which acted as liaison between the Resident and the Royal Navy in the gulf. Cox always had a rough idea where his man could be contacted at sea, though the desert was usually safe from his messengers. On earlier occasions the first lieutenant of H.M.S. *Sphinx* merely conveyed the Resident's instruction by loud hailer. This time he came alongside and handed him a wire: 'Return immediately. Cox.'

They turned course for Bushire across the water. But they did not hurry. Why should they? The alarm was almost certainly due to the desert meetings between Ibn Saud and other Arab chiefs which had been going on when they left Kuwait, and to the return of Sayid Talib from Constantinople. Shakespear could not understand the attitude of people who claimed to stand by a policy of non-interference in Central Arabia, and who yet jumped like scalded cats whenever the Arabs acted to determine their own policies.

As he suspected, the Government was in a state of jitters over reported desert meetings which seemed to anticipate the schemes of London and Constantinople. The two events were not unconnected and the Foreign Office was taking an unusually keen interest in the proceedings. Shakespear had already told the Resident, who in turn had told the government, that if the Arab leaders were left to their own devices they would unite in an effort to rid their country of the Turk. Now the three most important figures in the drama, Ibn Saud, the sharif and Ibn Subhan, the Regent of Hail, were conferring to that end, and the Sultan of Turkey, astutely aware of the danger, had approached Britain with the suggestion of an Accord or Convention which would give mutual recognition to the rights of the Ottoman in Central Arabia and Hijaz and to Britain in the gulf.

Ibn Saud would be recognized as Mutasarrif of Najd and Britain's part of the deal was to elicit Mubarak's support in bringing together the other princes of Arabia in friendly accord with the Ottoman power. Turkey for its part would withdraw from the Hasa coast and permit Ibn Saud to reoccupy his lands. It was not the first time that the sultan had gone with the prevailing wind in Arabia and Shakespear doubted that it would be the last. He doubted, too, whether Ibn Saud would take kindly to the title of Mutasarrif, thus recognizing the overall authority of the Turk.

The Resident told him to talk to Shaikh Mubarak as soon as he could, to find out what Sayid Talib was up to, and keep a close eye on the tribal shaikhs.

The shaikh was away again on Failaka Island in late August. Shakespear and Craufurd took the *Lewis Pelly* across to his holiday resort, where the Political Agent learned that Ibn Subhan was having trouble with his own family at Hail and was not expected to survive a new power struggle in which the hand of Turkey was barely concealed. As for Sayid Talib, he had arrived back at Basra with an escort of Turkish naval vessels and he was proposing to visit Ibn Saud as soon as he could contact the amir. Mubarak's private Intelligence service was the best in Arabia; there was not much that he did not know.

Other matters called for Shakespear's attention as the year progressed.

There was more trouble between the Foreign and India Offices over travel in Arabia. Over both political and ordinary, everyday issues, these two departments of the British administration behaved as though they represented opposing powers. The right hand seldom knew what the left was doing. Leachman was once again the culprit. He had gained the support of the Royal Geographical Society for another exploratory journey, but such support did not carry much weight with an administration which was particularly keen to keep the peace with Turkey. The paths of Shakespear and Leachman crossed repeatedly in Arabia. They had some curious qualities in common, not the least of which was an aptitude for upsetting authority. Strangely they never met. In September the Foreign Office had repeated its opposition to any officer travelling in Turkish Arabia. In October, Leachman made a direct appeal to Sir Percy Cox – who had been knighted in the Coronation Honours List – to aid his plans. Arnold T. Wilson, later to achieve fame as the historian of the gulf and then Second Assistant Resident, wrote to Shakespear on October 26th, 1912: 'We have had a request from Leachman. Cox thinks we should do everything possible, privately, to help him, but before doing anything he [Cox] thinks we should mention the matter to you as he knows you have ambitions in that direction.'

Shakespear's reply was terse and unhelpful:

I don't exactly burn with affection or admiration for Leachman after his masquerade here ... Judging from Leachman's previous trips and what I have heard of him (I have never met him) he will probably attempt the present trip again in disguise ... as to which I have the strongest objection so far as the badawin tribes around Kuwait are concerned. They trust me more-or-less and have become used to me knocking about the place as a 'sahib' who does not wish to pinch their country ... Raunkiaer the Dane, though he admittedly wore kaffiya and abba, could not be disguised and did not speak Arabic ... Lastly, I haven't forgotten my fall from grace re. the Dane, though the Resident wrote very nicely to the Government in his official letter.

Sir Percy wrote back in conciliatory mood, on December 21st: ' ... one necessarily has a fellow feeling for these wanderers, and realises the Quixoticism of discouraging our own men, while we assist foreigners.'

Before Shakespear could raise further objections, Leachman had settled the argument. He was several steps ahead of everyone. Some time before, Cox had wired Damascus. He had a feeling that Leachman might be in the desert while officialdom was deciding whether he should be allowed to travel. The consul at Damascus informed the Resident that Leachman had left Damascus on December 3rd, making in an easterly direction, 'whence he goes SSE to map the route between Najd and Basra'.

It was mortifying for Shakespear, who already had much of that route marked out in his notebook. But he began to realize that a dog-in-manger approach was not going to get him very far. He wrote to the Resident asking if his earlier letter could be regarded as private and not be put on file. 'I will treat it as demi-official and place it on record,' replied Cox. 'I presume you have no objection.'

On December 23rd, Shaikh Mubarak told Shakespear that there was an English traveller in the desert. He wanted to know who it was. Ibn Saud had sent horsemen to fetch the wanderer to him.

'I hope he doesn't play the fool or disregard what Ibn Saud tells him,' exclaimed the Political Agent. 'He will certainly get into trouble if he does.'

On Christmas day, Mubarak told him that the European had arrived at Buraida accompanied by a servant and interpreter and that they had been there for some twenty days. He had been taken to Ibn Saud's camp and was well received and hospitably treated. His route had been impressive, from the Hamad in the north to Riyadh, covering some of the most difficult and little-known regions between. By the New Year, Shakespear had changed his tune.

> Dear Sir Percy,
>   You will have seen Leachman, I suppose. It is a jolly fine journey and I am awfully pleased Ibn Saud did him so well, though I rather envy all those other travellers going to Riyadh when I am the only one who really knows the king.

The Resident played for time in reporting back to the government. Travel in Arabia was now only possible by virtue of conspiracy among the officers of the Indian Government. Tell Whitehall after the event, tell it as little as possible and disclaim all knowledge of and responsibility for the explorers, became the guidelines.

Shakespear's response to Leachman's impressive achievement was to get on with the preparations for his own journey, and to involve himself in yet another scheme, flying. Following his tuition at the flying school at Aldershot, he was convinced that, given official support, he could assemble his own aircraft and use it to speed up communication in the gulf. He applied to the Resident for permission to import parts of a flying machine. The Resident was sympathetic but he had to refer the matter to the Viceroy, which he did with tongue-in-cheek formality since the Indian Government was never quite sure what Captain

Shakespear would do or propose next. The reply was as matter of fact as the request. 'No.'

Another and equally predictable announcement came at about the same time. Dorothea wrote to tell him that she had become engaged to a young officer of the Indian army, Captain Lakin. It was not an unexpected letter. He wrote her a letter of good wishes and resigned himself to the loss; though he carried her photograph with him to his death.

In December Shaikh Mubarak had returned at last from Failaka. He left almost immediately in his refurbished yacht to join his closest friend, Shaikh Khazal of Muhammerah. He opened the new *madrasah*, thus beginning the process of formal education in Kuwait, and set in motion another fund, this time to extend the boat harbour, a scheme expected to cost some 40,000 rupees. Craufurd had returned to Kuwait to spend Christmas with Shakespear and they followed Shaikh Mubarak to the Shatt-al-Arab and Shaikh Khazal's little principality on its right bank.

The two rulers were the greatest of friends and spent a lot of time in each other's territory. Shaikh Khazal had built a fine residence of his own in Kuwait, a two-storey structure with *diwaniyah* and harim facing each other across a courtyard. Both were inordinately proud of their yachts and Shakespear spent much of his time arranging improvements and repairs to their vessels. He also found amusement in the rivalry of the two men, each determined to outdo the other in the speed and furnishing of his boat. When they arrived at Muhammerah the place was in a mild state of uproar. The shaikh had sought the help of a Scot by the name of Sam Biggam, an engineer with the British India Steamship Company. Biggam was one of a colourful band of characters who made their way around India and along the coastlines of Persia and Arabia in those days, aboard the 'fast' and 'slow' mails. He knew everyone of any importance, including the shaikhs of the Arabian coast, whom he called sultans, and the leading citizens of the ports of Mesopotamia and Persia. He had a dry humour and the pride of an engineer who could mend anything mechanical. But the task set by Shaikh Khazal presented problems even for him. The repairs to his boat demanded a dry dock. The shaikh promptly supplied a group of African slaves, who proved good workers; but the Scot was angered to find that his usual method of disciplining, by cutting their pay, was impossible since they did not receive any pay. He was complaining bitterly of his false position when Shakespear and Craufurd arrived on the scene. The loquacious Biggam was worth listening to when his temper was roused. He had another complaint too, which he voiced to the shaikh as soon as he appeared on the scene. One of the Arab merchants had tried to invade his sleeping quarters. The shaikh found no difficulty in resolving that problem; he ordered Biggam's sleeping quarters to be locked at night, more concerned that his boat engine should be repaired than that the Scot's sanctity be preserved.

Biggam's stories of encounters with Arab chiefs had become part of the folklore of the pirate coast and the gulf ports. He confided in Shakespear that he did not care much for the Shaikh of Muhammerah who had descended to the unspeakable trick of engaging an assassin to kill his brothers in order to secure his position. Mubarak, on the other hand, was a gentleman. He had killed his own brothers in order to ensure his hegemony. Biggam did not speak Arabic but his Hindustani was good, and his conversations with the shaikhs were usually conducted in the latter language since it was easier to find interpreters who understood his version of the Indian tongue than the broad Scots dialect with which he amused the English-speaking community.

In the end a suitable hole was dug in the bank of a creek, the shaikh's yacht was run into it and then the end was filled in and the water pumped out. Biggam could set to work and everyone was happy.

Shakespear's seamanship was by now a byword along the gulf coasts and as he made his way back to Kuwait aboard the *Lewis Pelly* his skill was put to the test. A fierce *shimal* blew up suddenly and the normally calm water was whipped into a frenzy. Giant waves battered the launch and the howling gale forced its navigator into some hair-raising manoeuvres. As Shakespear fought to bring the vessel under control one of the big British India mail ships came on to the scene, and its captain and passengers lined the decks to see the smaller craft fight for survival. They watched it pitch and yaw and eventually plunge into an ocean trough. They decided that it had gone under and prepared to move to rescue its crew. But it reappeared and as it came into view again the captain noticed that a signal had been hoist. It read 'Do you need assistance?'. The captain thought at first that the wrong signal had been hauled up. Then he roared with laughter at the impertinent gesture. A. T. Wilson, Shakespear's contemporary in the Indian Political Service, was among the passengers, and he recalled the incident in his book *Loyalties, Mesopotamia*. 'Such men are the salt of the earth', he wrote.

15

Interlude

The sixth tour was to be the second longest so far, and in more ways than one it was to prove the most difficult.

Shakespear had to wait until the very end of the travelling season before setting out. Delicate negotiations were going on in Constantinople and Basra, and Cox was talking of arranging a meeting with Ibn Saud which he would attend along with Shakespear. The Political Agent spent most of January and February of 1913 at Bushire following the grand strategy of Turkey and Britain, and the fluid battles of the desert. Several skirmishes had recently taken place involving the Ajman, Mutair, Muntafiq and Rashaida tribes. There was an ominous quiet between Riyadh and Hail, and the Saudi leader was confined to his capital. The Resident had been told that he was not to contact Ibn Saud until the Convention with Turkey, still under discussion in Constantinople and Whitehall, was settled.

A few days after his return to Kuwait, Shakespear boarded the *Lewis Pelly* again and took himself off to Kubbar Island. He had already planned his journey across Arabia and had spent a good deal of time completing maps for it and assessing his requirements. He would not be able to leave for another year but he was already immersed in its problems and possibilities. Cruising in the gulf gave him an opportunity to work at his maps and make his arrangements undisturbed. He spent two days on the island and returned to Kuwait at the end of February. He then collected his caravan together and marched off in the direction of the Dahana sandbelt which he had not so far explored and which was one of the most interesting regions of the desert, forming a long, crescent-shaped link between the Nafud in the north and the sandy regions of Najd in southern and eastern Arabia.

It was March 8th when they left, trotting and walking their

camels through Kuwait towards their old encampment at As Safa. The hot season was approaching and the thermometer already registered a temperature of 80° in the shade but rain came to cool the air and slow their pace. The ground was soft and muddy after a day of uninterrupted rain and Dhabia made her displeasure apparent, refusing to move at more than a leisurely walking pace. Only Shalwa seemed to be enjoying the trip, resting peacefully on his master's wrist, or on his stand when they pitched camp. They went across the Shaq depression which they knew so well by now, and down into the Summan where Shakespear had already noted the strangely confused earth and flat-topped hills. There was little grazing on the way and as they trudged through the desert they made poor progress between camps. But once they reached the Dahana sandbelt progress quickened and they completed their 300-mile outward journey in 17 days, good going by any desert standards and especially so in view of the heat and intermittent rain. The Dahana confirmed everything Shakespear had heard about it. Its deep crimson and orange sand, sweeping down from Nafud like a fiery tongue, supported plenty of vegetation and teemed with wildlife. *Arfaj* and the fleshy *ausaj* bush grew in profusion, and gazelle roamed across it in great numbers. It was here that the Amir of Najd kept his great camel herds. Ibn Saud's *rafiqs* kept watch for more than a hundred miles and any intruder was soon sent packing. Only Pelly and Raunkiaer had travelled this route, but neither had taken the same path as Shakespear to the oases of Sudair.

Men and animals were equally pleased to reach Majmaa, the fertile town in the well-cultivated Sudair where they found refreshment and hospitality. Shakespear left his men at Camp XV and went off to the nearby village of Harma to meet a man he had come to know well in Kuwait, Abdullah ibn Askar. He was well entertained and invited to smoke his pipe – a sure sign of acceptance in Najd – and he learnt that Ibn Saud was engaged in some heavy raiding in the desert and was presently camped at Khafs, some sixty miles to the south.

The government was sensitive about unplanned and unapproved contacts between its officials and Arab leaders. But Shakespear could not resist the temptation. The going was hard between Majmaa and the Saudi camp, but he was determined to pay a courtesy call on the amir. They battled for three days along craggy hillsides and ridges, to Tamair and across the Khazza ridge and finally to Khafs. They arrived at Ibn Saud's camp in time for evening prayer, though prayer in the amir's presence had no particular hour; it was obligatory response to every mishap, good fortune and hope. The ritual was unvarying. At camp the men had no *gibla* or place of prayer. They simply formed a line facing Mecca. But first came the ritual cleansing, squatting on the ground and rubbing the palms of their hands in washing gesture over arms, feet and other exposed parts. Then, with Ibn Saud in front, the apex of a squat triangle, leading the chorus of Koranic phrase and incantation, they offered up their prayers with utter devotion. Each phrase, each *salah* of prayer accompanied by the proper symbolism, standing, bowing from the waist, kneeling, sitting back on heels and offering forehead to the ground. At last the amir rose and said 'Salaam alaikum' over his right shoulder, then over his left, acknowledging the symbolic angels of Islamic prayer, and the men returned to their tasks. Even when they were engaged in battle the men of the desert found time to pray, though always with rifles at the ready, laid muzzle to butt before them.

He was greeted with obvious pleasure by the amir. They embraced now as comrades in arms and were soon chatting in Ibn Saud's tent. Shakespear arrived at the camp on March 30th; he did not leave until April 4th five days later. In that time he was locked in conversation with the amir for hours on end, but what he learned it is impossible to know. He did not record his conversations in his notebook, neither did he report them to the government when he returned. In the light of subsequent meetings, and of Shakespear's own reports, it is hard to imagine what was said during those five days. But whatever it was it produced a stark reaction in the listener. One thing is fairly certain, that a visit by Sayid Talib to Riyadh had something to do with it. It may be that by this time Ibn Saud had decided to give up any hope of an agreement with Britain and that Talib had told him that Britain was to back Turkey in offering to make him Mutasarrif of Najd and to recognize his authority over the coastal province of Al Hasa. That at any rate was the substance of discussions then going on in Constantinople. Shakespear knew roughly what those proposals were from his discussions with the Resident, but he did not know that Turkey was going to make them to Ibn

Saud before the Government of India had so much as expressed
an opinion on the subject, neither did he expect the amir to accept
them. Perhaps it was the last fact – that in his exasperation with
Britain Ibn Saud had decided to come to terms with the Turks –
that infuriated Shakespear.

He left the Saudi camp at Khafs on April 4th, leaving some of
his old baggage camels behind and accepting a gift of fresh
animals from Ibn Saud. From that moment he travelled at speed
and in some anger. His travel log books, kept immaculately for
some 1,600 miles of desert journey over a period of nearly five
years, suddenly became illegible. Usually he would sit in his tent
at night and transcribe his rough notes into a perfectly kept
master notebook. He no longer bothered. His notes ceased
altogether on April 20th when camped at Wafra outside Kuwait.
For the sixteen days of a long and difficult return journey he had
scribbled haphazardly as if he had lost interest.

Whatever justification there may have been for his sudden change
of attitude, his own journey was still to be looked forward to and
almost as soon as he returned he resumed his planning and preparation for the trip. But his meeting with Ibn Saud might well
have put it at risk; had this been so, valuable information would
have been lost. Already he had made a major contribution to the
world's knowledge of Arabia. The records of his journeys to date
had already enabled the cartographers in India to build up a
detailed picture of eastern Arabia. His maps and notebooks were
models of accuracy and thoroughness. But much remained to be
done. Of the 1,554 miles so far covered, less than a third was
known territory. It was not merely a matter of using the correct
survey techniques, of having the tenacity to take readings and
sightings in heat that blistered the flesh, or in howling gales that
blew a man off his feet and required two or three others to hold him
down while he worked with sextant and other instruments, and
that filled his mouth and lungs with sand as he worked, or in
torrential rain and cold. These were the conditions of desert
exploration which others, before and after Shakespear, were
prepared to face. The factor that distinguished this Englishman
from almost all others in Arabia was his ability to gain the confidence and absolute trust of the badawin. And because his Arabic
had a native perfection he was able to discuss features of terrain

with them in minute detail and make exact transliterations of the names they gave to the uninhabited regions of the desert. He would argue for hours on end with badawin companions or people he happened to meet on his journeys, in order to establish a correct place name. Single-mindedness is the quality which constantly comes to the fore in following Shakespear's life. Others, from the highly imaginative, quick-witted Palgrave to the immensely painstaking Doughty, had moved among these people and come away with striking, perceptive impressions. He set out to explore, and nothing, except at that last moment on his journey back from Khafs, diverted him from that purpose. Not an hour of a single day till then had gone unrecorded. Yet, as with the looks and manners of the desert people, he made no note of speech. He did not, like Doughty, find 'Attic sweetness' in the Najdi tongue; he was not a gifted writer, and had no literary ambitions, save the satisfaction of getting a place name right. He did show a certain interest in anthropological matters, questioning his badawin friends on customs of circumcision and the marking of their bodies, but he seldom noted what they said except for an occasional very general remark. He was much too intent on getting his noon sighting or the bearing of a sandhill. The tribal *wasms* were another matter: the distinguishing marks which each tribe, sub-tribe and clan used to denote its ownership of animals were listed with immense care and precision. Each mark was drawn and its point of application noted. Thus: '*Wasm* mishab: *place of applic*: off-side neck close to head: *tribe* Sbei: *sub-tribes*: Bin Mijfil and Samala.' Altogether he ascertained the marks of over eighty tribal divisions and shaikhs, making sketches of them as he went. He also showed a keen interest in the natural history of the desert, naming plants and animals as he went and preserving many specimens of snake, lizard, spider and other creatures, often sacrificing his precious reserve of whisky when he ran out of formalin. If he shot a wildcat or killed a snake he would measure it precisely and go to any length to establish its correct Arabic name. But nowhere is there a human description, an assessment of looks or speech or manner. The Government of India, from the viceroys of his period to the Foreign Secretary Sir Henry McMahon and Shakespear's immediate chief Sir Percy Cox, knew that of all its men he could be relied on most assuredly to reach the most distant places and bargain for the most difficult of objectives, so long as they did not expect him to procrastinate; when delaying tactics or subtle bargaining were required they usually sent somebody else with him, as they proposed to do at the next meeting with Ibn Saud. Shakespear, like all men, had his Achilles' heel. He was generally a poor judge of mood and character and he was sometimes unjust in his assessments.

It does not seem to have occurred to him that the meeting with Ibn Saud at Khafs would cause trouble. His friend the amir was nearby and it was only natural that he should pay a courtesy call, despite the fact that the government was at that stage in the midst of delicate negotiations with Turkey regarding the future of Central Arabia, and a battle between his own chiefs and the Foreign Office was in full swing. Certainly he was not prepared for the explosion that greeted his admission of the meeting. Cox informed McMahon straight away when he heard what had happened. The reprimand was immediate and fierce. The Political Agent was told that he must not meet with Arab chiefs in future without the prior approval of the government 'at any time, in any circumstance'. He protested that he had made a social call without a word of official business passing between him and the amir. The record does not show whether or not they believed him. He did not say that he had spent four days with the amir, a lengthy social call, but it could be that his seniors' anger derived as much from the fact that he may have discovered the truth of their plans as from their concern at a breach of protocol.

Shakespear's main worry, however, was that his indiscretion might have serious consequences for his proposed journey. He aimed to set out at the end of the year and now he relied heavily on an embarrassed Sir Percy Cox to see him on his way.

Before leaving for the trek to Majmaa and Khafs he had found Shaikh Mubarak in the best of spirits. When he returned even the row over the meeting with Ibn Saud was overshadowed by the alarming news that the old man was on his death bed. Although the two men had gone through a lengthy and often angry period of disagreement, they retained a healthy respect for each other.

Mubarak, for all his artful and unpredictable behaviour, was a mighty force in Arabia and an unshakable ally of Britain.

Shakespear would be sorry to lose him. Now, in April 1913, he was suffering from bronchitis, with severe cardiac and renal complications. The physician of the American Mission, Dr Harrison, and the assistant surgeon to the Political Agency, Dr Kelly, attended him and took a grave view of his condition. But as soon as they left the patient, Mubarak's favourite medical adviser appeared – a 'Najdi quack' Shakespear called him – and put aside the medicines and advice of the qualified men and prescribed various potions of his own. To everyone's surprise, the patient recovered.

With the ruler out of danger and Ibn Saud busily engaged in desert raids, Shakespear was able to settle to tidying up the affairs of the agency and making final arrangements for his planned journey across Arabia and then home to England. He had still not received official sanction, but he had almost completed the usual five-year term as Political Agent, and the Resident had agreed to find a replacement for him in Kuwait. If the government proved intransigent, Shakespear intended, like Leachman and Raunkiaer before, to make his way without permission.

Meanwhile, there were several official functions and social activities to attend to.

In July a portrait of George V was unveiled at the shaikh's palace. The ruler threw himself into the event with enthusiasm, draping his palace in bunting, raising the Union Jack on the flagstaff and ordering all boats in the harbour to be dressed. The European communities of all the major gulf ports were invited and the court poet was instructed to write a verse in praise of the King Emperor. Shakespear made a formal address in Arabic and English and unveiled the portrait. Then the laureate read his eulogy. He went on in archaic and unintelligible Arabic for half an hour. When it was all over Shakespear returned with the European guests to the agency for a stiff and much needed whisky.

The pearling season came again and he took once more to the sea. He cruised off the coast, perhaps for the last time, following its course from the bay of Kuwait past the promontories of Adjusa and Ardh, Jilai'a and Zor, Bardhelk and Khafdji and then steaming back to the islands of Umm al Maradin and Karu and Kubbar, and to the pearl banks where men dived so deep for their quarry that they often died in the process, for they had no breathing equipment. He seemed to be saying farewell to many places and people in this his thirty-fifth year.

When he returned to Kuwait he was just in time to greet a visitor of some historical importance. Admiral Sir Edmond Slade, who had been honoured at the Coronation durbar for his enterprising work in stopping gun-running in the gulf, came to call on the shaikh. The old man, though recovered from his illness, was still unwell and his son Jabir took the admiral out to Burgan, 'the place of bitumen,' which the shaikh especially wanted him to see. More than twenty years later that was to prove to be the site of the biggest single oil discovery of all time.

The political tasks of Shakespear's term of office were not quite at an end; there was still the meeting with the amir to be fixed up. More reports were coming in of meetings between the Arab chiefs. In May Ibn Saud had retaken Hasa and much of the coastal district from the Turks. The amir was clearly not waiting for Britain and Turkey to concert their plans; he had also, presumably, had second thoughts about accepting a nominal role under Turkish authority. Events began to move fast. Turkish troops from Basra were transported to the scene of battle in a British ship, the *John O. Scott*. Other vessels chartered by the Turks were on their way to pick up troops from Aden and Bombay. In July the Ottoman claimed to have retaken Katif, but it turned out that a few officers and men had gained a foothold at Uqair, whereupon the officers had retired to Bahrain with British approval. Ibn Saud wiped out the small Turkish force left behind and promptly demanded of the Political Agent in Bahrain, Major Trevor, that he eject the officers from British territory. The Government of India waited on the Foreign Office. Cox decided that the projected meeting with the Amir of Najd must take place as soon as possible. But on August 11th he received a wire from the Foreign Office, pointing out that discussions were still going on between Britain and Turkey and containing the sentence: 'Shakespear is in future to confine his activities strictly to the limits eventually assigned to Kuwait under the Anglo-Turkish Convention.' September and October went by with talks still going on in Constantinople and the Turks and Ibn Saud battling for position along the eastern coastline. The Turks occupied Qatar and Ibn Saud demanded their withdrawal. The Indian

Government knew that more Ottoman troops were on the way from Basra to reinforce the garrison established there, and asked for urgent guidance.

Sir Edward Grey hoped that ratification of the treaty 'would not be long delayed' and then all would become clear. It was apparently held up by negotiations between the Turkish Government and the Baghdad Railway Company. But the Foreign Secretary could not see 'such urgent and paramount necessity' for withdrawal of Turkish troops from territory 'which has been theirs since 1872'. Sir Edward's interpretation of history was somewhat pedantic, for Riyadh had controlled the coastline effectively prior to that time and had reoccupied it on several occasions since. The importance attached by Britain to the events of this period is indicated by the fact that Sir Edward Grey's most trusted assistant, his one-time Private Secretary and Permanent Under-Secretary at the Foreign Office, Sir Louis Mallet, was at this time appointed ambassador to Constantinople. On November 4th Sir Louis told the government that Turkey was about to recognize a *fait accompli* in Najd by appointing Ibn Saud its mutasarrif.

The Resident had the gravest reservations about the policy that was emerging from the Anglo-Turkish Convention. He decided not to attend the forthcoming meeting with Ibn Saud but to send Major Trevor from Bahrain along with Shakespear. Whatever the government might think about confining the latter to the affairs of Kuwait, he was the only man who could hope to persuade the amir to accept the fact that Turkish rule in future was to have the wholehearted support of Britain and that the Anglo-Turkish accord would be binding on him.

The meeting finally took place at Uqair in December. Ibn Saud told Shakespear and Trevor that he was still negotiating with the chiefs of Muscat and Yemen and that he had been in consultation with Husain of Mecca and Ibn Subhan the Regent of Haíl. The Turks, aware of these meetings, were trying to force him into treaty arrangements. Again he said that he wanted an agreement with Britain and that he would gladly accept British suzerainty over his territory. He was told that such an arrangement was out of the question now. He must come to terms with the Ottoman. Ibn Saud accepted the title conferred on him by Constantinople reluctantly. Perhaps he and Shakespear knew that the matter was not quite settled, for neither appeared to take the meeting very seriously. They spent much of their time together arranging a visit to Riyadh in the course of the Englishman's crossing of Arabia.

Before leaving for Uqair, Shakespear had written to the Resident:

Dear Sir Percy,

I am enclosing my last despairing effort re. my trip to Central Arabia. I have written it as a sort of private letter to you, which you can send off in original if you think it will be any use, to Sir Henry McMahon, with a covering letter of your own. I leave it entirely to your judgement so please tear it up if you think that advisable ... If I leave it until Lorimer takes over [Cox was about to return to India and Lorimer was designated to take over the Residency] it may be too late to get an answer and a solemn official application would take months to get any sort of reply. What I thought was that if you could back it up to Sir Henry, asking him to send me a line direct in answer and at the same time told me you had forwarded it to him, I could, after the confab with Bin Saud, write to him direct giving Bin Saud's 'no objection' (I am certain of getting that all right!).

Of course, I shall be careful to avoid all politics in my trip and really all I want is a hint from Foreign that they have no objection to the trip as a geographical effort ...

Yours sincerely,

27.11.13.   WHIS.

In the accompanying letter for Sir Percy to send on to the Foreign Secretary at Simla, he wrote of his special knowledge of the interior. He was still under a cloud, however, and felt it necessary to explain that his previous meeting with Ibn Saud at Khafs was an accidental confrontation.

... This all sounds rather like blowing one's own trumpet but I can't show in any other way what an exceptional oppor-tunity exists now for me to go and do some really good geographical work. Leachman in his journey hurried through on dhaluls with, I think, only a small prismatic compass and aneroid:— I have not seen his map but unless he was able to make astronomical sights his estimates of a day's march will be liable to considerable error: at least such has been my own experience. Barclay Raunkiaer the Dane has just sent me the result of his trek (in Danish and therefore unintelligible to me): but his map, which I can check, looks like the work of a schoolboy; anyway he has taken the positions of Buraidah and Riyadh directly off Hunter's map of Arabia and has marked out his own route in between to fit, leaving out a lot of geographical features in between which he must have traversed; however, as he did not know Arabic and had only a small pocket compass, shade thermometer, and pocket aneroid, perhaps he has not done too badly. I would not make these rather disparaging remarks were it not for the fact that I have marched backwards and forwards over a good deal of the country with ample leisure to take bearings, sights for latitude etc, and know the country of which I am speaking really well ... I fancy the Intelligence at Simla would give a good deal for the information which I shall be able to produce not to mention the geographical section of the War Office at Home. After all, the whole of the risk and expense is mine, while Government stands to get all the profit and benefit of the results ...

Having made his point to Sir Percy and the Foreign Secretary at some length, he went off to Uqair.

When he returned, he sat down to write to every useful contact he possessed. By this time Lorimer was settled in at Bushire as the new Resident while Cox returned to India as second in command to McMahon, and he wrote to him knowing that he would receive a friendly response:

On returning here I found a letter from Lt. Col. F. R. Maunsell re the compilation of a new map of northern and central Arabia, also one from Murphy our intelligence officer at Simla, asking me to revise a whole stack of articles dealing with Kuwait and Central Arabia ... if I could do the trek as I want to I could do vastly more accurate and reliable work which would, besides, have some permanent value.

The letter was dated December 24th.

He wrote to his old friend J. B. Wood at the Foreign Department, Simla, and to Major-General W. R. Birdwood at the Army Department in Delhi, also on December 24th.

> Dear General,
>
> You were rash enough to say, when you were here, that you would lend me a hand towards my proposed trek across Central Arabia if I wrote to you. Now you see the result of your kindness. I am just back from negotiations with Bin Saud and have just applied through the Resident at Bushire to do the trek. Bin Saud was most affable and offered me no end of help if I came along to his dominions, so that there is really nothing to stop me doing any amount of exceedingly useful work (all at my own expense and risk of course!) if Government will only let me go.
>
> Sincerely,
WHIS.

In December 1913, the Viceroy decided to send a personal letter to the Secretary of State for India, Lord Crewe.

> Captain Shakespear, now the Political Agent in Kuwait, who is proceeding on leave early in January, has asked permission to attempt the journey through Arabia to the Red Sea. He has received an invitation from Ibn Saud, who is a personal friend, to visit him at Riyadh and he proposes to proceed then in the direction of Hail. Shakespear, who has long been preparing himself for such a journey, knows Arabic well, is personally acquainted with the tribes as far as Najd, and is thus exceptionally well qualified to undertake a task of this description. His exploration would be most useful from the military, political and geographical points of view.

The Viceroy went on to explain that the Turks had recently recognized Ibn Saud's authority in Central Arabia, it being essential to allay any fears in Whitehall that Ottoman susceptibilities might be injured. 'It will be most unfortunate', he concluded, 'if for political reasons, Englishmen are always to be excluded from exploration in Central Arabia while the field is left open to foreigners.'

While these last-minute appeals were doing the rounds,

Shakespear was sailing the *Lewis Pelly* between Bahrain, Basra and Muhammerah on a final bout of farewells.

It was necessary for the Foreign Department at Simla to wire the India Office again, telling it that Captain Shakespear was about to leave his post, in order to provoke a reply. On January 20th, 1914, the government finally gave in, subject to a warning from the ambassador in Constantinople that the Ottoman Power could not guarantee his safety and that the Vilayat of Hijaz was closed to him and all other non-Muslims. It was also made clear that the explorer would have to pay his own expenses.

Before he left a letter came from Lorimer, dated January 20th, 1914:

My dear Shakespear,

I have just received your private letter of 12th. When it was written, you did not know that your journey would be sanctioned, and now you have got permission I think it is your duty to your country and yourself to start without delay.

Kubbar beacon and the marking out of the Bandar Shuwaikh plot will be done all right, though your local knowledge would have made both easier and I am sorry to lose the benefit of it.

God speed you in your great enterprise.

Sincerely,
LORIMER

It was the last communication Shakespear was to receive from the new Resident, one of the most able men in the Indian Government service. Shortly after Shakespear's departure he shot himself while cleaning a loaded gun.

16

Across Arabia

'Arabia is a hard, barren mistress and those who serve her she repays in weariness, sickness of the body and distress of the mind.' – Lord Belhaven.

There was a good deal of clearing up to be done in his final few days in Kuwait. His successor, Colonel Grey, had arrived and though he and Shakespear had met years before when the latter took over at Muscat, they knew little of each other. They soon discovered a natural antipathy. Grey fussed, and Shakespear quickly came to look on him as 'an old woman'. He introduced him to the shaikh and to local men of importance and began to fear for the future of the agency he had established as perhaps the liveliest and most talked about outpost of H.M. Government in the East. He presented the shaikh with his salukis and his hawk, parting with them with great reluctance, but he could not take them on the journey.

His last, semi-official act was to patch up a quarrel between Shaikh Mubarak and his friend Shaikh Khazal of Muhammerah. As they got older the two men argued about almost anything. But the rival claims of their yachts caused the fiercest disputes and they were at each other's throats when Shakespear called to say farewell. He patiently pointed out the superior qualities of each boat in turn and in the end convinced them that their vessels were of about equal merit.

The politics of Arabia continued to ebb and flow in the aftermath of the Anglo-Turkish Convention. The Wali of Basra had asked Mubarak for an interview to see if anything could be done to bring Ibn Saud to heel and stop him attacking the Turks. Mubarak confided in Shakespear that he thought it unlikely now that Britain would do anything to help the amir. An official of the

Turkish war department was also trying to get Mubarak to arrange a meeting with Ibn Saud. Shakespear left the legacy of desert politics to Grey with some misgivings.

He returned to the agency on his last night in Kuwait to entertain a few old friends. He had become a popular figure with the merchants and sea captains and the local shaikhs. Some came to offer their salaams, others to enjoy his widely renowned hospitality. The party went on all night and he retired to bed at 6.30 a.m. An hour and a half later his servant Wali Muhammad woke him.

Rain fell generously in early 1914. *Arfaj* flowered miraculously, as if in instant response, and all over the desert camouflaged creatures came to life. They seemed to disappear when the land was dry, though the badawin knew their habits and could find them in their underground hiding places, under the thorny *ausaj* bush, under stones and in remote lairs. The burrowing jerboa, lizard and hare, snake and shrike and bustard, the bigger animals, cats, wolves and foxes, scavenging hyena and vulture; when the rain came they could feed from the sprouting vegetation and the badawin would offer up a prayer to Allah for his munificence – until the locusts came to eat every leaf from every bush for hundreds of miles. Even then the wandering men of Arabia would see the hand of God at work and make a meal of the swarming insects.

Dhabia was reluctant to leave. She watched the baggage animals being loaded in a cold drizzle and when all was ready she made her protest by lying down and refusing to get up. Her owner was almost as reluctant to set off. But at last his camel was persuaded to rise and it came to the moment for final handshakes, a last look at the agency and at his yacht moored along the harbour. 'Sahib' led his caravan towards the desert.

It was a small caravan by the standards of Arabian travel: Abdul Aziz ibn Hassan, his camel jemader, and two unnamed badawin to help him with his duties; Mathi ibn Hazaim of the Sbei tribe, his head *rafiq*, and three other *rafiqs*, Ghanim of the Mutair, Hadi and Ali, both from the Ajman; and an unnamed Mutairi herdsman. Then there were his personal servants, Wali Muhammad, the little Punjabi, and Awayd, an Iraqi from the Shatt-al-Arab. Abdul Aziz and the *rafiqs* had their own *dhahuls*.

Servants and the Najdi men rode as best they could on the baggage camels. Thus, including the leader of the expedition, there were eleven men, seven riding camels, eleven baggage camels, and four sheep bringing up the rear. Much the same party that had gone with him on earlier journeys.

They had not gone far before it began to rain in earnest. They went along the Jahra road, past Bandar Shuwaikh where he caught a last glimpse of the *Lewis Pelly*, and on into the desert in the wake of the Buraida caravan. The rain made the going sticky and tiring for animals and men, so it was decided to camp early that day and make up for the previous night's loss of sleep.

They awoke early, but the tents were too wet for them to strike camp, so Awayd served a late breakfast in his master's fifteen-year-old tent. Shakespear had built up his canvas home over the years as a suburban house-owner would improve his property. To the bathroom section, which he had added in his first year in Kuwait, was now joined a verandah divided by a curtain, as in the badawin tents, embroidered by an old woman of the desert. They were away by 9.30 a.m. and soon they passed the Buraida caravan on the way to Rigai wells. The rain clouds cleared to reveal a locust invasion.

> At first they were in wisps on the lee side of the bushes and looked like the shadows thrown by the sun either at early morning or late afternoon. Next we ran into them, flighting; so thick that you could not wave a stick without hitting several. The men say they should be cooked, after taking off the head, wings and legs, in water, boiled apparently, with a lot of salt.

The meat, the badu told him, was like the yolk of an egg in colour and taste. But he could not make up his mind to try it. Ibn Saud had told him that in Najd whole villages would turn out to destroy the young locusts, digging trenches and driving the young insects into them, before they could fly, and making great bonfires of them. Even so, they came every year in clouds which blotted out the sun and reduced the vegetation of entire regions to bare twigs.

The first two days were peaceful and happy. Then Ali the Ajmani took fright. He decided that he was being taken to the end of the world. He blandly announced that he was not going a step further. Shakespear had little patience with men who neglected their duty, whether from fear or cowardice. He gave Ali a severe talking to, and the Arab seemed fairly content again. By the end of the third day they were 60 miles from the wells of Rigai and had left the Buraida caravan behind. It was stormy, windy and 'beastly cold'. They were glad to settle for the night, after Shakespear had taken his religiously punctual readings of bearing, height and temperature. The aneroid reading showed 29.6 inches, or 1,270 ft., the thermometer 60°F, boiling point 211°F. Watches were set at 8.10 p.m. when they went to bed.

When they awoke on the morning of February 6th, Ali the Ajmani had bolted, taking Shakespear's spare suit of clothes with him, but leaving his rifle and cartridges behind. The Englishman regretted that he had not punished him in good time, for there is no greater crime in the desert than for a *rafiq* to desert his friends. 'It is precious little satisfaction that all the other men execrate him and his action.'

The march that day was tiring and unpleasant. A fierce *shimal* followed them relentlessly. The landscape was flat and featureless. They marched for just over seven hours and then, exhausted, camped by the main track to Rigai. At night the wind dropped and so did the temperature. It was 58° inside the tent. They were now, according to Shakespear's earlier mapping, 38 miles from Rigai wells, where they hoped to find water, for the rain had ceased and they were running low.

February 7th was another cold, dull day and the route again uninteresting. There was not a single feature on which he could obtain a bearing. 'Camels a bit done up by starvation. However, we did over seven hours and 22 miles, so tomorrow ought to get us to Rigai, and with luck a rest day for the camels,' he wrote. Fortunately, the wind had dropped.

Next day, Sunday, produced an event that relieved the monotony of the trip. A baby camel was born. The birth took half an hour and within the hour the infant was being carried across the desert by its mother, in an artificial pouch at her side. Neither camels nor men can wait on nature in the desert.

Eventually they arrived at Rigai, only to find that Mutair tribesmen were gathered round the wells, rifles at the ready. Shakespear was not a man to take a threat lying down, but, after heated argument and threats of violence, he was forced to make do with

one skin of dirty water. They went on along the Batin across the
desert of Dibdibba, thirsty and tired, their animals suffering badly
from lack of food.

They were forced to halt along the Batin because Shakespear's
camel harness gave out, the hanging straps falling away. He spent
several hours splicing stiff manilla into the straps, cutting his
finger badly in the process. They had lost sight of the Buraida
caravan.

On the sixth day they awoke to find their tents and the sands
around them drenched. They decided to stay where they were and
rest their camels. By 6.30 a.m. the wind had changed direction
and a cyclone hit them. They had to hold their tents down, while
water rushed past along the dry course beside them. The foul
weather was a mixed blessing: at least water would not be a
problem for some time to come. Despite his tent blowing away in
the middle of cooking, Awayd served his master with a good meal,
cooked by Wali Muhammad; 'A marvel,' said Shakespear. The
rest of that day was spent in projecting map sheets for later stages
of the journey.

The next day too they were halted by rain. Shakespear occupied
his time with photography. Not until the 11th could they get on
the way again, by which time they heard that the Buraida caravan
was north of them and that Faisal ibn Dawish, paramount shaikh
of the Mutair, had intercepted it and demanded payment of £70 in
Turkish money before it was allowed to move on.

'Good for Faisal,' said Shakespear. 'I wonder if he is as fat as
ever. I haven't seen him for over two years.'

On February 11th they battled through more greasy mud and
squelching sand. They camped after completing eighteen miles,
and lit the coffee fire. Then the badu guides began to entertain
Shakespear with their interminable stories and desert riddles.

'Tell me,' said one of them, addressing their leader, 'two men
bought eight measures of clarified butter from a badawin, in a
skin. They had two skins of their own which would hold three
measures and five measures in turn. Before taking leave of each
other, they wanted to divide the clarified butter evenly.

'How did they do it O Gonsul?'

Shakespear replied that he had no idea, so the badawin told him.

'First fill up the five-measure skin and from it fill up the three-
measure skin. This leaves three in the eight-measure skin, two in

the five and three full. Pour the full three back into the eight-measure skin, making two in the five and six in the eight and none in the three-skin. Now pour the two from the five-skin into the three-skin and fill up the five-skin from the eight, leaving the five-skin full, the three-skin with two and the eight-skin with seven. Fill up the three-skin from five-skin leaving four in five-skin, three in three-skin and one in eight-skin. Then pour three into eight-skin and you have four in each of five and eight-skins.'

'Q.E.D.' murmured Shakespear. The Arabs looked at each other and shrugged their shoulders.

At 9.15 p.m. watches were checked and they went to bed.

They were still in the featureless region of Dibdibba, traversed by Knox in 1906. The Batin, which passed through it, descended to 200 feet below the level of the surrounding desert. On the ninth day of their journey they moved on to Kasr Ballal. Shakespear found that his old map, based on his own and Knox's earlier calculations, had the place inaccurately plotted. Kasr Ballal was marked by the remains of a walled enclosure about ninety feet square, with a gateway at the southern end. Alongside were the remains of an old well and reservoir.

Several stories were told to Shakespear of the old man who was supposed to have set up a permanent home here. It was said that a shaikh of the Bani Hilal, the 'first people', whose name was Ghailan, had a favourite slave named Ballal, and that the slave after a time amassed great wealth in camels. He collected dues from passing caravans, extracting from each a skinful of water with which he made mud-mortar for his *kasr*. Then he dug a well and found excellent water, which he would exchange with the passing caravans for the youngest camel foal they had, and so increased his herd and his wealth, which in the end became vast.

On along the Batin to Hafar, where they could replenish their water. Shakespear used the last skin of old water for a bath, his first since they left Kuwait. Then he ate a hearty meal and lay on his bed reading Palgrave. 'Shall hope to get some more bearings and a good noon observation tomorrow,' he wrote before going to sleep. It was Friday, February 13th.

Every now and again he fancied a 'Europe' morning, which meant lying in bed until 8.15 a.m. and breakfasting at about 9. Saturday was such a morning.

There were about forty wells at Hafar, distributed over a circular plain, and Shakespear measured the depth of the water as fifty fathoms. This may have been the scene of the Battle of the Chains, in the early days of Islam, when the Persians under Hormuz met the Arabs in battle and suffered a great defeat at the hands of Khalid, the 'sword of Islam'. It was then a frontier station of the Persian Empire.

Shakespear was more concerned with the mounting problems of the moment than with contemplation of past battles at this historic site. 'Altogether a very poor day,' he noted. The next was not much better. The rain had not touched the region they were now entering. It was as dry as bone. They got into the bottom of the valley of the Batin, an extension of the Wadi ar Rummah beyond Hafar, and it broadened out as they went along it. They marched for twenty-five miles on Sunday and caught up with the Buraida caravan again. One of their camels had gone lame and they bought another from the caravan. The Batin began to narrow again and more rain came so that they had to move along the high bank of the depression. On Tuesday, February 17th, they were off to an early start. It was dead country now and there were obvious signs of old buildings and disused wells. A new religious asceticism had come to life in a place about a hundred miles south of their present position – Al Artawiya – and it had caught up with the tribes they met on this part of the journey. Its adherents were called *Ikhwan*, 'the Brotherhood', and they were soon to enlist Ibn Saud to their cause.

Sharper bends appeared in the dried-up waterway of the Batin, plants grew in profusion and the red sands of Nafud began to appear. They camped at Qulban ibn Towala, where again there were dry wells, ruined limestone buildings and a graveyard, the work of the early Caliphs and, nearby, the ruins of a summer camp which the Bani Towala section of the Shammar tribe had tried to establish twenty-five years before. They had not been able to survive the grim terrain and in any case the Shaikh of the Bani Towala was convinced that a giant dog lived at the bottom of the water well and threatened to eat his men. One of the ancient wells was measured by Shakespear: 238 feet from bottom to lip. His Hurricane lamp burnt all the way down.

That afternoon someone shot a hare, so they had fresh meat for the first time in several days.

By February 18th they were behind the Buraida caravan again, and the valley along which they had progressed so far was beginning to fill up with red sand. There were more signs of old habitations, mud brick buildings and a great *birka*, a huge circular reservoir, between 70 and 80 feet in diameter and made of lime concrete. An arm extended from it at either end with watering places along its length. The walls of the main tank were as much as eight feet thick, but there was no dome as on the Persian *birkas*. It was patently a considerable feat of engineering in its day. In the surveyor's language that Shakespear often adopted, the *birka* was 'athwart the debouchure of a valley from the north west'.

They trudged through the red sands for several days and arrived at the wells of Ajibba on February 20th. Shakespear was too tired even to make his customary observations. He decided to rest for a day to water the camels and give the men a well-earned respite. They had moved through almost perpetual wind and rain for seventeen days now.

They went in search of sand grouse. There was a lot of shooting but nothing to show for it, for the birds were shy and they merged into the deeply coloured foreground. Shakespear went to develop his film of the ruins and the ancient wells and buildings that they had passed recently, only to find that the roll of film stuck and was ruined beyond redemption. He could not remain unoccupied, so he tried his hand at flower-pressing.

Now they were passing across the neck of the great Dahana sandbelt that he had touched on his journey the year before, some 600 miles in length. The Batin was shut off by a bank of sand, almost as if it had been raised artificially.

On Sunday the 22nd, they turned south, at right angles to their route so far. They camped at the lower level of the wall-like ridge along which they had travelled. It rose in steps, and Shakespear climbed the first two rises to find that he was over 100 feet above the camp.

They ran into camel tracks here, which the men looked on with some apprehension, believing them to belong to Mutairi. But Shakespear sighted some sheep grazing and sent Abdul Aziz off to see if he could buy one or two. They turned out to be the property of Anaiza tribesmen but since the owners were not in sight they could not do business. To steal sheep would have been to invite disaster.

Now they had to cross the Sairayat ridges which run into the Nafud or red sands of Al Asiyah. They tried a number of short cuts but each time the steep, heavy sands defeated them. Eventually, they succeeded in climbing one of the ridges with their baggage animals, but they only just made it. Again they were exhausted early in the day by soft sands and foul weather. After dinner rain came again and the wind began to howl around them. They had to roll up the bedding, shut tight all their boxes and hold on to the tents from inside. Shakespear wrote his diary entry for the day sitting on a box on the bare sand.

One of the Najdis had a raging toothache and Shakespear doctored it with alcohol and cotton-wool pads, finding that he had forgotten to bring laudanum with him.

The soft sand and foul weather made the going heavy for several more days. Occasionally they would alight on an unexpected well. Otherwise, ironically, they were forced to wet their parched lips by cupping their hands to the rain. Still it rained with cold, piercing ferocity and a howling gale blew. The men had trudged through mud and shifting sand for three weeks now and they dropped in their tracks exhausted, their animals as weary as they.

On the 25th, after a hard day's march, they were within striking distance of Zilfi, the rich oasis at the head of the Sudair. The weather improved slightly and they camped in the shadow of the Tuwaik escarpment, the 'Caucasus of Arabia' as Palgrave called it. Shakespear took a 'light meal' and wondered as he prepared for bed if anyone else had ever enjoyed sparkling Moselle and marrons glacés in the desert.

By February 26th they stood at the top of the Tuwaik, the entire valley spread out below them patched with the green of date plantations and the gold of cornfields, a vignette framed by the frowning yellow ochre stone of the escarpment and the crimson and orange of Nafud.

They were looking on Zilfi.

In fact, there were two Zilfis, both walled towns, about a mile apart. The correct name of the older one was Shamaliyah, a fortress town designed to defend the villages at its rear. The other, Jambra, had the date gardens and was newer.

'Palgrave's account, at least in the small edition with me, is not at all bad of the valley, though meagre as to the villages, and

exaggerated as to the height etc. of Tuwaik.' He was so entranced
that he arrived back at camp too late to make his noon observation.

He prepared the next morning to call on the local amir, Ali
ibn Badr, assuming that he would get an invitation to do so. But
no invitation came and the amir did not call on him. Abdul Aziz
was despatched to draw the amir's attention to the fact that his
master was a friend of Ibn Saud and Shaikh Mubarak, and that
courtesy demanded an exchange of calls. A message promptly
arrived from the distinguished and aged Najdi, Abdullah ibn
Suleiman, whose family had played host to Palgrave. It suggested
that Shakespear should call on him and the amir at the latter's
diwaniyah.

Eventually, the amir, who turned out to be a boy of eighteen,
visited him. The young man was obviously afraid of the old sage.
He explained that Ibn Saud had killed his uncle, the former governor, when he took the Sudair towns from Ibn Rashid. Ibn
Suleiman had then become Governor, but Ibn Saud had recently
made the boy the amir, though he lived in the shadow of Abdullah
ibn Suleiman. Abdullah sent a gift of two sheep to Shakespear and
the Englishman returned the amir's call before leaving next day.

If the initial reception was too cool for Shakespear's liking, the
young amir made up for it next day.

> Ali's house is close to the gate and he met me in the street
> and took me through a courtyard and down a couple of steps
> into the diwaniyah, which must be quite three feet below the
> street. Walls mud inside with rough crosses and things meant
> to be palm trees I think, done in whitewash or juss. Place
> nicely furnished with carpets and a big row of coffee pots. He
> seated me in the place of honour next to him by the coffee
> hearth. Then the local people came in. Sweet tea and coffee
> served and everyone affable and polite, while Ali was a perfect
> host. Stayed about twenty minutes and parted in the odour of
> *aod* with many *fi aman Ullahs*.

It was February 28th and time to move off along the trough
between Tuwaik and the Nafud and into the gorge of Ghat, a
few miles south of Zilfi, where they camped. Here the reception
was very different. The local chief, Saad ibn Abdul Mehsin as-
Sadairi, met them on arrival with gifts of sheep, firewood, food

and the offer of dinner. He was a relative of Ibn Saud's on his
mother's side, and was leaving nothing to chance.

Next morning, Shakespear made the mandatory call. The amir,
a thin, wizened man of about forty-five, had no less than fourteen
coffee pots on the boil. All the town had been invited to call and
see the Englishman, who sat at the chief's side while they viewed
him from every angle and exchanged pleasantries. The amir
wanted him to stay for lunch, but Shakespear was anxious to get
on his way. So they were given dates to take with them and, for
the first time since Shakespear had come to Arabia, cow's milk
butter.

'These people go in for cattle more than sheep and camels. The
cattle are very small, tiny, like the men and equally wizened and
dried up looking.'

Fifty of the local men had gone off to fight with Ibn Saud
recently. The amir himself had fought with the Saudi army at the
taking of Hasa and Shakespear recalled that he had noticed him at
Khafs the previous year in Ibn Saud's camp.

Shakespear had sent his party on ahead of him while he was
entertained by As-Sadairi. He caught up with them later in the
day of March 1st after toiling along the gorge and climbing out of
it 'by a fearsome place with an overhanging ledge on the top of
Tuwaik'.

Again he noted: 'Palgrave's account of pomegranates and
other fruits in Ghat is buncombe. Dates only but a lot of fields if
they have rain.'

It was a weary journey to Majmaa, the town at the head of
Sudair's long string of habitations where Shakespear had been
just twelve months before.

Nobody from the West, so far as he knew, had made the journey
through the gorge between Ghat and Majmaa: he had begun to
map virgin territory.

Wali Muhammad surpassed himself that night. They were all
tired but the sight of a meal of soup, sardines, chicken, peas,
potatoes and apricots revived Shakespear's flagging spirits. They
ate and talked and drank coffee until 9 pm. and went to bed
content. 'Shall halt tomorrow to try to get the latitude really
certain.'

Next day he had another 'Europe' morning and after breakfast
went to see his old friend Abdullah ibn Askar. They met in the

Arab's *kahwa*, built sixty years before by his father. It was typical of some of the finer pavilions of the rich men of this fertile and prosperous part of the land and the Englishman describes it in detail:

> A fine big room with two stone columns in the middle to support the roof which is quite 15 to 18 ft up. The walls were jussed for about six feet and had alcoves in them. There were two holes in the roof and three or four in the upper parts of the walls to let in light and air and let out smoke. The door wall was only about eight feet high, the hall being just outside.

Talk and coffee and the belching smoke gave an air of languor to the morning and Shakespear was made more than usually welcome by these generous people. But he had to get on. He had heard that the warrior king of Riyadh was planning another *ghazu*. He had recaptured Katif in a see-saw battle with the Turk and was on the rampage. The Englishman was making a detour of 900 miles in order to meet up with his old friend. He did not want to miss him.

The time had come to write his last letters for despatch to Kuwait. Ghanim and Hadi, his two most reliable men, had to be sent across the desert with them, for the others would not survive the journey alone.

The string of villages through which they passed, eighteen in all, presented some of the loveliest views in all Arabia. It was a pleasant part of the journey. Shakespear was able to take accurate sightings and to make detailed barometric and hypsometric observations as he took in the view.

He provided the first accurate description of the tributaries of the dry water-course of Sudair. It was earlier thought that these drainage beds rose on the Tuwaik heights. He demonstrated that they originated at the borders of Washm and Aridh, stretching north for 100 miles until they were blocked by the Dahana sands. Shakespear's account of the topography and demography of the area was so precise that it was possible for later geographers to draw a complete map and survey of the region, down to the smallest detail, and to make accurate estimates of population.

'It feels home-like, meeting people I know,' he wrote as they passed through the villages of Sudair, and he acknowledged the

greetings of men he had met in the company of Ibn Saud, Mubarak
and other chiefs.

By March 4th rain and wind had returned to hamper their
progress. The men Shakespear met could not remember such
disturbed weather over such a prolonged period in Central
Arabia.

At Audah, the last of the Sudair villages, they came upon more
ruins, the remnants of Ibrahim Pasha's occupation of Najd. But
Shakespear was more interested in the news of Ibn Saud's movements. The amir had not, it seemed, called in his own camels from
the Dahana, where they were kept, so it looked as though he would
still be at Riyadh by the time the Englishman arrived. They progressed to Hasi where they met the local amir, 'a ragamuffin
badawin with barely enough clothing', who reigned over thirty
households. They camped in a depression beyond the settlement.
After dinner Shakespear was working on his maps when he heard
the patter of feet past his tent and the clicking of Martini rifles.
He grabbed his own rifle and roused the camp. Men were running
around the rear of the camp and a dozen or so camels were spotted
on the skyline.

'What are you?'

'*La'ab* (friends), we have only been to buy dates. We are Sbei
friends of Mathi.'

The visitors camped with them for the night.

By March 8th they were proceeding due south over flat, bare
land with only the occasional dry water-course to relieve the
monotony. Again the animals were tired and hungry and they
slowed down. To while away the time on these featureless stages,
Shakespear treated his companions to sermons while they related
the history and folklore of the desert.

The Arabs nodded, but not necessarily in agreement, for they
were half asleep as they rode. When the 'Consul' had finished one
of his diatribes, those who were still listening would look at each
other knowingly and say, 'Maktub.' It is written. The badawin
answer to everything.

That day they reached Banban where there was a water well,
together with six houses, ten men and a few wheat fields by
Shakespear's estimate. Tempers were frayed, for the dreadful
weather lowered the men's spirits, and Abdul Aziz and Mathi had
a blazing row. Next day, however, they were in sight of Riyadh

and morale improved. One of Ibn Saud's men passed them on his
way to bring in the amir's fighting camels from the Dahana.
They camped outside the capital at the date gardens of Shamsiyah.
Mathi was sent ahead to warn the amir of their arrival.

As usual, Shakespear described everything in and around
Riyadh except its appearance. Fortunately, Palgrave had been there
before him and as they approached from the same direction the
scene facing Shakespear must have been much the same as that
described in *Central and Eastern Arabia*:

> Before us stretched a wide open valley, and in its foreground,
> immediately below the pebbly slope on whose summit we
> stood, lay the capital, large and square, crowned by high
> towers and strong walls of defence, a mass of roofs and ter-
> races, where overtopping all frowned the huge but irregular
> pile of Faisal's royal castle, and hard by it rose the scarce less
> conspicuous palace, built and inhabited by his eldest son
> Abdullah .. All around for full three miles over the sur-
> rounding plain, but more especially to the west and south,
> waved a sea of palm trees above green fields and well-watered
> gardens . . .

Shakespear had not finished washing and dressing for his entry
into Riyadh when men and ponies arrived to escort him. Ibn
Saud sent his apologies for not coming in person but he had a
cold and was confined to his palace.

The Englishman's diary tells of their meeting.

> . . . went by moonlight along the Shaib until we crossed a bit
> of rising ground and the whole east wall of town with its
> bastions was in front. Taken through East gate along a wide
> road, past a lot of ruins and some big houses . . . built on a
> palatial scale. Greeted warmly by Abdul Aziz and Saad and
> then taken into library or office. Tea, coffee, and sweets and
> talk until evening prayer and then again afterwards until
> nearly 9.30.

The rain had ceased and the wind dropped. The night was
relatively warm. He finished some sketches before he went to
bed in his tent outside Riyadh. The amir asked him to stay at the
palace but he declined as he felt he would be able to get on with

his maps and diaries better away from the constant interruptions of the amir's court.

Next day he was too late for Ibn Saud's *majlis*, so he took coffee with his father, Abdur Rahman ibn Faisal, imam and grand old man of Najd. He roamed the town with his camera, the first ever to take photographs there, making a unique documentary record of the walled town as it was in the days when its king was said to be able to carry the entire wealth of Central Arabia in gold pieces in his saddle bags.

'Palgrave's plan of Riyadh is exceedingly good,' he wrote that night, 'though the palaces of Al Saud were all demolished by Ibn Rashid, excepting a square sort of fort in Abdullah's Kasr which was the Rashid Governor's house until Abdul Aziz killed him in 1902.'

Since the young Ibn Saud's dramatic return and murder of the Rashid governor, he had been busily rebuilding the *kasrs* of his family and friends. 'Quite a third of the town is taken up by the homes of the Saud family,' Shakespear noted.

Each day while he was in Riyadh, Shakespear spent hours on end in conversation with the amir and his father and brothers. Sometimes they would come out to his camp in the palm grove of Shamsiyah, the garden made by the Circassian Mahbub, Faisal the Great's prime minister and reputed son, who had been mentioned by both Palgrave and Pelly. Those two travellers and Sadlier were the only Europeans of note who got as far as the Najd capital before Leachman reached it less than two years before. But none saw as much of it as Shakespear. Like most European travellers in Arabia he was assumed to possess limitless medical skills and was usually surrounded by a mob of prospective patients pleading for the alleviation of their ills.

On the morning of March 11th, the entire Saud family joined him at camp. They walked around the date gardens together and played with the amir's young children Fahd and Muhammad, and the older boys Turki, Saud and Faisal, Shakespear constantly taking photographs. None of the members of the royal household had been photographed before or had even seen a camera apart from the Englishman's. But whereas in Kuwait and at Thaj they had been slightly suspicious, the princes of Riyadh posed for him and would even form into family groups.

Ibn Saud was always pursued by crowds when he walked around

the town and often had to bolt into his secretary's house after his *majlis* in order to escape them. He was in hiding when Shakespear sought him out to say his farewells. In private, Abdul Aziz was able to speak freely to his old friend and to tell him how much he valued their friendship. Not for the first time the king stressed that Arabia's future resided in an alliance with the 'Great Government', and he saw in Shakespear the one man capable of bringing that alliance about.

Next day Abdul Aziz was to leave on a raid, and the two men arranged to ride out of Riyadh together. No outsider in Arabian history had ridden with the Sauds under the war standard of Riyadh.

The amir mustered the men, dividing up the camels and mares, giving orders in all directions, and frequently cursing his warriors. Then he led them in prayer, as if in atonement for his hasty words. Shakespear left them and went back to sleep in preparation for a busy day to follow. The amir's brother Saad had taken a great liking to his rifle and he left it with him as a parting gift.

As Shakespear led his own contingent into Riyadh on the morning of March 12th, the central square seethed with camels and men. Abdul Aziz was squatting in the midst of the confusion, cursing loudly. Shakespear went to say farewell to Abdur Rahman. He went back to join Ibn Saud who was seeing off his fighting men as the Englishman appeared. The banner of Riyadh went first, fluttering in the breeze and carrying the white *kalima* on its green cloth – 'There is no God but Allah' – and the war cry, 'Victory is of God: success is near'. The king and the Englishman brought up the rear. It was a unique sight and marked a high point in the friendship they had forged out of a meeting at the court of Shaikh Mubarak, four years earlier.

Shakespear's party travelled with the *ghazu* for two days on the journey northward. It was a rewarding experience, since he was able to attend the *majlis* of the amir and the senior shaikhs of his party and join in the discussions of the chiefs and their people. The Englishman talked to the assembly about wireless telegraphy, warships and other modern aids to war and communication and the men listened with rapt attention.

The last night was spent in conversation with the amir on matters of religion and politics, 'another long buck with Abdul

Aziz'. Then he made his farewell calls. Abdul Aziz would be off
before him next day.

The amir had left him three experienced guides, Thami the
Shammari and a Mutairi and an Ataybi. They moved back in the
direction from which they had come, to Banban, where they
passed by their old camp of March 8th. Then they took the
Malham road to Shaib Fajna. It was a dull march, but the monotony was relieved by the appearance of a particularly deadly
snake, which Shakespear labelled a 'Hanasch', probably a desert
viper. He bottled its head most reluctantly in the precious remains
of his whisky. He had no other pickling fluid. The creature was
3' 10" long with a fat body and very thin tail and a huge mouth. Its
colour was generally orange and it had dark-brown splashes down
its back.

That night as on many others, conversation round the coffee
hearth was devoted to the degeneracy of some surviving practices
of the tribes. After one of the Englishman's lectures on their bad
habits, Thami admitted that he knew of young girls being killed
on their bridal night. The thermometer read 73° and the watches
10.45 p.m. when they went to bed.

During early March they passed through almost unknown
territory. Reinaud, Sadlier, Pelly, Palgrave, Raunkiaer and Leachman had wandered by, but it remained one of the great empty
spaces on the maps of the West, undescribed and undefined.
Shakespear noted the features of the Malham oasis with his usual
attention to detail. Extensive palm groves surrounded the two
villages, set on either side of the *shaib*, the depression formed by
the dry wadi near by. The inhabitants were mostly Sbei and
Atayba. A few were of the Bani Khalid. Near by were the villages
of Jarina and Haraimla, which Palgrave had said contained 10,000
souls, but Shakespear could find no more than 3,000, assuming a
generous 7 or 8 to each of the 400 neat and tidy houses. It was a
small paradise. Lemons, oranges, figs, pomegranates and dates
grew in profusion. And there was the castle which Ibrahim Pasha
built and which so astonished Palgrave, though Ibn Saud had
recently demolished it to use its stones for dam building. Here was
the birthplace of the most important religious personality in the
history of Arabia since the Prophet himself – Muhammad ibn
Abdul Wahhab, the motivating force behind much that had

happened in the desert for the past 150 years and the power behind much that was still to happen.

From Haraimla they went on to Thadiq, and again Shakespear's observations differed from Palgrave's. To Palgrave, it was 'a large and busy locality'. Shakespear found it to be a high, bare plateau, the crest of the Tuwaik which stretched far to the south and disappeared in the unexplored wastes of the Empty Quarter, the Rub al Khali.

They proceeded by way of a steep gorge which was said to be the easiest path across the Tuwaik. 'I should hate to negotiate the worst,' said Shakespear.

By mid-March they were across the depression of Shaib Um Sidr and the Nafud sands beyond it, and could look down on the villages of Shaqra and Qarain. They camped at the former and a crowd of small boys immediately gathered round. Shakespear was not feeling too well but he summoned the energy to make the mandatory call on the local chief, the Amir Mahad ibn Saud. Mahad insisted that his English guest should spend the following day with him. It was an opportunity for the Amir of Shaqra to tell of his people's heroism when they had held out for 45 days against Ibn Rashid some time before. He had not been able to tell his story to a stranger since the battle.

Thami the Shammari guide was proving a burden. Not only was he idle, but also, as they went along their north-westerly path that led through Haraimla, Thadiq and Shaqra, and now on towards Juraitha across more red sand, he picked up a growing mob of friends, like a Pied Piper of the desert. They became such a nuisance that Shakespear had to use force. Thami was loafing behind the caravan all day and merely deigned to sleep with it at night.

On March 22nd, in one of their talks around the coffee fire they discussed the habits of the tribes. The western or Harrat section of the Atayba, it seemed, did not clothe their children until they were about to marry; the women wore only a 'horse's eye' fringe about their private parts, even when their breasts were fully formed and menstruation had begun. Iraqi badawin circumcised their women, according to knowledgeable members of the caravan, but this was not a practice permitted among the badu of Arabia proper.

After finishing his journal entry and reading, Shakespear went to sleep, only to awaken at about 10.30 p.m. with the flap of his tent blowing in the night breeze. He shouted to Awayd for a hammer. While driving in the tent peg he noticed that things were disarranged and that his *khanjar*, or dagger, was missing. His *abba*, which he wore in cold weather and otherwise used as a pillow, was missing too, while his British army overcoat was deposited on the basin in the bathroom of his tent. Abdul Aziz and Talaq the *rafiq* found tracks in the sand and followed them while the rest of the party, including Shakespear, pointed their rifles at the night and waited.

After a while they heard Talaq shouting: 'We are Bin Saud's men. No-one must pass near this camp. If you are Atayba, I am the rafiq, I Talaq . . .' There was a chorus of yells from behind every bush within fifty yards. 'You are not Bin Saud's men, you are townsmen. We know Talaq. You are not Talaq. If you are Bin Saud's men speak truly.' Talaq and Thami swore and shouted that they were what they said, inviting one of the unseen intruders to advance to identify Talaq. In seconds a mob of men were among the tents shouting and yelling in confusion, grabbing each other, swearing, demanding and denying. Then a rifle went off.

There was much cursing but fortunately nobody fired a shot in reply. Curses gave way to words of recognition and welcome. They were Atayba of the Burga section, and soon coffee fires were lit and the pestle and mortar began to ring merrily. The stolen property was returned, and Shakespear went to bed while the most villainous crowd he had set eyes on for many a day made itself at home around his hearth.

The visitors turned out to be young raiders of the Atayba who were out learning the business of the *ghazu*. Had Shakespear not discovered the theft they would most certainly have attacked the Englishman and his companions in their sleep. At best they would have lost their belongings. As it was, they were able to continue their journey across the sand barrier of Nafud Es Sirr. It took them six hours of measured camel stride to travel sixteen miles, through scattered villages and past fortified farmhouses in this salty, unhealthy region. The only other European likely to have seen Es Sirr was the German Baron Nolde who penetrated to Anaiza in 1893 and was escorted south to meet Muhammad ibn

Rashid at the time the Amir of Hail had displaced Ibn Saud's father Abdur Rahman. It was now March 25th and they were making remarkably good time through 'pestilential' weather; they stopped at the village of Mudhnib for sweet water, crossing a 'beastly' stone plateau covered with flat chips of slate-like limestone, to their next camp at a deserted place called Shaib Laudhan.

Next day they sighted Anaiza, the great town set on the boundary of Qasim at the eastern extremity of the Wadi ar Rummah, one of the major dry waterways of Arabia, which still ran more than a mile in width and from six to nine feet deep after heavy rain and thus supported some fine plantations and provided the badu with a huge source of water.

Shakespear carried with him a sheaf of letters of introduction, some from Ibn Saud and Mubarak, others from princes of Arabia who enjoyed a position of nominal neutrality between the warring houses of Riyadh and Hail. Anaiza at this time was governed by the Amir Saleh ibn Zamil. The Englishman and his party entered Anaiza by the east gate and camped under the wall in a part of the enclosed town reserved for the people of Zilfi. Thami was sent off with a letter to the amir from Mubarak: 'To all the people of Anaiza. God keep them safe. We, the shaikhs and you, are obliged by the will of God to guard the Englishman and protect him from any unfriendly hand.'

Before Shakespear was able to wash and change his clothes, the letter brought the amir in person and a host of local shaikhs to see him.

They had travelled through the night and were able to spend a full day in this 'civilised place . . . so different from the rest of Najd'. In the afternoon Shakespear strolled through the market place to the amir's palace to make a return call. Suddenly he was back in the world of commerce and politics, of cosmopolitan men and sophisticated habits. When he was with Ibn Saud or with the people of the desert whose lives were guided by the strict code of their Wahhabi faith, he did not openly smoke or drink. It was pleasant to relax in the company of Saleh ibn Zamil, to talk freely of matters of politics and religion, smoke his pipe and listen to talk of business dealings in India, Egypt, Mesopotamia and the Hijaz. He met the distinguished merchant Mahad al Suleiman, and had coffee at the house of 'a dear old deaf man'. He also came face to face with the 'Najdi quack' who now made loud claim to having cured Shaikh Mubarak of his illness the previous year.

Two of Shakespear's *agheyls* (the neutral caravanners who were supposed to protect wayfarers from molestation in Arabia), Abdullah and Muhammad, decided they could go no further just before he moved on towards Buraida, the other great township of Qasim. The amir found him two substitute men and he moved off on Saturday, March 28th, though departure was delayed by a seething crowd of visitors who had come to wish them well. They loaded up with fresh fruit, sweet water and the many gifts showered on them, and Shakespear gave Saleh a Mannlicher carbine and doctored his brother who was yellow with jaundice.

Rain and cloud had given way to intense heat and a glaring sun. The journey was only eighteen miles in length but they were weary and almost blinded by the time they arrived at Buraida. Even the freshly watered camels wilted.

Doughty had looked down on the green gardens between the two towns 'in their winding sheet of sand' and when he saw Buraida for the first time, coming upon it from a brow of the Nafud, he found 'Jerusalem in the desert'. Like his predecessor, Shakespear was overwhelmed by the sight. Whereas Doughty found words to convey its enchantment, 'a little oozing water ... by the tamarisks', and to describe the course of the wadi across the sandy plain of Qasim, 'sometimes hardly to be discerned by the eyes of strangers', Shakespear did not stand and look; he unpacked his survey equipment to take measurements of height and distance and depth, to measure rainfall and make boiling-water tests.

They camped at a place described by Palgrave, a sandy plain under the fort in the north face of the town wall. 'The north face of the town must be nearly, if not quite, a mile long.'

Thami had been sent on ahead to warn the Amir Fahad ibn Mu'amar of their arrival. In fact, Ibn Saud had already sent a messenger to tell Fahad – who had fought with him in the 1912 battle with Husain of Mecca – that his English friend would be calling on him. As they pitched their tents, Thami and an old friend from Kuwait, Abbas al Falaiji, came galloping towards them to bid him attend the amir's *majlis* which was in progress at that moment. After introducing himself to Mu'amar Shakespear went back to his tent to rest, only to find that the amir had pursued him in the company of a noxious, fat Arab, one Abdullah al Khalifa, who insisted on talking in very bad English which he had acquired in New York.

Buraida fell far short of its promise in terms of hospitality. It was the loveliest and greenest place Shakespear had found in his travels. But Fahad and his cronies were, he said, 'fanatic, inhospitable and shameless in their dealings'. Leachman had remarked that it was one of the few towns in Najd where he met discourtesy. For Shakespear, it was a great disappointment after the first impact of the 'great clay town built on waste sand'.

They were less than a third of the way across the peninsula. More camels and guides were needed and they wanted fresh *agheyls*. Ibn Saud's rascally old ally proved to be a hard bargainer: a shifty and shameless dealer who demanded eight Turkish pounds per camel and money in advance. The Englishman handed over his deposit, only to find that the amir was set on a new round of bargaining. Fearing that the contract would be broken by the unscrupulous Fahad, he asked for his money back and suggested that the amir should take another look at Ibn Saud's letter sent to him by special messenger and at the letter which Mubarak had written:

> The person who is calling on you is called Shakespear, the English Consul. If God wills when he arrives with you he will be kept in care and comfort until our son Abdul Aziz bin Saud contacts you. This is required of you.
> God keep you safe. Salaam,
>
>   MUBARAK

Shakespear left him to reconsider his attitude. Later Thami hurried back to camp to say that the amir promised to keep his bargain if the money was sent along. Next day a new round of negotiation was necessary since the amir had conceived an all-in scheme whereby the Englishman would pay Ali al Ribdi, a camel dealer, sixty Turkish pounds for the services of an expert *agheyl* and six camels to take his kit to Damascus at the end of the journey. He was running short of money but it seemed to be about as good a deal as he could hope for. In the end he had to provide his own saddle bags and load the new pack camels himself, with the aid of Abdul Aziz and Awayd. His new helpers,

supplied by Ibn Mu'amar, appeared when the caravan was ready
to move off. Their names were Abdulla and Suliman. There was
also a 'slab-sided' youth, the brother of the camel dealer Ali al
Ribdi, who did not appear to have a name. He missed his old
rafiqs and had little faith in the new men. He had caught a bad
chill. His throat was sore and his head had ached for several days.
But they had to move on.

They passed out of settled Qasim into land that was the traditional preserve of the badu.

The easier routes from Buraida would have taken them either
northwest through Hail or west through Taima. Instead they took
a new, unexplored path to Jauf, through the plain of Asiyah and
El Bittar, which they had traversed on the first part of the journey,
through the eastern region of Jabal Shammar, the closed and
unwelcoming territory of the Rashids, and along the entire
eastern and northern boundaries of the Nafud desert.

A *shimal* blew as they set out and Shakespear's throat became
unbearable as the swirling sand penetrated the mask of his kaffiya,
which he was forced to wear when the wind was up. For hundreds
of miles now they could look forward to wild, uninhabited
country and none but the badawin to keep them in touch with
mankind. The northern part of Qasim was barren and devoid of
interest. Shakespear was sick and all the men were weary from
poor food, hard terrain and salty, brackish water. But they were
forced to keep on the move. There is no mercy for the straggler or
the weakling who stays to nurse his wounds in such places. They
kept themselves going with endless conversation, Shakespear
listening the while for his throat prevented him from adopting
his usual role of philosopher to his desert-bred companions. As
they passed by Arabia's Stonehenge, which Palgrave had said was
near Ayun and which they found to be called Hassat-an-Nasala,
one of the new men told them the story of the fat Abdullah al
Khalifa whom Shakespear had instantly disliked when they met at
Buraida. Abdullah, now a very rich man, had owned a shop in
Cairo which went bankrupt, so he stowed away aboard a ship
which took him to New York. There he drove a cab for six
years, saved £1,000 and became a rich merchant before returning
to Buraida. The previous year he had gone on the hajj. After
visiting the Holy Cities and acting out the ceremonies and rituals
of the pilgrim, he could not resist the temptation to take ship to

Bombay to add to his fortune. He returned from the hajj the richer by £400. 'Now he is one of the biggest men in Buraida,' they said. By Sunday, April 5th, they were deep into the sands of El Bittar, at Mudaraj, where Al Ribdi the Buraida camel dealer kept his animals. They were surprised to see the merchant himself galloping out of a swirling sand cloud to complete his side of their bargain. From here they would have fresh animals and *agheyls*.

The weather grew less friendly as they went. Now the wind was bitterly cold, and as Shakespear's sickness worsened and his stomach became raw with the effects of brackish water, he turned to more map projection and to brushing up his French to keep his mind off his woes. Their remaining water looked 'like urine' and he could not wash or even develop his photographs in it. 'Had a look at the sun at noon but miles too high for the sextant now.'

Now they moved into the Nafud proper, earlier red sands being tongues of the great desert which licked deep into the territory of Najd. Sandy waves, 300 feet high, formed an endless vista of ridges. They were, according to Shakespear, of different sand from that of El Bittar, though Leachman had linked them on his map while showing them as separate dunes. They were now twenty-eight miles from the point where they had begun their ascent to Riyadh on the first stage of the journey several weeks before. The Batin was below them to the east stretching almost to Basra and Kuwait.

They passed the last waves of the Bittar sand steppes, making for Zarud, a station on the Darb Zobaida, the pilgrim road from Persia to Mecca. Water was still a nasty, straw colour and tasted even worse than it looked. Shakespear's stomach still felt sore and his head ached. He found it difficult to decide on the road to take now that he had picked up his *agheyls* and a seething mass of camels, some 400 in all: Al Ribdi had decided they would have to take him and his animals along with them. For more than a week now a fierce *shimal* had blown in their path and it was bitterly cold. Shakespear wore his army overcoat and woollen gloves, but the cold went from his throat to his chest and caused him to cough. They made slow progress northwards.

They nearly took the diagonal route across Jabal Shammar to Jauf, their immediate northerly destination. But in the end they decided to skirt the Shammar country, along the edge of the

Nafud desert. The country was not as he had expected, with a sand wall providing shelter and an easily defined path. Either his own map projection was wrong or the information on which it was based inaccurate. There was a continual rise and fall of dunes, radiating eastwards towards the Dahana belt. They had to go another 150 weary miles before they found the protective wall of Nafud. With Shammari and Ruwala guides leading the way, Shakespear was forced to leave direction-finding to them, for his maps were now useless, and in this wild country only the badawin could find his way with assurance. The Shammar and the Ruwala, principal tribe of the great Anaiza confederation, were the bitterest enemies in all Arabia, but the *agheyls* have their own code of conduct and the two guides who now led them appeared to get on well enough with each other, though in a tribal feud they would have had little fellow feeling.

Al Ribdi was proving a menace on the journey. He appeared to interpret the contract with Shakespear liberally, deciding which camels the party could use and refusing to have any part of water-gathering and other chores which everyone else shared. Shakespear upbraided him, whereupon he changed his tune and swore eternal friendship. Meanwhile, one of the guides had disappeared and several camels went astray. Progress was still slow and painful. The Englishman was just finishing his map projection for the final stages of the journey when a *zarag* snake slithered across the floor of his tent. The same evening he killed another poisonous specimen, 'a vicious little brute called *Um Janaib*, like a horned viper, without the horns, about 15 inches long.'

In the second half of April they were deep into Shammar country. Ibn Rashid's men even appeared in the night to count their camels. Water could only be obtained now with the approval of the Rashid guards who were stationed at the wells and relieved once a year. Another *rafiq* left them, Husain the Harbi, deciding to return to his people. Life was becoming hard for the faithful Abdul Aziz, Awayd and Wali Muhammad who had to do most of the donkey work now that the original *rafiqs* had all gone. To make matters worse, Dhabia became ill and had to be rested. Shakespear treated her with medicines as though she were an ailing human.

When they reached the wells of Haiyaniya they heard startling news; nine days before, the homicidal family of Rashid had engaged in another bout of murder. The young Amir Saud ibn Rashid, now just about twenty years old, had decided to kill his Regent Zamil ibn Subhan. He and the son of Saleh ibn Subhan, another Saud and nephew of the regent, planned the coup. When the Shammar army was on the march near Abu Ghar with the regent at its head, they instructed a slave to follow Zamil and shoot him in the back. When the regent's brothers and others of his supporters jumped on their mares and made off, they were pursued and killed too. While all this was going on the two young Sauds rode past without paying the slightest attention. Zamil ibn Subhan and his cousin before him had saved Saud ibn Rashid from almost certain death as an infant and had protected him for the best part of his twenty years.

Shakespear carried a letter from Shaikh Mubarak to the Prince Saud ibn Abdul Aziz al Rashid:

An Englishman named Shakespear is visiting you in order to buy horses. He requires from six to eight animals for adornment and according to the ties of friendship between our two great nations, our Happy Arabian State and the Great and Glorious English State, it is our duty and yours that we guard this man and help him. As his intention is to come to you with his men to visit the fortress of Shammar and Harb, and on his way to see the Arabs of the north, then going into Egypt, we hope that you assist his journey and protect him. My son and brothers salute you.

Salaam.

MUBARAK

It was a cleverly worded letter, but not much use to Shakespear. As the friend of Ibn Saud, a fact widely known by now among the tribes, he would be ill advised to seek an audience with the young king.

The Buraidi guides were proving more nuisance than they were worth, and to make life even more difficult the Shammar tribesmen were stealing their camels and charging two pounds in Turkish money for their return. To complete the misery of this chaotic part of the journey Ali al Ribdi and his Buraidi friends somehow obtained the carcass of a sheep and promptly devoured the best meat off it, offering Shakespear and his hungry companions the bones, with a few miserable pieces of fat on them.

The Englishman found some solace in being able to take his first bath for three weeks and in trimming his rapidly growing beard. 'If only we can get to Jauf without losing all our camels I shall be thankful,' he wrote.

Rain and heat came alternately at this stage; even Dhabia was giving Shakespear trouble. She decided to pretend lameness, 'as artful as any pretty woman would be', and he was compelled to let her follow at her own pace while he rode one of the *agheyl dhaluls*.

By April 22nd tempers had improved, the men were treating Al Ribdi's bad manners and meanness as a jocular subject for their coffee-hearth soirées, imitating his evil gestures and deriding his laziness. And Dhabia was improving. But by the next day, the mood had changed again. A fierce wind blew up in the night and tents had to be taken down hurriedly. The men were forced to sleep in the open with a wicked gale blowing. Amid this constant discomfort and apparently endless adversity, Shakespear never failed to make his barometric readings and his boiling-water tests.

As they marched north-eastwards on the last stage of the journey to Jauf, they encountered the Anaiza people, and at their first coffee halt they were approached by a fine old Arab from Damascus who offered to give them reliable men, as many as they needed to see them to Egypt; and he would accompany them on their way. 'A most delightful change after the ignorant Buraida swine.' The old man was in complete charge of the tribesmen with him and they ran about 'doing his bidding like small boys'. Shakespear decided to lie in bed in the morning. Soon he would be able to tell the Buraidi *agheyls* and Ribdi to go to the devil.

They had left the wells of Khub Labba and several deserted townships behind, including Kasr Adhfa, with a single well beneath its north-west tower which Muhammad ibn Rashid had filled in to discourage Ruwala raiders. They were treading sand covered in the larvae of locusts when they met the next wayfarer. He was another old man, who at first took Shakespear for a railway official looking for a route from Suez to Kuwait – an astute observation since the Political Agent, in his inevitable role of Intelligence agent, had been asked by Craufurd to look at the territory with precisely that possibility in view. The newcomer's

name was Muhammad al Rawaf and he had been in charge of
camels at the Chicago exhibition fifteen years before and had
afterwards travelled in Brazil. In virtually unexplored regions to
which few Europeans had hitherto gained access Shakespear had
now heard of two Arabs who had been to America. His aged
companion told him that another European Christian had passed
this way not twenty days before. He had come by rail from Constantinople to Tabuk, and from there by camel to Taima and Hail
to see Ibn Rashid. Finding the Amir of Hail away, presumably on
his recent mission of murder, he went on to Kerbela. 'Government business,' said the old man confidentially.

As they trod the relatively easy path through the Nafud sands of
Hadjara on the last stages to Jauf, the discomforts of the recent
past were fading. It was April 25th. Eight days before, when the
wind had forced them to abandon their tents and sleep under the
stars, a badawin found a deserted wolf earth with eight cubs in it.
The badu distributed the young animals, yelping for milk, and
Shakespear took a female and fed it on goat's milk. He nursed his
pup, and it came on well, becoming a favoured member of an
increasingly bizarre caravan of animals and men. Now he was
offered an ostrich chick by another badawin. But his menagerie was
full, and he declined the offer.

He still had health problems, for which the veterinary equipment
of the camel men came in useful. He had a bad toothache and
borrowed a guide's rusty forceps in order to remove one of his
own lower molars.

By Sunday, April 26th, they were at camp on the edge of a flat
plain within sight of Jauf. Locusts had eaten every piece of
greenery for miles around. Insects infested the tents and the men
itched. Shakespear's whole body ached with exertion and his
neck had swelled with insect bites.

On the following day they made a 'silly' march of $2\frac{1}{2}$ hours'
duration to find grazing and await a visit from Ibn Shaalan, the
venerable Amir of Jauf. But the locusts arrived before them and
they had to spend most of the day in a frantic effort to keep the
insidious creatures out of their tents. The wolf cub had become
lame and Dhabia, who was much better, was resting herself in
her master's *mizwada*, or baggage tent. His camel was much
indulged and usually couched under a tent of her own at night.

The diary notes of Tuesday, April 28th, tell the story of the entry to Jauf:

> Off early over very flat plain until we reached top of Jauf basin. Got some bearings to hills etc. Descent into Jauf drops over four successive ledges, a white limestone, and red slatey-looking close-grain stone, similar to that at Majmaa, and greyish close-grain stone, almost a green colour, and again limestone or chalk. This is the order of descent. In the basin immediately struck three new plants (or rather not seen since Kuwait), a red Hamth, Shigara and a useless though pretty shrub called . . . (must find out what that one is) . . .

And so on. Normally, after so long and tiring a journey, Shakespear would have rushed into Jauf to seek the comfort and sanctuary of a town which boasted at least the basic amenities of civilization. But he was in a solitary mood and he stayed behind with his botanical specimens while Al Rawaf led the others into the town.

> The agheyl did not wait for baggage to arrive but rushed off direct to Bin Shaalan's deputy, a semi-negro called Amar. He was very pleasant and hospitable, largely due I think to Muhammad al-Ruwaf having preceded me by some minutes. Fed with dates and ghi, coffee and tea until evening, then a terrific dinner of a whole sheep and rice. Young Sultan, son of Nawaf bin Nuri bin Shaalan, a ripping little chap of ten years, took special charge of me, and was not a bit scared, but chatted away like blazes.

Jauf, the home of the Shaalan, hereditary amirs of the immensely powerful Anaiza confederation and of its principal tribe the Ruwala, was a place of staunch independence. Nuri ibn Shaalan, proud and determined leader of his vast tribe, was a cornerstone of Arabian politics, and his friendship was sought by the princes of Arabia and the Turks alike. In the shifting alignments and the ceaseless battle for ascendancy among them, his support was often vital, and in years to come he was to prove an important element in the Arab struggle for independence.

Shakespear was the first outsider to woo and win his favour. For Ibn Shaalan, Ibn Saud was an important ally, for though the Amir of Jauf could lay claim to kingship of the greatest tribal alliance in Arabia and was, therefore, in some ways as powerful as the Amir of Najd, his position was weakened by eternal conflict with the Shammar, who came close to the Anaiza in number and probably excelled them in strength of arms and the discipline of their men. The Anaiza and the Shammar were hereditary enemies and their feud had lasted for centuries. Hail and much of Jabal Shammar was rich in pasture lands, watered by the Wadi ar Rummah and its tributaries, rich in horses, sheep and camels, as were Riyadh and the dominions of Ibn Saud. Though Ibn Shaalan was not so well off in material terms, and Jauf, his capital, had diminished in size and importance over the past century, he still led the numerically strong and widely feared Anaiza, and was thus the lord of something like a third of the black tents of the desert. His own tribe, the Ruwala, were proud custodians of the *Markab* or Abu Duhur, the Ark of Ishmael; elaborately gilded and embroidered, the ark passed from tribe to tribe by right of con-quest, but it was in a sense the common property of the badu who made votive and thank-offerings before it. It had been in the possession of the Ruwala for the past 150 years. The federated tribes of Anaiza – Ruwala, Fidan, Amarat and Saba – accounted for over 12,000 tents and 60,000 people in Shakespear's time.

It was two days before Shakespear met the amir. In the mean-time, he talked with Nuri's son Nawaf and was looked after with touching concern by the chief's grandson Sultan; when he could escape the lad's attentions he engaged in the usual round of bargaining for *rafiqs* and pack camels. With eyes and ears open as he went, he learned of yet another example of European inter-ference in Arabia. Through the agency of a doctor who used the name Musa Namisu, the Austrians were arming the Ruwala and providing the tribe with considerable food supplies, to help them in their fight against Turkey's ally Ibn Rashid.

On the second full day in Jauf ('which is properly called Jauf-al-Amr after Omar the second Caliph', he noted) he bargained feverishly with Shaikh Amar, a camel dealer; in the end he gave him Craufurd's rifle, left with him after their last voyage on the *Lewis Pelly*, in the hope that it might soften him up. Amar merely complained at the small number of cartridges that went with the gift. They settled for two *rafiqs* and two camels at £10 each, Shakespear preferring to wait until he met the next Arab chief, Audah of the Howeitat, before buying more camels.

It was not until their final day in Jauf, Thursday, April 30th, that the Englishman met Ibn Shaalan. The amir called at his camp in the afternoon just after Shakespear had discovered that the hired *rafiqs* wanted to call off their escort duty, though the money had been paid. That matter was resolved with hard words, and Shakespear was not in the best of moods when Nuri ibn Shaalan arrived at his tent. He presented Mubarak's letter to the amir, explaining that Ibn Saud had thought it best not to send a communication in case it was intercepted in the desert. Then, with his remarkable ability to bring the Arab chieftains to his side, he turned from the customary polite exchanges to the amir's favourite topics, guns and medicine. He explained the curative effects of the drugs he was carrying and Ibn Shaalan listened with rapt attention. Then he presented a carefully prepared medicine chest to the amir. Nuri became a practising doctor from that moment. But he was not immediately confident enough to try his hand at curing the insane. He brought a lunatic to Shakespear for attention and the Englishman shook his head and admitted that the case was beyond even his curative powers. Then they turned to firearms. Shakespear carried a veritable armoury with him and the amir tried one gun after another. They set up a target and Nuri shot off each gun in turn, showing himself to be a good marksman. Then he asked Shakespear to try. He hit the target first time. The amir suggested a competition, and Shakespear, determined not to be beaten, tried for all he was worth and won a close-fought contest.

They departed at 6 a.m. next day, stopping at the amir's palace on the way through the town to breakfast with the chief, who joked about the Englishman's victory the day before. Farewells were prolonged and affectionate. Young Sultan asked for a coin from the Englishman, as a token rather than a bribe, and burst into tears at the moment of parting. But Arab being Arab, and incapable of passing up an opportunity to make money, one nobleman of Jauf brought eleven eggs, offered them as though he was making a presentation, and then asked some six times the market price for them. 'You blighter,' said Shakespear in English as he paid up.

They had to trot to catch up with the baggage camels. They were now out of the Nafud proper and approaching the stony Harra desert. They found difficulty in keeping to the road plotted by Shakespear on his maps; they were in unknown territory and the guides seemed to be at odds with their tribes so that they afforded no protection and very little directional assistance. Advised by Al Rawaf, who had decided to accompany them further, Shakespear told one argumentative *agheyl* to go to the devil and made do with the others in the hope that they could reach the Shaikh of the Howeitat before their throats were cut. The Howeitat *rafiqs*, who had joined him at Jauf, even tried blackmail, demanding loans as a condition of going on whenever they struck especially dangerous territory.

By May 3rd they were on a totally uninhabited and uncharted road leading north-west through a painful flint plain. Shaikh Audah was normally reckoned to be two days' march from Jauf. They had travelled for two days and were still a day's march away from the source of camels and *rafiqs* that should see them through the last stage of the journey to Aqaba.

Next day they ran into territory that was alive with rascals, apparently encouraged by the Howeitat *rafiq* whom Shakespear had dismissed at the start of the journey from Jauf. Soon they were under attack. They were forced to camp at 10.30 a.m. and to set up an armed fortress to ward off the raiders. By the afternoon they decided to break for freedom, with the strongest members of the party and the best shots leading the way. Shakespear and the most trusted of the guides galloped on their *dhaluls* towards Shaikh Audah's camp. The rest found a bunker and hid in terror, to follow the next day when the raiders had dispersed.

Parched by the hot, waterless desert and worn out by the effort of evading the wild men who came after them, they arrived at Audah's camp a day later than they had expected. Shakespear's throat was too dry and swollen to eat with comfort, but he swallowed as much as he could and made the obligatory appearance at the camp fire of the Shaikh of Abu Taiya.

This was the point at which Abdul Aziz and Wali Muhammad had to leave him. They were to take the main part of the baggage to Damascus, and return from there to Kuwait. It was a sad parting, for they had been the mainstay of his journey, faithful and attentive. Of the men who had set out from Kuwait, only Awayd and Ali the Ajmani now remained with him.

Shaikh Audah, whose renown went before him in the northern deserts, was all that Shakespear expected. He lived up to his
reputation by rousing Shakespear from his bed to announce that
he could not accept the apology of the practically penniless
Englishman for the absence of a suitable present. The suggestion
that he should name a gift which would be sent to him from Egypt,
and take £10 on account, was nothing short of an affront. Eventually, Shakespear was forced to empty his entire belongings before
the scoundrel; when he realized that every worthwhile possession
had already been given away and the Englishman had a meagre
£27 left in money, the shaikh reluctantly decided to take £20,
leaving his guest with the remaining £7 to see him to Egypt. As
a final gesture, he took the finely braided camel girths and coloured
halters with which Dhabia was dressed. 'Poor Dhabia will look
very naked now,' said her dejected owner. In return for all this
Audah did at least provide the *rafiqs* and camels needed to see the
party to Aqaba. But he was a ruffian if ever Shakespear had met
one, red kaffiya covering a mane of black-grey hair, dirty *dishdasha*
over his erect, martial body. He was husband to twenty-odd
women and father to uncounted children. But nearly all the
members of his vast family had been killed in wars which he had
provoked and in the tribal raids that were his *raison d'être*. He kept
count of the Arabs he had felled, but not of the Turks who were
his favourite prey.

They set out on May 7th at sunset, to make the final, fearsome
stage of their journey under cover of darkness, for the region
through which they were to pass was the most dangerous in all
Arabia. The guides insisted that from now on Shakespear should
wear Arab dress, for all their lives were at stake. For the first
time since he entered the desert five years before, Shakespear
packed away his Indian army greatcoat and topee and donned the
kaffiya headdress and the *abba*.

On the first night they slept for two hours under bushes of
ghada, then they crossed the Wadi Sirhan where the British
explorers Aylmer and Butler had been in 1907, and halted at the
wells of Arfajiya. They washed and filled their water skins but
they could not pitch tents for fear of being seen. Without cover
Shakespear could not work at his maps. It was the first time that
anything on the entire route had been allowed to interfere with
his survey routine.

They went on in bright moonlight, keeping as far as possible in the shadows of the sandhills that dotted the lip of the Sirhan until they came to Basaita, flat as a pancake, bare of vegetation and covered by gravel. They bivouacked when they were too tired to go on, scraping a place in the gravel on which to sleep. They had marched for forty hours and had about four hours' sleep.

The night of May 8th was too cold for them to journey on. While Shakespear slept for a few hours there was a calamity. The camels, perhaps disturbed by intruders, panicked, and in the rough and tumble that ensued his wolf cub was trampled to death. He had nursed her with great care and devotion and by now she was tame and had become a lively companion. When he was aroused by the noise, she lay dead on the gravel.

His body was 'one huge ache'. The sun was intense by day; the cold penetrating by night. Without his topee he had a touch of sunstroke and was reeling for part of the day; but they went on for fourteen hours on camelback, by foot when the going was too rough for the animals to carry their human burdens. He decided to wear his topee again and to keep the kaffiya by him for emergencies. No sooner had he changed headdress than a rider appeared on the horizon. But Ali the Ajmani chased him away. Now they had to find natural shelter wherever they went and eat scrap meals from tins. They could not pitch camp or light fires. They marched only at night, usually in the face of a fierce gale. They were in wild country of red and black stone ridges, without grazing for the animals. Shakespear's nose was blistered by the sun. They found a half-dry well and washed in its putrid water. But it made them feel better. As they ate a hurried meal under a huge rock, they were visited by a scorpion. It came within two feet of Shakespear before he caught sight of it and killed it.

On May 10th his diary read:

Got off early and did a good trek in the cold moonlight, bivouacking in a dry nullah perished with cold, with forbidding looking rock hills all around. Not a vestige of grazing for camels. Head, eyes, mouth all full of sand. We are in the Tubaik hills. Men undoubtedly good guides. Got a couple of photos to try and show kind of country . . . Ascended a terrific pass in afternoon at junction of rocky Tubaik and the sandy Sanam. Much against the men's will pitched kitchen and

Abdul Aziz's tents to try to get a little food cooked and do some map plotting. Just finished plotting when tents had to come down. Men still scared to death of Shammar raiders. All this country is so desolate as to be no use for grazing and is only traversed by raiding parties . . .

Although they had made some progress the previous afternoon, they were still travelling mainly by night.

Monday, May 11th:

Started early before the moon was up and after some good going reached a place which looked like the side of a house. Here the camels panicked at the squawking of some young crows and refused to pass, so we had to go round and had fearful time in the cold wind wandering about among hill tops in a half light, tripping over stones, slithering about in sand hollows.

The road towards the Hijaz railway which they now took was probably the most dangerous in Arabia – thick with natural hazards and rogue tribesmen. Every step had to be considered, every sand track investigated before they could move on. In the hope of getting out of the region as fast as they could they travelled by day and night, sheltering and sleeping for an hour or two whenever they found a suitable place and then going on; but all the time, whatever the danger, Shakespear recorded and noted. They passed some Howeitat tents and a little while later the scouting guides came to tell them that the tents had been raided soon after they passed. The *ghazu* would now be following their sand tracks. They hurried on and finally found a deserted place called Bawaib where they bivouacked on a sand slope. It was a fortunate halt for the camels, for *ghada*, a succulent tree of the tamarisk family, grew there and the animals were able to eat for several hours.

On May 12th they were able to light lanterns for the first time since leaving the *agheyl* camp in Audah's territory six days before. They were at the summer headquarters of the Howeitat, and the water was excellent. Herds of oryx inhabited the area, but it was too dangerous to pitch camp. Shakespear plotted his maps and they moved on towards the railway.

A four-hour march by moonlight took them to the Hijaz

railroad, a single, metre-gauge track, with wooden telegraph poles along its length. They were approaching civilization, but there were dangerous regions still to be negotiated between here and Egypt. Shakespear kept his notebook ready to sketch in natural features and the place names which were known only to his companions.

The plain beyond the railway was utterly bare, with numberless tracks running from north to south. It was the old hajj road from Damascus which pilgrims had used for more than a thousand years and along which an élite of Europeans had travelled during the four hundred years since the Italian Varthema had made the first recorded visit of an outsider to Mecca in the early sixteenth century.

They dropped into a broad valley with awe-inspiring slopes to either side of them. The hajj route from Cairo passed this way and they began to meet groups of Arabs. They turned into a cool gorge and found a cave where they could rest without having to pitch tents. On Friday, May 15th, they left the gorge and soon found spring water coming from a cleft in the rocks. They made for Wadi Ithm but found that it was wrongly marked on existing maps. They could not find a way through to Aqaba and they could find no Arabs to tell them the way. They decided to sleep on the problem.

Next morning an Arab came by who was known to one of the guides. Shakespear, wearing his Arab dress, affected to be a sick *agheyl*, while the men bribed the newcomer to show them the way.

It was the worst day of the entire journey. They went easily across the Wadi Yatun, the Englishman still sick and wrapped in his *abba* and double kaffiya and pretending to be speechless until they reached Naqab, at a height of over 4,000 ft according to Shakespear's aneroid reading. They glimpsed the sea and a haze in the distance above Aqaba. The descent was hair-raising. Shakespear turned one ankle three times and the other once. He was in great pain but found that it was even worse when he tried to mount Dhabia so he trudged on for an hour until he could stand the agony no longer. They halted at 9 p.m., but the guides wanted to go on so that they could be clear of Wadi Musa and its dangerous inhabitants before daybreak. Shakespear's shoes had come away from his feet and two camels were badly lame. The only course open to them was to jettison a large part of their load and make their way by night on full stomachs and a prayer. They consumed the rest of their food and left behind chairs, several tents, spare poles, Shakespear's wooden bathtub and four water skins. The remaining load redistributed, they marched through the night in a stumbling effort to reach the bottom of Wadi Musa. They went on a slow, downward path for five hours. Their feet were bruised, camels were lame, and the men were exhausted. When finally they reached the base of the Wadi, running through mountainous sand and rock, they had to find the road up the next range of hills. Some of the men simply fell asleep in their tracks. Those who could keep awake went in search of their road. Shakespear's *shedad*, a silver-mounted acacia-wood camel saddle, slipped from Dhabia's back and hung sideways. He tried to adjust it, but a strap had broken, and so he walked, thankful for the better going. At 4.30 a.m. they were progressing along the soft bed of a stream on a rising gradient, until they came to another gorge and a well-defined track running north-west. At 5.30 a.m. when daylight broke, one of the Howeitat guides decided that he could go no further. Never before had Shakespear sympathized with a deserting *rafiq*, but now even he could understand the man's reluctance. He paid him two pounds and let him go.

They were feeling fairly safe from pursuit, and a cool wind blew. They halted for breakfast at 7.30 a.m. after clambering over the roughest terrain they had encountered for nearly twelve hours without rest. They were still surrounded by mountains, but they felt that the worst part of the journey was behind them.

They had only dates and camel milk to sustain them now, and soon they found that their optimism was ill placed. As the heat became worse, so did the road. The camels trudged on bravely but they were in poor shape. None of the guides knew the territory they were in and finding a way out to the north seemed more hopeless as the hours passed and their weariness grew. Then, suddenly, they came on to a plain, and the road to Kontilla in Egypt stretched before them. When they reached it they had travelled for twenty hours with only two brief stops. All the camels were lame or tender. They pitched one of their remaining tents for cooking purposes, and slept under bushes, grateful for the mercy of clement weather and safe passage. 'I would like to sleep for ever,' he wrote. 'It was the worst day of my life and one I shall never forget.'

Despite the need for sleep, they were off before breakfast on Sunday, May 17th, and they crossed the boundary into Egypt before halting for more dates and milk. At about 11 a.m. they sighted the police post of Kontilla, and hobbled towards it. They decided to have a full day's rest, the first since leaving the domain of old Audah Abu Taiya.

A bath, taken while the men did their washing and generally gave expression to their feeling of relief, was followed by a bottle of Moselle, his last but one.

Awayd was sent into town to purchase food and the ingredients of a genuine meal. The menu that night was the realization of many a desert dream: 'Vermouth. Consommé Bovril. Saumon à la Worcester sauce, sparkling Moselle (the last bottle). Pilau of mutton with carrots and celery. Tapioca. Blanc Mange à la vanille. Port wine and sugared rice. Floured dessert cakes.'

All cooked by Awayd to his master's instructions and solemnly noted in the diary. A night cap of whisky and bed. They still had several days' march across Sinai ahead.

Monday, May 18th, was a real 'Europe' morning, beginning with a shave and ending with photographs of the Kontilla post and the local inhabitants, who, to his surprise, spoke English. He had heard hardly a word spoken in his native tongue for $3\frac{1}{2}$ months.

They repacked their *yakdans* and prepared to leave in the evening. Meanwhile the Egyptian boss of Kontilla had shown an interest in Dhabia. Her owner was reluctant to let her go but he could not take her to England. Almost as if she knew that something was afoot she decided to go lame again and the Egyptian lost interest.

They left Kontilla in the early evening but all the camels were so lame they bivouacked at 10.30 p.m. and began the march again next morning at 5 a.m. There had been no rain in this arid juncture of Arabia and Egypt for four years, and so the animals went hungry again. They went on through Bir Abbas on the hajj road, the men determined to stop for coffee wherever possible, their relentless leader pushing them to the limit, for he was now determined to reach civilization as quickly as he could. There were occasional stops for rest and two or three hours' sleep and the inevitable halts for prayer. Otherwise they travelled through torrid heat to Nakhl, where they arrived at 6 a.m. on Thursday, May 21st. The influence of the British was everywhere. A guard of honour turned out to welcome them and the district commissioner, or mudir, Captain C. E. Barlow, gave Shakespear the run of his office. He wrote letters to friends and relatives telling them of his safe arrival, brought his notes on the journey up to date and prepared for the final four days' march to Suez. Barlow arranged for enough money to be made available to see him home. By May 24th they were in sight of Suez. The guides and camel men had been paid off with the exceptions of Ali and Awayd. Dhabia, along with the remaining camels of their caravan, was taken into compulsory quarantine, and Shakespear paid the Egyptian official in charge to see that she was found a good owner. The proceeds of the sale of the others was given to his two loyal servants. Shakespear took the ferry at Kubri and then a cab to Suez. He had a haircut and then caught the train to Ismailiya, falling into the company of an 'affable old Buster, an out-of-work dragoman' by the name of Johnson. He went on to Port Said and stayed at the Hôtel de la Poste on the recommendation of Mr Johnson. Before leaving Egypt he called at the Residency to apprise Lord Kitchener and Sir Reginald Wingate of the political situation in Arabia. He found the 'local big-wigs' inclined to 'exaggerate the influence of the Sharif' and, he said, they had only 'sketchy information on Central Arabia'.

He had covered 1,810 miles, roughly two thirds of which was unmapped and unrecorded until his journey. *The Times* of London reported his arrival in Cairo, and said that he had promised to deliver a talk to the Royal Geographical Society.

His achievement is best conveyed in the words of Douglas Carruthers, himself a noted Arabian explorer, who wrote the only account of it ever to appear in print, in the *Geographical Journal* of May 1922:

Shakespear's trans-Arabian journey covered about 1200 miles of unknown country. Only for one-third of the whole traverse between Kuwait on the Persian Gulf and Kontilla, the first Egyptian outpost on Sinai, was he on ground already covered by Europeans. For the whole distance, 1810 miles, Shakespear kept up a continuous route-traverse, checked at intervals by observations for latitude. He also took, as on his previous journeys, hypsometric readings for altitude, which give a most useful string of heights between the Gulf and the Hijaz railway. The initial results of Shakespear's last journey may be summed up as follows: the first complete traverse of the Wadi ar Rummah in its lower course – as the Batin – between Hafar and Ajibba, where the great fiumara is blocked by the Dahana sand bed, and also the region southwards to Zilfi; the first reliable map of the Tuwaik settlements between Zilfi and Audah, and of the new route onwards to Riyadh; a great deal of new detail between Riyadh and Buraida; a complete new route from Buraida to Jauf, and also between Jauf and the Wadi Araba on the frontiers of southern Palestine. For the eastern limits of the Great Nafud sand-bed we are indebted to him; also for the true bend of Jebel Tubaik, and for much information on the various sand belts which seam Kasim and Sudair. But even where he was on old ground his surveys were of much value. He crossed at various times the traverses of Sadlier, Pelly, Palgrave, Knox, Wallin, Guarmani, Blunt, Huber, Nolde, Butler, Aylmer, Leachman, Raunkiaer, Bell, and my own, and by doing so helped to pull these, in many cases, rough traverses into shape. Routes which had hitherto been merely conjecture could now be drawn more or less correctly, many errors put right, and many a problem solved.

Within a few months Shakespear's notebooks were being used by the War Office to construct maps of the desert terrain so that others could follow in his footsteps, though for very different reasons.

17

The Hot Summer

In London, the government was deep in the throes of the Irish troubles and was not interested in the Arabian problem. Britain was bound by treaty to back Turkey as the governing power and Ibn Saud was its representative in Najd. That was the end of the matter. Shakespear took a room at Dawson Place Mansions Hotel and from there conducted an almost daily correspondence with men who had little interest in what he had to say.

Not even the war clouds gathering over Europe in the middle of the hot summer of 1914 could jolt the Asquith government from its preoccupation with home affairs. The enthusiasm with which he came home was quickly extinguished by officials, whose only reaction to his long and informative reports was one of terror lest he should make any public pronouncement.

He called at the Royal Geographical Society's headquarters and deposited his photographic negatives, maps and notebooks. He also called on Sir Arthur Hirtzel, permanent secretary of the Political and Secret Department at the India Office, to show him correspondence between Ibn Saud and himself. He had written from Cairo to Ibn Saud:

I started with the agheyl from Buraida and we marched by the route Labba, watering at Haiyaniya, to Jauf-al-Amr ... On the road we heard of the murder of Zamil ibn Subhan and I grieved for he was a good man ... God knows what will now happen to the affairs of Ibn Rashid. Doubtless you are aware that the Turkish Government has sent many thousands of rifles and magazine arms to Hail and it is commonly reported by the badawin in the north that Ibn Rashid will shortly make war on your tribes. The matter is with God Almighty and I trust that he will strengthen your arm if there is need. The great ones of my Government here are much interested in your news and I have told them all I know, also our friend the Resident at Bushire, Sir Percy Cox, whom you could not meet and in whose place I came with Major Trevor to Ujair to meet you. He is now in India with the Viceroy and he will certainly keep an eye on your affairs, which, God willing, will continue to prosper. After Jauf I reached the tents of Audah Abu Taiya, Shaikh of the Howeitat, and he gave me two rafiqs to take me west to the Egyptian border, but he was different from all the other shaikhs I met and was very greedy. However, we reached the border in safety, without seeing any Turkish soldiers or officials and thence I came on to Suez where I took the Egyptian railway to Cairo. My journey was a very long one and we took 111 days from Kuwait to Suez with 87 camps, but thanks to God all the men and camels arrived safely.

I have only been a few days in Cairo, and not yet able to obtain the Arabic barometer you wanted but I shall not fail. The field glasses will be sent on to you from London where I shall be in a few days.

I would like to thank Your Excellency for all the arrangements you so kindly made to ease my journey, and beg to send my salaams to your father the Imam, Abdur Rahman al Faisal, and to your brothers Muhammad, Saad, Saud and Abdulla, and to your sons. May Your Excellency's affairs prosper and may you be preserved. Your friend.

SHAKESPEAR

He had written another letter to the amir while on the journey, using French instead of Arabic for fear of interception. Ibn Saud's reply eventually arrived in London:

Our friendship will never be affected by being away from each other because it is mutual and is based on respect and sincerity. I was pleased to receive your splendid letters telling me of your journey and safe arrival. You mention the assistance given you on the way by the Shaikhs. That is but their duty. As for your thanks to me, it is because of your great merits that we are happy always to offer you our help. I am especially glad that Major Trevor whom we met in Uqair and who is now in the company of Sir Percy Cox and

the Ruler of India, will be supervising our interests. My
beloved friend, our dependence is first in God, then in Your
Excellency ...
My father the Imam, my brothers and sons send their
compliments, and I send my best wishes for permanent and
everlasting friendship. God bless and guard you.

Abdul Aziz, prince of Najd and chief of all its tribes.

3 El Keeda 1332 [3 May 1914]

The journey Shakespear had planned and thought about for three
years or more had been accomplished. His political mission, by
contrast, had not come to much, but he could hardly be blamed
for that. He had expressed his views honestly, and he had won
the respect of Sir Percy Cox and the Viceroy. He began to wonder
what, if anything, his next assignment would be, for he remained
in the service of the Indian Government.

The suffocating heat of London, so different from that of
Arabia where mud-brick dwellings and tents seemed to provide a natural cooling, may have contributed to his feeling
of being stifled and isolated. But there was undoubtedly another cause. Earlier visits to England had always been tinged
with the expectation of meeting Dorothea. Now she was married
and in India. His brother too was in India, with Dorothea's
sister Winifred. Apart from his ageing parents in Brighton he
was very much on his own. Even his motor car, hardly used
since his visit to the Coronation durbar, was garaged in Bushire.

But he was not given to introspection. He worked at a tremen-
dous pace in his hotel room, completing his journals of the
trans-Arabia journey and labelling his natural history specimens,
corresponding with friends and relatives and keeping up an
exchange of letters with Ibn Saud and the desert shaikhs who
had shown him hospitality in his travels. He was proposed for
fellowship of the Royal Geographical Society by Lieutenant-
Colonel F. R. Maunsell who, as military attaché at Constantinople,
had come to know him well. The collection of plants that
he made on his way across the desert and carefully preserved,
was presented to the Natural History Museum. His botanical
specimens were in many instances the first of their kind to find
their way to a British, or indeed a western, museum; and
they remain to the present day as evidence of his wide-ranging

From: your friend Captain Shakespear

To: Sheikh Abdul Aziz bin Abdur Rahman al Faisal
Ruler of Nejd.

a/c.

and after Your Ex: will see from this letter that by the grace of God your friend has safely reached Cairo and by the kindness of one of the great ones of the government is able to write to your Ex in Arabic.

I wrote to Y.E. in French from Buraidah & hope your relative Ahmed bin Thanyan will have made clear to Y.E. how grateful I was for all the & kindness which your Amirs evinced for my affairs.

I started with the Agheyl from Buraidah and we marched by the route Labba, watering at Hacyaniyah, to Jof-al-Amr. The Agheyl were very kind to me while with them particularly Saleh al Mutawah, Bin Khalaif & Al Garawi of Anaizah and Mahd Bin Rawaf of Damascus, also many others whose names I cannot remember correctly.

On the road we heard of the murder of Zamil Ibn Sebhan and I grieved for he was a good man & your friend — God knows what will now

Shakespear's translation of the first page of his letter to Ibn Saud written after his 1914 journey

scientific curiosity and his thoroughness as an explorer. Another collection, left with Douglas Baird in India, was presented to the same museum in 1916, and in 1920 the Bombay Natural History Society sent it the wildcat he shot near Kuwait which became the named example of the sub-species *felis ocreata iraki*, or as the badu call it, *hurr*.

His main task remained, however, to convince the India Office that there was still room for manoeuvre in Britain's relations with Ibn Saud. The early encounters with his immediate contact, Sir Arthur Hirtzel, had not been encouraging.

On June 18th Sir Arthur told him in a letter delivered to his hotel:

> I enclose a set of correspondence about Ibn Saud received from India since February. In noting upon it and making any suggestions ... please bear in mind the fixed policy of HM Government to assist the Turkish Government to consolidate itself in Asia. It is quite certain they will not do anything which they think tends in the opposite direction, and it is no use beating the air. If HMG are to support Ibn Saud, his interests must somehow be harmonized with those of the Turks, or at least shown not to conflict with them.

He added a postscript:

> In view of the letter we have had from the Foreign Office, I had better put in writing their request that anything which you may contemplate publishing should first be submitted to them. If and when the time comes, perhaps you will be good enough to send us two copies – one for Lord Crewe and one for Sir Edward Grey.

Shakespear replied the next day, June 19th, promising a report on the situation in Central Arabia, and reaffirming that he would bear in mind what he had been told regarding British policy in Arabia. 'Also, if anything for publication does materialize, you shall certainly see it first,' he wrote.

On June 26th he sent the India Office his promised report, a synthesis of his various statements and short reports to the India Office since his arrival. He stressed his close relationship with the Amir of Najd:

> I would add that being on especially intimate terms with Abdul Aziz and his whole family he frequently showed me the confidential correspondence passing between him and other Arab chiefs, among them Sayid Muhammad al-Idrisi, the Imam Yahyah of Sana, Ibn Shaalan the premier Shaikh of the great Anaiza tribe and others of lesser importance, as well as his communications with the Turkish authorities. I did my best to discourage his confidence, seeing that I had

no official status, but as he insisted they may now be useful.

He went on to demonstrate a grasp of affairs which came from the closest possible contact with the leaders of Central Arabia and an understanding of the complexities of tribal and Turkish ambitions. Everything he had learned from his discussions with Mubarak and Ibn Saud, with the chiefs of the Mutair and Ajman and other important tribes, was set down at length and with clarity. His report showed that Ibn Saud had learned of Turkish plans to reoccupy Katif, Uqair, Hasa and other important bases in eastern Arabia, despite the agreement with Britain which recognized this area as part of Najd; and the amir had mobilized his townspeople and the badawin to meet the challenge. Shakespear set out the meetings of desert chiefs that preceded and followed his meeting with Ibn Saud at Thaj in 1911, leading to the potential alliance between the amir, the Sharif of Mecca, the Regent of Hail and the chiefs of Asir and Yemen, in 1913; a threat to the balance of power in Arabia which assuredly precipitated the signing of the Anglo-Turkish Convention. Neither Turkey nor Britain relished the thought of an Arab rebellion at that time. He also set out the role of Sayid Talib the Basra deputy in these proceedings, and the continuing perfidy of the Turks in arming and abetting Rashid. Inevitably he pleaded again the cause of Ibn Saud, though more to keep the record straight than in the hope of convincing his superiors. He stressed the military efficiency of the Amir of Najd, though assuring them that he had no aggressive intentions, and underlined Ibn Saud's most recent assertion that he would not commit himself to Turkey while there was a slender chance of arriving at an arrangement with Britain. He was, said Shakespear, exceedingly anxious about British plans in the event of Turkish attempts to reoccupy his coastal territory. The report was able to detail Turkish troop movements and arms traffic with some precision, for he had made careful notes of conversations with local badawin round the Hijaz railway. He concluded:

I am convinced that present Turkish methods in Arabia, if persisted in, will end in disaster – Turkey has not the power to coerce Arabia and should matters ... come to a head the probable result will be a combination of all the Arab tribes, the expulsion of Turkish troops and officials ... and the establishment of an independent Arabia with a loose form of confederation of which Ibn Saud will be the head ... I have heard the subject discussed so often along these lines, and by so many widely separated chiefs, that I cannot avoid the conclusion that the Turkish Government is riding for a very bad fall ...

By August 1914 he had finished his various tasks. Whitehall, having received and acknowledged his report on the state of Arabia, maintained a resolute silence. At least the War Office took an interest in the information be brought home from his journey. Its geographical department was busily updating older topographical studies on the strength of his notes.

War came almost as a relief. The purposeless months of waiting, the lassitude inspired by heat and dusty streets and the inaction of officialdom, were over. But Britain, as always at moments of crisis, behaved phlegmatically. For five weeks he went from one recruitment office to another. He was a trained army officer, a veteran of the desert, as fit as any man could be. Yet he could not find anyone willing to take him on.

Eventually he found a sympathetic listener, and after five weeks of frustration he was sent to Aldershot, where he was left entirely to his own devices, a situation which suited him admirably. He found a squad of men who were only too glad to be scooped up by an officer of apparent enthusiasm. They were subjected to a rough and vigorous training programme and within a few weeks they and their self-appointed commander were, in their own view at any rate, ready for active service. They let it be known that they would leave for the battlefields of Europe as soon as their orders were drafted.

Meanwhile, Whitehall came to the sudden realization that if Germany persuaded Turkey to enter the war – and it looked like doing so at any moment – the door to its eastern Empire was wide open, as indeed were the eastern corridors of Europe. Dusty files were opened and barely read documents started to shuttle between the India and Foreign Offices. Sir Edward Grey and Lord Crewe decided that no time could be lost in finding a reliable ally in Arabia and a knowledgeable emissary to go to him with their plans. A frantic search for Shakespear began. He had been breathing down their necks for the best part of five months. Now he was nowhere to be found. They eventually traced him to Aldershot and ordered him back to Whitehall. His men made their way to France without him.

18

War and Death

War-Confidential.

There is not a moment to lose if Bin Saud is to make arrangements in time, so will you kindly take Shaikh Mubarak into your confidence but impress on him that secrecy and despatch are essential. If he adds a letter of his own exhorting Bin Saud to do what is required of him speedily, I think it would be excellent, but I feel sure he will do it almost without being asked. Our embassy at Constantinople is evidently very weary of the Turk.

6.10.14.   KNOX
Acting Resident, Bushire

That message to Grey, the new Political Agent in Kuwait, was preceded by a sealed packet for delivery to Ibn Saud and a telegram from the Secretary of State for India dated October 4th.

Bin Saud should receive from you by way of Bahrain and Kuwait the following message which should be translated into Arabic. Begins: 'Your friend Captain Shakespear will arrive at Bahrain about 4 November (i.e. middle of Zil Hajj) and begs that you will arrange for camels for him at Ujair on that date. He is coming from England to visit you on important business connected with the British Government.'

CREWE
Secretary of State

When Shakespear was called to Whitehall in September 1914 he was no longer the meddling nuisance who sought to change Britain's entire policy of détente with the Ottoman Empire in order to further his scheme for an alliance with the Central Arabian leader. He was welcomed with open arms. His personal friendship with Ibn Saud, his experience in dealing with the desert princes and his knowledge of places as yet uncharted on War Office maps marked him out for a task of the utmost importance. His views were sought by the India and Foreign Offices and by the War Office. He repeated the opinion that the only hope for Arabia was for Britain to recognize the independence of Ibn Saud under British suzerainty and to arm the amir so that he could deal effectively with the Turkish-supported Ibn Rashid. The government may have seen a glimmer of light, but it was not yet ready for so radical a change of course. He was briefed by the India Office during the first few days of October. He would go back to Arabia with the title of Political Officer on Special Duty, responsible directly to Sir Percy Cox, charged with the task of ensuring that Ibn Saud and the tribes of Central Arabia were made ready to take Britain's side if need be. But he was to do his utmost to prevent the Arab leader from taking any action against the Turks unless they came into the war; even then no action was to be taken until the intentions of H.M. Government were made clear.

It was, in effect, the position as before. He went over his old reports with government officials; he pointed out that the Turks, though despised by Ibn Saud, remained the keepers of the Caliphate, and that it would take more than vague promises to counteract the work of the holy men if they started to preach the cause of war against the infidel. He protested just as vainly that the Amir of Najd was a man of stubborn independence, faced by a ruthless and well-armed adversary, whose ability to survive depended on help from outside. If he did not receive at least the promise of a binding treaty of alliance with Britain, and immediate material aid, he would eventually be forced to come to terms with the Turks, if indeed he had not already done so. Shakespear was told that at this stage Britain could offer nothing more than a non-committal treaty of friendship and he was given authority to negotiate such a treaty, for approval by the government. The Political Officer's movements were now in the hands of the Foreign Office and on October 9th Sir Edward Grey asked the India Office to relay his plans to Simla and Bushire:

The S.S. Arabia, sailing tomorrow (10 October), will bring out Shakespear as Political Officer on Special Duty.

He will tranship for Bushire at Bombay. As soon as possible he is to place himself in personal communication with the Amir of Najd and exert his influence with that chief with the object of 1) Preventing our proceedings from causing disturbance among the Arabs 2) In the event of war with Turkey, to make certain of Arab goodwill.

While these hurried arrangements were being made, the new ambassador at Constantinople, Sir Louis Mallet, advised caution, and the Turkish Government, already aware that a British mission was afoot, promptly made overtures to both Ibn Saud and Mubarak. The ambassador reported:

That Enver Pasha and others have been in communication with the Shaikh is only natural. Personally, however, I do not think that Turkey means to take an active part in the war on Germany's side. It is doubtless advisable to make a bid for Ibn Saud's friendship, but I consider it would be unfortunate to allow him to imagine that we are in particular need of it.

The government, though maintaining a negative attitude towards the Arab leader, was taking no chances. On October 9th the Secretary of State for India wired Bushire, confirming Foreign Office instructions and continuing:

Meanwhile, in anticipation of Shakespeare's arrival, it is considered advisable by HM Government that Shaikh Mubarak should at once communicate to the Amir a message to the following effect. 'The Shaikh is aware that the Germans are doing their best to persuade the Turks to do something that will entangle Great Britain and her allies in war, which we are all anxious to avoid. Great Britain, the traditional friend of Islam, is especially reluctant. Owing to the attitude of the Turks, however, certain military precautions have had to be taken by HM Government, but they wish that the Arabs should clearly understand that it is only in the event of Turkish aggression that we will contemplate taking action. Material assistance can be afforded by Ibn Saud and Shaikh Mubarak in the maintenance of peace if they exercise their influence over their own tribes. Their powerful friends, the Sharif of Mecca and Bin Shaalan might be led away by specious promises of reward or inaccurate statements and here again the friendly influence of our two friends would be invaluable. Captain Shakespear is being despatched by HM Government in order that he, well-known already to the Arabs, may explain the wishes of the Government, who rely on Ibn Saud and the coastal chiefs to take no action until they have been informed of the intention of the British Government in more detail. This, even in the event of the outbreak of war.'

It was not the most positive of statements, and Shaikh Mubarak translated the hesitant language of Whitehall into less feeble terms:

My son,

May God keep you safe! I send you herewith a message from Sir Percy Cox, the former Agent at Bushire who is now Foreign Secretary of the Government of India, and he is a man whom both you and I know to be a friend. You should read these words carefully and consider their meaning well. According to what I hear this war is entirely the fault of the Germans, and they are inciting the Turks. May God abase them both! Otherwise, my son, they, the Germans, will give the Turks control over you and me and all Arabs ... They, the British, do not want to fight the Turks and will do so only in case of the Turks declaring war or committing some act which will necessitate it. The Turks will go and the English will rule Turkish territory; the punishment of God for their bad treatment of Arabs. Therefore, my son, you and I must follow the wishes of the Glorious Government, for therein lie our interests.

There was another letter, dated October 14th, in the same parcel, and despatched by special messenger to Buraida where the amir was engaged in punishing the Bani Harb for a recent raid.

After repeating that for some time the Germans had been urging the Turks to commit actions that would result in war, Mubarak wrote in the second letter:

Now the Glorious Government needs our help to maintain peace. It is sending to you Captain Shakespear whom all Arabs know, that he may explain to you the objects of the Government and her intentions. He arrives at Bahrein on 15 November. You will welcome him, please God, and will give him a reply which will please him so that he may return from you happy. Because, my son, the road to comfort for you and me is one and the same, to follow his wishes.

Meanwhile, Mubarak's first message to Ibn Saud, following the new Resident's communication in early October, had brought a response. He had sent it in the care of Abdulla ibn Jiluwi. The reply, undated, said:

I have understood all you say. You told me about the war between the nations and that the English and those with them would be victorious eventually. Now you tell me the Turkish Government is very nervous. I hope God will give the victory to those from whom advantage comes for you and us. You say that the Turkish Government is sure to be affected. Know then that relations between you and me are unimpaired and I will follow your orders in regard to any change from the present state of things. My dependence is upon God, then upon you.

The shaikh showed the letter to Grey on October 12th. He wired Knox immediately: 'Ibn Saud is with us.'

It was a premature note of joy. On November 5th, Ibn Saud was told in a message from Mubarak that Great Britain and Turkey were at war. The Turks were putting pressure on all the Arab leaders to join them in their struggle for the defence of Islam, inviting them to join their holy war against the infidel and promising arms and money in return for their support. Britain, for its part, still offered nothing but vague promises. The Arab leaders, Ibn Saud included, were biding their time, keeping both major powers at arm's length. Even the fervently pro-Turkish Saud ibn Rashid, when asked to supply armed men for the defence of Basra, dug his heels in; when Turkish officials arrived at Hail they found that all able-bodied men had mysteriously disappeared into the desert.

From Bombay, the Political Officer took the British India steamship *Chakdara* to Basra. The vessel had been diverted from Calcutta to pick him up and take him on to the gulf. He eventually arrived at Muhammerah, where he stepped ashore in late October. The Turks attacked Fao on the night of his arrival, following the landing of British troops. Next day Shakespear witnessed the first casualties of the Mesopotamian campaign being carried aboard the *Chakdara* to be taken to hospital in Bombay.

The Political Officer arrived in Kuwait on December 7th. A message awaited him from the amir, who at that moment was in Riyadh playing reluctant host to Sayid Talib.

The letter was friendly but guarded. It suggested that they should meet soon and that Shakespear should take a path familiar to him from earlier travels, the Batin road to Hafar. 'We will meet you on the road. We will find you,' the amir told him. 'My hopes are strong that matters may be resolved so as to protect

11 . 12 . 14.

Dear Grey,

In case I should get snuffed out in the desert, would you be so good as to post the enclosed two letters as soon as you hear.

You might also write or wire would perhaps be better to my Mother :—.

      Mrs W. H. S. Shakespear
      c/o H. S. King & Co
      65 Cornhill, London E. C.

As far as my Kit is concerned, it might remain until you hear from my brother — he is my executor & will let you know what he wants done about it.

I think I have left everything squared up so as to give as little trouble as possible, any way have tried to.

       Yours sincerely,
       W.H.J. Shakespear.

Shakespear's last offical letter, to his successor
Lieutenant-Colonel Grey

our religion and honour, and please God when our meeting takes place, the real objectives will be disclosed on both sides.' While in Mesopotamia, on his way, Shakespear had met Sir Percy Cox, who had now assumed the title of Chief Political Officer with Indian Expeditionary Force 'D' in Mesopotamia, and General Sir Arthur Barrett, at army headquarters. They discussed his proposed meeting; but since at that time they saw the prospect of an easy victory over the Turkish forces the general had seen no great urgency about the mission to Ibn Saud. They announced that the Viceroy would be coming to Kuwait in December and thought that perhaps Shakespear should delay his journey to Najd to await his arrival. Shaikh Mubarak, anxious to have Shakespear by his side when the Viceroy arrived, since he did not find Lieutenant-Colonel Grey easy to get on with, also pressed him to delay his trip. But he refused. He wanted to join up with the amir as quickly as he could.

He had sent a message to Grey from Bushire asking if his old retainers could be made available to go with him to Najd. The new Political Agent promptly found other duties for most of them so that of his old team only Abdul Aziz the jemader and Hadi the Ajmani *rafiq* were available. He eventually borrowed a dozen camels from Shaikh Mubarak, found servants by the names of Khalid and Ambush to take the places of Wali Muhammad and Awayd as his cook and personal servant, and set out along the Batin on December 12th.

Perhaps he had a presentiment of trouble. He left a note for Grey:

Dear Grey,

   In case I should get snuffed out in the desert, would you be so good as to post the enclosed two letters as soon as you hear. You might also write or wire would perhaps be better to my mother: Mrs W. H. S. Shakespear, c/o H. S. King and Co., 65 Cornhill, London, E.C. As far as my kit is concerned, it might remain until you hear from my brother – he is my executor and will let you know what he wants done about it. I think I have left everything squared up so as to give as little trouble as possible, anyway have tried to.

                              Yours sincerely,
                          W. H. I. SHAKESPEAR.

Camp XXI Central Arabia, January 22nd, 1915. He had been with
Ibn Saud and his army for three weeks. Now the warriors of the
desert and the townsmen of Sudair and Aridh were preparing
to move on. Thousands of camels were brought in from the
grazing country beyond the Plateau of Arma and the badawin
sat in groups, waiting indifferently to be sorted and allocated
their beasts, or beating their drums, though with waning enthusiasm, for they had worked themselves to fever pitch for days on
end, and now that the call to war had finally come their martial
fervour deserted them and their drumming subsided.

From the day of his arrival, December 31st, 1914, Shakespear
and Ibn Saud had conferred for hours on end and then the
Political Officer had gone to his tent and pounded his typewriter,
often working late into the night by the light of his Hurricane
lamp while an army he estimated to be some 6,000 strong slept
and snored around him.

Abdul Aziz had not been in a good mood the day he arrived.
Even his greeting, usually warm and confidential, was restrained.
Distant even. Soon the cause of the amir's anger became evident.
He felt that he had been tricked and deserted by Britain and that
even his benefactor, Mubarak of Kuwait, had turned his back on
him. Abdul Aziz was a man of generous instinct and of black
temper. He enacted the most terrible punishment when his anger
was roused and he seldom forgot or forgave an insult. Entire
tribal encampments had been destroyed and their inhabitants
killed and mutilated because they crossed the path of the Prince
of Najd. Now his ire turned to Britain and Shaikh Mubarak, and
Shakespear had great difficulty in calming his host. But in the
end Shakespear reassured him that he still had friends in the
Great Government and that he and Cox were on his side, but not
without much private cursing at the conduct of Knox and Grey
while he had been away in England.

When he sent his first report to Sir Percy Cox, he began with
the words: 'It is unnecessary for me to recall what passed between
Bin Saud and Grey ... ' What did pass, or so it transpired in talk
with his host, was that back in April of 1914, little more than a
month after Shakespear's visit to Riyadh, Ibn Saud had received
an urgent request to go to Subaihiyah, close to Kuwait, from
Shaikh Mubarak. Since Shakespear's disappearance from the
scene, the amir had kept in touch with Trevor at Bahrain, for he

did not like the terse and unfriendly Grey, and he kept Trevor informed of his movements, expressing the hope that he would be able to meet British officials when he arrived. He was not unnaturally surprised to discover on arrival that Shaikh Mubarak was unable to attend the meeting, and that Sayid Talib awaited him with an entourage of Turkish officials armed with a treaty of co-operation and the offer of an annual pension if he signed there and then. The amir asked that Grey should be sent for. Up to this time he had not formally accepted the title of Mutasarrif of Najd, though Britain and Turkey had assigned it to him without consultation. Now, when Grey reluctantly appeared on the scene, he made a final appeal. 'I do not want to sign,' he told Grey, and asked him what he should do. 'You can expect no help or guidance from Britain,' Grey replied.

Shakespear's anger blazed almost as fierce as the amir's when he heard the story. On January 4th he wrote:

Bin Saud was completely detached from the British Government when I arrived ... Abdul Aziz, who is animated by an intense patriotism for his country, a profound venera-tion for his religion and a single-minded desire to do his best for his people by obtaining for them lasting peace and security, now finds himself in a difficult position. He trusted the British Government as no other ... now he is asked to commit himself to open war with his most powerful and bitter enemies by a power which six months before told him it could not intervene on his behalf and left him free to do a deal with the Turks ... but as evidence of his desire to assist the British Government without hopelessly compromising himself he has kept Ibn Rashid to his ground and by his example and lead induced in the Arab world an attitude ... distinctly sympathetic towards Great Britain.

Only three men could sway Ibn Saud in political matters, Mubarak, his cousin Ibn Jiluwi, and Shakespear. Now the Englishman worked patiently to drag him from his high horse, carefully drafting a treaty which would please the Wahhabi chief and yet give his own government the promise of support in its desert war. Day after day he went through its clauses, explaining their meaning and implications for the future, and the warrior king sat and contemplated Shakespear's Arabic and discussed it with Ibn Jiluwi.

It was ready early in January and a messenger went off to Basra to take it straight to Cox. Britain had taken the southern Mesopotamian town by then and Barrett's men were investigating the Turkish archives there. Among their first finds was the treaty Ibn Saud had been compelled by Britain's indifference to sign, dated May 5th, 1914. 'Ibn Saud not having broken openly with the Turks, the treaty is presumably still in force,' wrote Cox.

Sayid Talib, never far from the scene of negotiations affecting either Britain or Turkey, was at Ibn Saud's camp when Shakespear joined it. Now the amir wanted him removed and he sought his English friend's help. Shakespear advised Ibn Saud to write a note to Cox explaining that Talib was on a mission from the Turkish Inspector of War Affairs and that he could not openly oppose the Ottoman or his family would be in danger, but that he was friendly to Britain. A note to that effect was sent with the draft treaty, and a covering letter from Shakespear made it abundantly clear that the time for a leisurely approach to the politics of Arabia was past.

The treaty began: 'That the British Government will acknowledge and admit that Najd, Al-Hasa, Katif and their surrounds and the ports appertaining to them on the Persian Gulf are to me and (are) the territory of my fathers and forefathers; that I am the independent ruler ... '

And the covering note said:

... nor will he move a step further towards making matters either easier for us or more difficult for the Turks as far as the present war is concerned, until he obtains in that treaty some very solid guarantee of his position, with Great Britain practically as his suzerain. Granted this he can be relied upon to use all his resources and immense influence in Arabia on our side, not only in the present war but afterwards. He begs for the earliest possible response for already his neutrality embarrasses him.

The letter went on to state the advantages to Britain of Ibn Saud's influence over Muhammadan opinion, especially with the tribes of northern Anaiza 'with whom our occupation of Lower Mesopotamia will bring us into close contact'.

Cox received the bundle of documents on January 10th. Next day he wrote to the government: 'Can I possibly be authorised to draft a treaty along the above lines ... ' He also said that he had received 'very satisfactory letters' from Shakespear, Ibn Saud and Sayid Talib. By the 15th he was reporting to Simla that events in Basra had taken a turn for the worse, Turkish influence in the area was still dangerously strong, and *jihad* was being preached openly and was taking hold of Arab loyalties. A few days later Talib arrived at his office and was told that Britain intended to send him to India. It was not long before the loquacious merchant of Basra was preaching *jihad* to the Muslims of India.

The young Saud ibn Rashid, now in charge of the fortunes of Hail, was marching southwards towards Zilfi. Meanwhile Shakespear grew more and more despondent, though his letters betrayed an occasional note of optimism. On January 5th he wrote to Gertrude Bell whom he had met in London in the summer of 1914 following her journey to Hail which crossed his own desert path at one stage of the trans-Arabian trek. 'I had got as far as Karachi when war with Turkey was announced ... so I went up to Bushire and the Shat-al-Arab ... saw in the distance the shell fire of the last engagement before we entered Basra – it was annoying having to go down the river in the mail-steamer while quite a nice little scrap was going on ... had some pretty hard trekking to find Bin Saud ... He is making preparations for a big raid on Ibn Rashid with a view to wiping him out practically and I shouldn't be surprised if I reached Hail in the course of the next month or two as Bin Saud's political adviser! ... It would be very jolly here now if it wasn't so horribly cold ... last night my water-skins froze ... I don't know how much longer this special duty job is to last but I trust not beyond a month or two ... If you aren't too busy and can spare a line about your doings and how the lecture went at the RGS [Gertrude Bell's promised lecture to the Royal Geographical Society, like Shakespear's, went undelivered] you can help my loneliness out here ... Christmas day was a 22 mile march and New Year's day I had my second bath in twenty days ... '

On January 14th, Shakespear wrote to his brother. It was a long, rambling letter, filled with scorn of his superiors, belabouring a government which even now, threatened by warring nations on all sides, could not distinguish between friends and enemies. The elder brother unburdened his own problems at length ... he couldn't get decent camels, had had to make a detour of 160 miles to find Ibn Saud ... his cook was useless and had almost done for his stomach. As for Grey: 'I don't know how I kept my temper ... at times I had to clear out of the room. Kuwait Agency fairly made me weep at the state into which he had brought it.' But his harshest criticisms were reserved for the government. 'They will probably go on messing about until they make Bin Saud so utterly sick that he will chuck his present friendly attitude ... Heaven knows what trouble may be in store for us and all the petty chiefs along the coast.'

It was a hurriedly composed letter, typed between far more urgent tasks. But it suggested a profound disillusionment on the part of a man who had left England only a few months before on a vital mission which had the blessing of the Foreign Secretary and the Secretary of State for India, and who now found himself, not for the first time in his dealings with Central Arabia, in a paddle-less canoe.

The ending was prophetic:

... Bin Saud has some 6,000 of his men here in tents and thousands of badawin all around and in a couple of days we should make a move for a biggish battle ... there is never any knowing what these badawin will do; they are quite capable of being firm friends up to the battle and then suddenly changing their minds and going over to the other side in the middle of it. Bin Saud wants me to clear out but I want to see the show and I don't think it will be very unsafe really.

He wrote his last letter from Camp XXI on January 19th. He had already told Cox that he would be leaving with the amir in a few days' time and that they would meet the Shammar army somewhere around Zilfi, outside which town Ibn Rashid was camped. They marched north on January 22nd.

The weather was cool, and pale sunlight lay on the grey rocks to their left. Theirs was a rag-tag army, maybe as many as 18,000

strong. Nobody had counted it. Nobody ever counted the badawin. They came and went and even now some dissolved into the
distant landscape and went off to join their families, while others
tagged on to the army of Ibn Saud. There were probably 6,000
townsmen and enlisted tribesmen, dressed for war, rifles across
their camel saddles, ready to hand, bandoliers across their chests.
Some rode on horses, lean and scraggy mares yet fast and tireless,
though not a great number for Riyadh did not have horses to
spare as did the Amir of Hail. At their head was Ibn Saud on the
finest black mare of the royal stables, a commanding figure of
desert war. Beside him, as he had been at Thaj and Riyadh in days
that now seemed remote, the khaki-clad Englishman on his
camel. The war banner of the Sauds fluttered in the breeze, the
kalima only partly visible, 'La ilah il'allah'. There is no God but
God. Behind an irregular throng of badawin, men of the Ajman,
Mutair, Bani Harb, Sbei and other tribes who by wish or necessity supported the Sauds, fanning out across the desert and filling
it with the cries of men and the thud and rhythmic beat of animal
hooves.

Shakespear and the amir had much to talk about and they rode
on alone but Saad and Ibn Jiluwi were never far away and every
so often Abdul Aziz beckoned them to his side to ask an opinion,
though he often dismissed the proffered word with a wave of the
hand. The Arab chief wondered what he should do if Britain
rejected an alliance. Already the Turks had sent paid Wahhabi
adherents to Riyadh to preach holy war. They had been put in
'honourable confinement'. Turkish officers had been to see him
to assign him his part in the war. The Turks were naïve, but the
British were not much better. Both tried to foster the most
improbable alliances. Shakespear nearly fell from his camel with
laughter as Ibn Saud recalled the plans of the Turkish officers.
The amir was to be made responsible for the protection of Basra
and Baghdad in the event of a sudden British advance. Ibn
Rashid's Shammar and Ibn Shaalan's Anaiza tribes were to join
forces in the region of the Hijaz railway ready to advance on
Egypt and Sinai. The Sharif, the Imam Yahya and Sayid Idrisi
were to guard the Red Sea littoral with the tribes of Yemen,
Asir and Hijaz.

They camped beyond Zilfi next day. Camp XXII. Ibn Rashid's
army was twenty-five miles away to the south-west, in the direc-

tion of Buraida. Ibn Saud's *rafiqs*, who had scouted the desert for hundreds of miles as the army moved slowly northwards, reported that there were some seven hundred townsmen of Hail with the opposing army and between eight and nine thousand Shammar badawin.

That night the amir came to Shakespear's tent. They talked for more than an hour while little Ambush nervously served coffee, for he was terrified of Ibn Saud. They went over all the old ground, of alliance and rebellion, and of the position of Husain of Mecca and his part in the war-time alignments of Arabia, Britain and Turkey; Ibn Saud said that he did not trust the old man of Mecca but that relations between them had been better in recent times and he told Shakespear that he had recently sent him a gift of horses which he had purchased from Shaikh Muba-rak. Before they parted at night Ibn Saud asked his friend once more to leave for the safety of Sudair, along with his son Turki. Majmaa was only a few miles away and he would be able to rejoin the Saudi camp after the battle. Abdul Aziz, Shakespear's camel man, was passing as the two men argued over the matter and he heard the Englishman say: 'If I go now, I desert not only you but my own country. I cannot do that.' Then Ibn Saud asked him to wear Arab dress. Again Shakespear stubbornly refused. They were both immovable men, and each respected the other for it.

The plain where the sea of tents now stood was flooded with the bright light of the moon when they parted, and as the Arab leader walked towards his own tent a *rafiq* galloped towards him followed by a breathless rider on a fast *dhalul*. Ibn Saud recognized him as one of his own men from Riyadh.

A hurried consultation took place in the open and Shakespear could barely catch what they were saying. But he heard enough. On receiving the news of the impending battle, the sharif's son Abdullah had collected his army together at Madina and marched towards Riyadh. They were camped at Shara, two-thirds of the way to Riyadh.

Early next morning, Ambush woke his master, who ate a hearty breakfast and watched from his tent as the Saudi army prepared for battle.

A mounted force of Arab tribes was a fine sight to behold. The mares were taken to the scene of battle tied to the cinches of the *dhaluls*, handsome and erect as they trotted beside the fast camels. At the command of the cavalry leader their riders would slip them from their bonds and jump from camel to horseback in single movement, racing into the fight almost prone and with nothing but instinct and a squeeze of legs to keep them aloft, for they used neither saddle nor bridle; only a rope halter. Shakespear watched enviously as the cavalry went off with Ibn Saud.

He ordered his companions to pack their belongings and prepare to leave camp. Ambush handed him his field glasses, camera and revolver. Then with Hadi he went off by camel at the tail of the war party. The rest of the infantry had assembled and the camels and baggage were left in the charge of Abdul Aziz his jemader. All around them were sand dunes of Al Bittar and in front the dry bed of the Wadi ar Rummah. Along the wadi to their left as it swept down towards Buraida were the battlegrounds of Tarafiyya and Sarif, where the army of the Shammar had routed the joint force of Mubarak and Ibn Saud's father in 1901, and where Abdul Aziz had destroyed the army of his namesake, Abdul Aziz ibn Rashid, in 1906. He was joined by a young gunner of Ibn Saud's army called Husain.

The amir and his horsemen from the towns and his camel-mounted men from the Ajman and Mutair and Bani Harb veered to their left, fanning out along the north bank of the wadi to meet the Shammar as they came from the west. Sandhills and plain in this salty region looked snow-clad in the early morning sun. Thousands of badawin swarmed across the pure sands, loaded rifles in hand, some sandalled, but mostly bare-footed, jostling for position on and behind the dunes.

There was a stillness except for the click of rifle bolts and the flapping of kaffiyas in the slight breeze. Shakespear stood on a sandhill with his field glasses trained across the plain to the south-west and Husain, his companion, on the next hill mounted his field gun and pointed it in the same direction. Their own cavalry were out of sight.

The Englishman took his camera from its case and started to take snapshots of the badawin army around him, waiting for the oncoming horsemen so that he could capture them on film. 'No white man has seen this sight before,' he shouted to Husain. At that moment battle opened. He clicked the shutter and put the camera back in its case.

The Shammar horsemen and camel riders came over the skyline, the ends of their spotted kaffiyas tied across their faces to protect them, their animals kicking up the sand so that it swirled around them and made them appear to be riding on a cloud. And just as abruptly they changed course as the Saudi army attacked from their flanks, squeezing them in mid-flight. The war cry *Allah-akhbar!* was shouted on all sides. Soon the mounted armies were engaged in man-to-man conflict. Guns and *khanjar*, the curved daggers of the badawin, were used indiscriminately, and many men died from stray bullets. As the main forces fought on the desert plain, part of the Shammar army broke away and made for the Saudi infantry, who had been shooting without noticeable effect from the cover of the dunes. As the enemy came towards them Shakespear started to take photographs. Then he raised his field glasses and gave Husain bearings on the oncoming horsemen. The Shammar came at them like the wind, lying flat on their animals and firing well. Already many of the badawin foot soldiers had taken fright and were running away along the wadi. Husain shouted to Shakespear to remove his topee and take cover, but he kept his glasses trained on the Shammar and shouted instructions to Husain, who went on firing until the overwhelming numbers of the advancing enemy made further resistance pointless. The rest of the infantry, seeing the enemy swarming towards them on foot, horse and camel, had taken flight. Husain jumped from his vantage point, buried his field gun in the sand, and joined his fleeing comrades. Shakespear stood alone on the hilltop. He had already been shot in the leg. He had removed his topee at Husain's request, and was bare-headed in the sun and armed only with his revolver. He went on firing at point-blank range until he was cut down. As he fell he was shot in the arm, then through the head.

Shakespear was thirty-six years and three months old when he lay on the battlefield he had named. Jarab.

19

Aftermath

'Such ponderous caution is never so charming as the youthful impulsive hopes it extinguishes, and when youthful judgements are proved by events to be right it is only too easy, in retrospect, to scorn the maturer judgements which were wrong.' – David Howarth, *The Desert King*

He lay among the dead of both sides, stripped of clothes and possessions except for a blood-stained Indian vest, as rare a part of the desert scene in death as he had been in life.

When Husain the gunner returned to the battlefield several weeks later, Shakespear and the Arabs around him seemed untouched by sun and wind, unmolested by vulture or hyena. A passing badawin found his compass and Ibn Saud returned it to Major Trevor at Bahrain. He had died before news could reach him that he had been made a Commander of the Order of the Indian Empire for his services in Arabia. His companions, whose possessions had been pillaged by the Shammar and the Ajman defectors, made a slow journey back to Kuwait where they were questioned by Grey and Sir Percy Cox.

There is, inevitably, a suspicion that Shakespear may have gone to his death deliberately. His disenchantment with the mission his government had sent him on was apparent from his reports and his last letter to his brother. The long political battles with the government, the indifference of the men of power, and the desert itself, had certainly wearied him. Yet nothing he said or did amounted to a suicidal frame of mind. The buccaneering Victorian adventurer was there to the last, gun and camera to hand, as contemptuous as ever of the traveller's disguise and the marksmanship of the foe. It was, perhaps, surprising that he had survived so long, for many a man who took greater care and precaution in the desert died before he had travelled any great distance. Nothing is certain in the fickle circumstances of desert war, but the most plausible verdict is that he died at Jarab on January 24th, 1915, for no better reason than that it was not in his nature to climb down.

But what of the indecisive battle? Ibn Saud's cavalry had achieved their first objective. While the Shammar were putting the infantry to flight, the camel-mounted troops had cut through the Shammar horsemen and were driving half the enemy force before them. They would surely have been victorious, had not the Ajman leader looked over his shoulder at the crucial moment and seen the infantry in disarray. With the fatal badawin habit of caring more for the day than the morrow he led his men over to the Rashid side. The battle had lasted for less than two hours, fought mostly between the cavalrymen on the open plain towards Sarif. It did not take the Shammar long to put the infantry to flight once they had broken through.

Both armies were mauled and the ultimate test of strength between the houses of Saud and Rashid was put off to another day. The main Saudi force turned from the battle and headed straight for Riyadh. Rashid's men turned back towards Jabal Shammar, but before they went the Ajman helped them to pillage the baggage camp at Bagar and to strip the dead of their belongings. It was not the first time the Ajman had changed sides, and Ibn Saud never forgave them. But for the moment they had done their worst.

Did Ibn Saud, when he realized that the Ajman were defecting, withdraw in the knowledge that the army of Husain's son Abdullah waited within striking distance of Riyadh? Had the Saudi army defeated the Shammar in what was to be a final show of strength, would Britain then have made up its mind and come to terms with Ibn Saud? Such questions occurred to others who came after Shakespear to forge an Arabian alliance and to promote a desert rebellion.

When Mubarak next saw Ibn Saud after the battle he remarked angrily: 'I told you what would happen. I told you,' and the amir replied with justice that there was nothing he could do to protect the Englishman from the consequence of his own actions.

Ibn Saud wrote to Cox on February 4th, 1915. It was the

familiar story of defeat, or at best stalemate, being turned to the
best possible account, and it told his version of his English
friend's death.

> Our declaration of war against Bin Rashid and our
> severance of relations with him, have already been com-
> municated to you. We fought against him at a place called Al
> Artavel and a great battle ensued. They were slaughtered
> and defeated; but our beloved friend Captain Shakespear
> was hit from a distance by one of the enemy's shots and died.
> I offer my sincere condolences. Please inform the Secretary
> of State of your exalted Government of my sorrow at the
> death of our friend. We pressed him to leave us before the
> incident, but he refused to do so and was insistent on being
> with us. He said, *I have been ordered to be with you. If I leave you
> now it will be a blemish on my honour, and the honour of my country.
> Therefore forgive me.* Accordingly we allowed him to come
> with us. Now I request you to advise the Secretary of State
> of what he told me in Arabic as to what is required. Perhaps
> you could delegate somebody familiar with the Arabic lan-
> guage in order that I can tell him what was agreed between
> Captain Shakespear and me, so that he can communicate the
> same to your illustrious Government. May God protect you.
>
> ABDUL AZIZ

Of eye-witness accounts of Shakespear's death, none could
throw much light on the crucial moments when he was left alone
to face the oncoming Rashid force. Hadi bin Saddi the Ajmani,
Abdul Aziz ibn Hasan, Ambush and Khalid were all questioned
closely, but none was around when the firing started.

Of all the statements, that of Khalid the cook was the most
informative, though his sense of time was awry:

> I went with my late master Captain Shakespear from Kuwait.
> There were about thirty men with him. We met Bin Saud at
> Khafs. Two days after our arrival Sayid Talib of Basra,
> who had been for some time with Bin Saud, left for Kuwait.
> Next day Bin Saud marched towards Jarab in order to fight
> Ibn Rashid ... on our way parties of badu joined us. Bin
> Saud was on a horse and Captain Shakespear on a camel.
> One day before the fight Bin Saud and his son, Turki, told
> the Sahib that he should not accompany them but the Sahib

did not agree ... I heard the talk myself as my tent was quite close ... Next morning at 6 am Bin Rashid's troops were sighted and in less than two hours the enemy came close. Bin Saud's forces dug ditches at a distance of about 500 yards behind the firing line and all the kit, tents and luggage were loaded on to camels which were made to sit in the diches. Sahib left all his servants but one, Hadi, in the ditches, and took his camera and mounted on a camel with Hadi. He instructed Hadi to keep the camel when he dismounted and wait for him while he went on foot. I was about 300 yards from the Sahib and saw him well. He went on to a mound and started to take photographs. Bin Saud ordered a general attack at about 8 am, cavalry being on the right and left flanks, infantry in the centre. On the right one gun was working between the infantry and cavalry. The enemy, however, had superior cavalry and more men and soon dispersed Bin Saud's army, causing a complete rout. As they fled back I lost sight of the Sahib ... everybody saved his life as best he could ... I was taken prisoner by Bin Rashid's men ... but the second night I managed to slip from the camel and hide under a bush. I learned from the Bani Shammar that Captain Shakespear at first received a wound in his right arm and afterwards was killed by two bullets, one in the head and one in the back. Next morning I returned to the battlefield. For several days I lived on grass till I came to the tents of the Mutair who asked me to stay in their service. When we reached the battlefield I went round the dead bodies and recognised Captain Shakespear. Everything had been stripped from him except a ganji vest. I found the marks of three bullets on him – one in his right arm, one at the back of the head, the third in the groin on the right side ... I managed to slip away and in a few days reached Zilfi ...

Of the many letters received by his parents and his younger brother, none was more generous than that from Knox to his mother:

Dear Mrs Shakespear,
I trust that you will permit me the sad privilege of writing to console with you on the death of your son; the news has just come through to me by the report of Col Grey. I was

very closely connected with your son during his official career which achieved so much and promised still more. He succeeded me at Kuwait and continued with far greater skill, zeal and energy the work that I had begun and had very much at heart. The news that I received today saddened me more than I can possibly express to you – not so much for the sake of poor Shakespear, for I can well imagine that he would have chosen a soldier's death by the side of his gallant Arab comrade Abdul Aziz Bin Saud, before any other but for the irreparable loss that I and the Department and indeed the Service have sustained ... I enclose some extracts from Col. Grey's report ... it will no doubt be some poor consolation to you that the cause of his friend Bin Saud, for which your son did so much, is by no means lost. We had our poor friend staying with us a few days before he left on his dangerous and most important mission. He was as cheery and full of health and strength as ever, full of all he had been doing at home in Kitchener's new army. I heard at first hand his account of that magnificent and adventurous journey across Arabia from Kuwait to the Egyptian frontier. The tale was told with the simple force characteristic of the teller; but we who know something about desert travel could appreciate, and follow with interest, the splendid story. His last letters from the heart of Arabia still showed that keen enthusiasm and buoyant confidence that carried him through toil and danger that would have broken ten ordinary men. I do not think your son had an enemy in the world and he had – and still has – the admiration of all of us, his fellow workers in the Persian Gulf. We simply cannot replace him and the fame of his travels will live long in our annals. Not a mother in England has more cause to be proud of her son than you in your explorer son. With deepest sympathy, believe me,

S. G. KNOX

Ps. I would not have known to whom to write, but my wife, who shares my intense admiration of your son, tells me that he often spoke to her of you and of the close companionship between yourself and him.

Messages of sorrow flooded to his parents' Brighton home.

The King and Queen, Lord Crewe and the Viceroy sent their condolences. Cox, Grey and several servicemen whom Shakespear had known in India wrote movingly of their admiration for the man, and their own sense of loss at his death.

The Times of London, its columns filled to overflowing with announcements of death on the war fronts of Europe, could spare space for no more than a factual obituary. Nearly a month later, on March 13th, the same newspaper carried a report from its Middle East Correspondent, dateline Cairo.

Severe fighting has occurred in Central Arabia between Ibn Rashid, Amir of Hail, to whom the Turks last year sent large quantities of ammunition for use against the British protégés in the Gulf, and Ibn Saud, Amir of Riyadh. The intrepid Arabia explorer Captain Shakespear, whose death is officially announced, is believed to have succumbed to wounds received in this encounter while on a mission to the Anglophile Ibn Saud.

The Times of India spoke more handsomely. On February 18th, in a leader headed 'A distinguished career', it commented:

The death of Captain Shakespear ... is greatly deplored in Delhi, where his outstanding ability and energy and open character were greatly admired, and it is recognized that the Foreign Department have lost an officer they can ill spare, and one who was destined for a brilliant career. He was possessed of wide oriental knowledge of the best practical kind, and his popularity among the tribes of Arabia was, in the words of the communiqué, remarkable.

It was this which rendered possible his brilliant journey across Arabia. His energy of mind was shown also in the occupations of his leisure time. He was a keen man of the water and had ambitions as an aviator. While at Kuwait he made several trips across the Persian Gulf to Basra in a small steam launch. Such visits were not unattended with risk owing to the sudden rise of the sea and mists which are characteristic of that water. With regard to the air, he told his friends some little while ago that he was experimenting on the building of an aeroplane in Kuwait ...

Colonel Grey, pedantic to the last, always insisted that Shakespear was killed by a stray bullet in a small tribal skirmish. He instructed the Agency Clerk, L. M. D'Mello, to put the requisite stamps on the letters Shakespear had left behind – 'I think the letter may go officially' he noted – and together they set about restoring Shakespear's posthumous finances. The clerk put in a bill for £13.9.0 for food sent to him in the desert and they assessed his other outstanding debts, finding that he was some £400 in arrears as the result of his careless habit of neglecting to account for his expenses. When his will was proved in the district court of Agra in July 1915, his estate was shown to be worth 280 rupees, roughly £16.

A Committee of Adjustment was set up on the order of the Commander-in-Chief. It consisted of Colonel L. W. Shakespear, a cousin, who was elected President, Sir Percy Cox, and Captain A. T. Wilson. They sorted out Shakespear's financial status, but could come to no conclusion about his death, apart from the obvious fact that he died in action, at the side of the Amir of Najd, Ibn Saud.

A question was set down in the House of Commons soon after his death, but ministers in wartime England had other matters on their minds. Hansard does not record an answer. There was talk of sinking a well in the desert in his memory, but nothing came of it. A later Political Agent in Kuwait, Gerald de Gaury, raised a memorial to him in the cemetery there, alongside which was later to be placed the grave of another distinguished servant of Kuwait, and friend of Shakespear, Dr Mylrea of the American Mission. His old school, King William's College, recorded his final deed on a plaque:

In Loving Memory of
William Henry Irvine Shakespear CIE
Captain, Indian Army
Political Department, Government of India
Killed in Central Arabia on 24th January 1915
Aged 36 years
Pro Rege et Patria

General Sir Douglas Baird, as Dorothea's brother became, went to his school many years later and presented it with the giant Union Jack that Shakespear had left with him in India in 1914.

Within two weeks of Shakespear's death Captain Gerald Leach-

man was appointed in his place as Political Officer on Special
Duty in Arabia. On March 26th a note from the Viceroy was
minuted by the India and Foreign Offices. 'Captain Leachman
has travelled considerably in Arabia, sometimes in disguise.
While not of the same calibre as Shakespear, he may do well under
Sir Percy Cox.'

An India Office minute filed by the Foreign Office at this time
marked the final official comment on Shakespear. Dated March
17th, 1915, it acknowledged Shakespear's last report to Cox. 'This
interesting report must be one of, if not quite the last, written
by Captain Shakespear before he was killed. It emphasises once
more the advantages of wholeheartedly supporting Bin Saud.'

The appointment of Leachman was the last noteworthy gesture
of the Indian administration before power was taken from its
grasp and Arabian affairs passed to the High Commissioner and
the Arab Bureau in Cairo. By the end of the year a new era had
begun in Arabia. Sir Percy Cox himself concluded the treaty with
Ibn Saud on December 26th, but it had been drastically watered
down at the last minute at the request of the new Secretary of
State for India, Austen Chamberlain. Leachman played no part
in further negotiations with the amir. Indeed, there were no
further negotiations worth speaking of. Shaikh Mubarak was a
sick man and he died the following year. Ibn Saud pursued the
Ajman into Kuwait where, to his great anger, Mubarak's sons
gave them refuge.

The idea of an Arab rebellion against the Turks first came to
British ears when Shakespear reported to his chiefs after his
desert meeting with Ibn Saud in 1911. By the time he met the
amir in 1913 and 1914 a tenuous notion had gained strength.
Had he been listened to more carefully it is possible – just possible
– that at the outbreak of war Britain could have united all the
chiefs and tribes of Arabia under the leadership of Ibn Saud,
brought hostilities in the peninsula to a speedy end, and negotiated a peace in Arabia that was honourable if not enduring. As it
was Central Arabia and its king were abandoned at the moment of
Shakespear's death, if not before.

The men of the Arab Bureau who took over lacked nothing by
way of qualifications or credentials. It was at this time that one
of their number, Captain T. E. Lawrence, conceived the notion
of the *Arab Bulletin*, a propaganda weapon of the bureau and

source of information for the senior officers of the political and
military services. The bulletin, later to be edited by Commander
D. G. Hogarth and Major K. Cornwallis, became the only
reliable source for those who tried subsequently to follow the
events of the war in Arabia. Early issues of the bulletin told of the
continuing jostle for position among the Arab chiefs and the
British and Turkish officials who moved among them with
promises and propositions. While McMahon, who had come
west from India to take over the job of High Commissioner,
flirted with Husain, Cox was given the unenviable task of keeping
the Amir of Najd quiescent.

'Bin Saud is being advised to come to a full understanding with
the Sharif and if possible to give him active assistance,' said a
note of August 15th, from Cox to McMahon. On August 15th
Ibn Saud told the Chief Political Officer in Mesopotamia: 'I
have received letters from the Sharif asking for an alliance, but I
will only enter into an agreement with Husain if he gives a solemn
undertaking not to interfere with my tribes ... [and] if relations
with the Sharif are of concern to Britain.' At the same time
McMahon was asking Husain to meet Ibn Saud 'half way'.

It was not until edition number 25 of the bulletin, issued on
October 7th, 1916, that the real drift of events began to come
clear. Cox had reported in the previous July that Ibn Saud took
strong exception to a British statement which talked of 'Arabs
as a whole' in the same breath as it spoke of Husain. The amir had
no desire for an alliance with the sharif, and he strongly recommended that Britain should give Husain just enough assistance to
ensure the protraction of the struggle between him and the Turks,
and thus prevent the latter from detaching troops to fight in
Mesopotamia. 'The Sharif's original intention', Ibn Saud told
Cox, 'was to play off Britain against Turkey and to get the Turks
to grant him independence which would be guaranteed by
Germany.' Britain's response to the amir's advice was to tell him
that he should 'come to a full understanding with the Sharif'.
No wonder, for by then McMahon had written letters to Husain
promising him the lordship of Arabia, of virtually the entire
peninsula, in return for his allegiance, though even the Foreign
Secretary seemed to be in considerable doubt as to *exactly* what
was promised in terms of space and time.

The wandering correspondents of the bulletin put together a

miniature history of the events that had occupied the most important years of Shakespear's life, capturing distant happenings with a literary vigour which contrasted forcibly with the pale documentation of the official record. On November 27th, 1916, Ibn Saud went to Basra to receive a decoration from Britain. The scene, described by Gertrude Bell, was: ' … no less picturesque to the onlooker than it was significant to those who have studied the course of Arabian politics … When Abdul Aziz was a boy of fifteen, and the power of the Rashid at its zenith, the great Amir Muhammad, Doughty's grudging host, drove the Saud into exile and onward to their capital Riyadh. For eleven years, Abdul Aziz ate the bread of adversity … ' And on to the battle of Jarab and the death of Shakespear. 'We lost in him a gallant officer whose knowledge of Central Arabia and rare skill in the handling of tribesmen marked him out for a useful and distinguished career. His deeds have lived after him.'

The most illuminating item to appear in the bulletin, as far as the story of Shakespear and the battle of Jarab was concerned, was published in numbers 45 and 60. There was still a good deal of interest among British officials as to the reason for the excursion of Abdullah's army into Najd at the time of the battle which caused Shakespear's death. On March 23rd, 1917, a note written on behalf of the sharif was published. It was a hopelessly inadequate account; Abdullah's intervention was designed to protect Ibn Saud and to warn Rashid not to continue into Najd, according to the sharif's witness, who gave the date of the battle as 1916. But Abdullah was 'obliged to halt at Shara south east of Anaiza', about 170 miles from the scene of the fight. On August 20th, 1917, the bulletin reported a meeting between Colonel C. E. Wilson and the sharif, at which notes were taken by Lawrence. Husain then insisted that he and his sons were on the best of terms with the Amir of Najd and that Abdullah had gone to Shara to protect Ibn Saud. In the same breath he mentioned that he was inviting Abdur Rahman, Ibn Saud's father, to Mecca, in an attempt to reconcile dissident members of the family. Colonel Wilson was anxious to show that Husain's assumption of a royal title – he was now known as the 'King of the Arabs' – was not intended in any way to suggest interference in the affairs of Central Arabia. Meanwhile, the Ajman, who had committed their ultimate act of treachery, resulting in the death of Ibn Saud's

favourite brother Saad, were now in alliance with the sharif's other
son Zeid. Husain hoped through the intervention of Abdur
Rahman to persuade Ibn Saud to make peace with the Ajman!
'It was evident throughout the interview that the Sharif had no
intention of adjusting the relations of the Hijaz Government with
the amirs of Arabia until after the fall of Madina ... his position
would then be sufficiently improved to give him the advantage in
negotiation ... '

The men of Cairo very nearly realized the Arab dream of
independence out of the manifest absurdity of promises they
had no right to give and no power to enforce. McMahon, Clayton,
Storrs, Allenby, Lawrence, Sykes, Hogarth, Wilson, Cornwallis,
Miss Bell – they brought great gifts of intellect and skills of
organization to bear on an Arab revolt. They chose as their
vehicle Husain of Mecca, keeper of the Prophet's birthplace, the
only prince of Arabia whose title was granted hereditary status by
the Ottoman and therefore suspect to all other Arab leaders. No
promises were too extravagant, no ideas too far-fetched, to bring
their plan to fruition. They promised him and his sons sovereignty
over virtually all Arabia, drawing boundaries that embraced
territories no Arab leader had ever claimed, and offering new
kingdoms to his sons which would, if necessary, be cut from the
desert.

The early disasters of the Mesopotamian campaign stood as a
reminder of the need for bold action, and if an Arab revolt could
be induced and the war shortened, a few gratuitous promises
were a small price to pay. But such disasters also showed what
might have been had Shakespear lived to fight with Ibn Saud and
rally the tribes of Central Arabia to the allied cause. At any rate,
by late in 1916 the die was cast. Lawrence had been sent to
Mesopotamia to see what he could salvage from the mess there,
but he was given a cool reception by the generals.

Lawrence's story of the events which led to the Arab revolt
will remain forever a testament to the highest literary skill and
the most questionable of political motives. In *Seven Pillars of
Wisdom* he gave a faithful account:

> The Cabinet raised the Arabs to fight for us by definite
> promises of self-government afterwards ... It was evident
> from the beginning that if we won the war these promises

would be dead paper, and had I been an honest adviser I would have advised them to go home and not risk their lives fighting for such stuff … I risked the fraud, on my conviction that Arab help was necessary to our cheap and speedy victory in the East, and that better we win and break our word than lose.

They pulled off their coup and achieved victory where there might have been disaster for Britain, her allies and Arabia. And predictably, no sooner had they turned the Turks out of Arabia than the chickens came home to roost.

Husain's son Faisal turned against his father and placed himself under Allenby's protection; he was eventually given his kingdom, first in Syria and then in Mesopotamia, or Iraq as it came to be called. Abdullah was also given his kingdom, carved out of Syria and called 'Transjordan'.

By the end of the war, Husain was loudly claiming that McMahon had promised that he would be 'King of the Arabs', but Britain said that it had promised 'limited recognition' and the return of the Caliphate. Certainly there is good enough evidence that in October 1915, McMahon, without informing Whitehall, had promised independence within boundaries drawn by Husain, with two reservations, British supervision of Baghdad and Basra, and coastal areas west of Damascus, Hama, Homs and Aleppo. Otherwise virtually the whole of Arabia, possibly including Palestine, had been promised to Husain. But the documents, if indeed there were any, never saw the light of day. And while the men of the Arab Bureau and the High Commissioner in Egypt made their plans, ministers in London were puzzled. 'The Government is getting into a great mess with these negotiations of McMahon's,' said Austen Chamberlain on December 29th, 1915. He added: 'Are we going to add the independence of Arabia to all the other objects we have pledged ourselves to secure, before we make peace?' In June 1916, Sir Edward Grey declared that he 'did not have a clear head about British promises and intentions in Mesopotamia'. He meant 'Arabia', but he could be forgiven the mistake for nobody, least of all the protagonists of the alliance with Husain, had clear heads about the promises either.

Lawrence contributed a note on the Sharif family to the bulletin

of November 26th, 1916: 'One can see that to the nomads the
Sharif and his three elder sons are heroes. Sharif Hussein ... is
outwardly so gentle and considerate as to seem almost weak, but
this appearance hides a deep and crafty policy, wide ambitions and
an un-Arabian foresight, strength of character and persistence.'

Two years later the same writer penned another note for
the bulletin, but it was thought inadvisable to publish it then.
A. W. Lawrence published it in *Secret Despatches from Arabia* in
1939:

> When the Sharif drew sword he told us what he wanted, and
> we raised no vital objection to his claim. Since then we have
> helped him manfully, and his kingdom has grown ... He has
> involved himself and all his friends in the threat of gallows if
> they fail, or we fail, and has pledged his honour to the Arabs
> in the magnificent ambition of adding Syria and Mesopotamia
> to his dominion.

The bulletin went on until August 1919, though the last
edition under the editorship of Hogarth came out in December
1918. No single issue better exemplifies the mess to which the
politics of expediency had led than that of April 1918 with its
supplementary paper no. 3. Sir Percy Cox was on his way to
England by way of Cairo and Sir Reginald Wingate, the High
Commissioner, made his visit the occasion for a meeting of the
Bureau. By now McMahon was 'broken', to use Lawrence's apt
word, and Wingate had inherited an unholy agglomeration of
promises and aims. With him, apart from Cox, were Clayton,
Wilson, Lieutenant-Colonel Jacob, Lieutenant-Colonel Symes,
Hogarth and Cornwallis. The meeting took place on March
23rd, 1918, and the bulletin reported agreement that if Ibn
Saud 'should find a way of taking Hail' they would put no
obstacles in his way, but Cox felt that 'the balance of power
would be better preserved if Ibn Rashid continued to rule at
Hail'. It was also agreed that there was little chance of the chiefs
of Yemen and Asir, or of Ibn Saud, accepting Husain as their
overlord. They wondered if Husain would ever be in a position
to 'crush Ibn Saud', and they talked of the possibility of the Sharif
being made Caliph of Islam. As for Mesopotamia, 'the people no
doubt expected some sort of Arab façade to the post-war administration ...'

It was one of the queerest debates ever to take place on the subject of Arabia. Tens of thousands had died, often needlessly, in Mesopotamia. Arabs had been fed on false promises and encouraged in vain hopes. Now these men sat and talked as if nothing had happened in the interval of the war. Cox had seen every report Shakespear ever wrote, warning his superiors that Ibn Saud enjoyed the support of by far the greater number of tribes and princes, and that he and only he could be relied on to form a strong and enduring alliance in the desert. Cox had supported his Political Agent in everything he said. But even he, in the end, became victim of the disease of self-deception which infected every British politician connected with Arabia. By 1918 only one man in this bizarre drama knew where he was going. Ibn Saud took matters into his own hands. Had the Foreign and India Offices consulted their own files, they might have anticipated the rest.

Three times in 1918 Husain's troops attacked the Saudi-held oasis of Khurma on the Najd-Hijaz border. Each time his army was thrown back. In 1919, he decided to try again, with British approval and support. This time his army was annihilated. The road from Najd to Mecca was open and Husain clamoured for British protection. Lord Curzon, once the protagonist of an understanding between Britain and the Wahhabi amirs, was now responsible for advising the government on its post-war policies in Arabia. And in the very year that the sharif made his ill-advised attack on Ibn Saud, he declared: 'Our policy is a Husain policy.' The War Office, in a closely reasoned document, argued that in conflict between the amir and Husain, 'the latter would win hands down against the Wahhabi rabble.' They were famous last words.

Two months later, in May 1919, Lord Curzon made it plain that nothing anyone could do would prevent the advance of Ibn Saud or deny him his rightful territories. The War Office, too, changed its tune.

Matters were coming to inevitable resolution in other parts of the desert at this time. In 1920, Saud ibn Rashid was the last victim of the royal house of Hail. Just as he had come to power by murder a few days before Shakespear passed by in 1914, so he died by it. Britain, seeking any avenue of escape from its own folly, had begun to toy with the idea of an alliance with Ibn Rashid to help bolster the frail regime of Husain.

The three great leaders of Central Arabia, Ibn Saud, Faisal ibn Dawish, the chief of the Mutair, and Ibn Shaalan, the Ruwala leader, moved on separate fronts. By 1921 the kingdom of Shammar and its royal house at Hail were no more. The Shammar were driven to seek refuge in Iraq. Ibn Saud was the acknowledged master of Central Arabia. Indeed, by late 1921, Abdul Aziz was in command of the entire heart of Arabia, with Britain's Hashemite or Sharifite puppets in Hijaz and Transjordan.

Britain, following the 1921 conference in Cairo, presided over by Churchill, was no more certain of its position or policies than it had ever been. The Foreign and India Offices were at odds again, and now the Colonial Office joined the battle. Sir Percy Cox was trying to pick up the pieces of Whitehall's grandiose schemes in Iraq, where he was dealing with the omnipresent Sayid Talib, who was now Minister of the Interior in the Provisional Government. Nuri Shaalan, soon to be immortalized by Lawrence, had handed power to his grandson Sultan, the little boy who had wept when Shakespear left him in 1914. The old man retired to Damascus, where he made sure that despite his great age he would not die in ignorance of such carnal pleasures as had so far escaped him.

Husain and his sons ruled over stretches of desert to which, in the view of most Arabs, they had no right. Ibn Saud's patience was at an end. In 1924 he attacked Hijaz and in December of that year he entered Mecca, donned the pilgrim robes for the first time in his life and began to impose the puritanism of the Wahhabi creed on Islam's holy city for the second time in history. In the following year he took over the rest of that country, and Husain was exiled first to Aqaba and then to Cyprus. In November 1925 Sir Gilbert Clayton, who nearly ten years before had set the seal of his authority on the wartime deal with Husain, went to Bahra, between Jidda and Mecca, to meet the *de facto* King of Arabia.

It is arguable that the sons of Husain proved reliable allies of Britain even if their father was, in the end, an insupportable burden. But theirs was a costly legacy.

No more than two years before the deal with Husain was made, Shakespear had told the government in his report of June 26th, 1914, to Hirtzel: ' ... the Arabs have now found a leader [Ibn

Saud] who stands head and shoulders above any other chief and in whose star all have implicit faith.' Ten years later, when that leader took matters into his own hands, nobody in Whitehall was particularly anxious to produce Shakespear's testimony.

Ibn Saud found a staunch champion in Shakespear's successor at his court, H. St J. Philby. He too, sharp-tongued apostle of Arab causes, found that his slender resources of tact and patience were heavily taxed by his chiefs in the years of Anglo-Hashemite intrigue. But he lived to see his own and Shakespear's views vindicated, to see the lean years of the desert king give way to plenty, and – in the end – to excess. He wrote:

> It was left to Lawrence and the army of the Hijaz to accomplish what in other circumstances – with a little better luck and a little more imagination on the part of the authorities responsible for the Mesopotamian campaign – might have been accomplished by Ibn Saud and Shakespear.

And again:

> While India was generally right in its appreciation of the Arabian situation and lacked only the habit of action which had been petrified by decades of ponderous routine, the vigorous methods and enthusiastic originality of the Egyptian authorities were almost enough to carry a fanatic and utterly impossible experiment to the desired successful conclusion. Only one man, indeed, stood in the way of their triumphant success ... Ibn Saud ...

Of others who followed Shakespear to the Arab lands and who heard tell of his exploits from tribesmen, several became life-long admirers, but inevitably there were detractors. Some lacked a taste for his political rigidity while others had little enthusiasm for his championship of Ibn Saud's cause. Before and after Shakespear, the motives of desert travellers were many and varied. Sexual adventure, scholarly enquiry, espionage, curiosity, self chastisement – the list is long and not all the men who followed in his steps could be expected to understand the nature of his close ties with the Badu, or to see eye to eye with his unbending disapproval of the policies of his superiors. Neither could they all expect to find a recognisable echo of their own ambitions and peccadilloes.

Sir Arnold Wilson, who eventually became Civil Commissioner in Iraq and the far from universally popular strong man of Britain's post-war administration, never lost his youthful admiration for his contemporary in the Bushire Residency. There may, indeed, have been a note of reminiscence in his own final grand gesture when, at the outbreak of the second World War, he induced friends in office to help him join the Royal Air Force, to become one of its earliest – and oldest – casualties as a rear gunner. Field Marshal Lord Wavell, whose cousin H. J. B. Wavell made a pilgrimage in disguise to Mecca in 1908, and who himself became a considerable student of Arabia, often spoke of Shakespear's desert adventures. Sir Reginald Wingate greatly admired the weather-beaten young man who dismissed him and Kitchener as ill-informed 'bigwigs' after calling on them on his way through Cairo in 1914. And his son Sir Ronald Wingate learned of the still-glowing legend of Shakespear among the new men of the Indian Political Service when he joined its ranks after serving in Mesopotamia during the first World War.

Yet it was the sensitive and articulate Lawrence, self-proclaimed hero of Britain's wartime involvement in Arabia, who captured the essence of Shakespear's desert magnetism.

Many of the Ageyl of ibn Dgheithir had travelled with him, as escort or followers, and had tales of his magnificence and of the strange seclusion in which he kept himself day and night. The Arabs, who usually lived in heaps, suspected some ulterior reason for any too careful privacy. To remember this, and to foreswear all selfish peace and quiet while wandering with them, was one of the least pleasant lessons of the desert war: and humiliating, too, for it was a part of pride with Englishmen to hug solitude; ourselves finding ourselves to be remarkable, when there was no competition present.

Perhaps alone among those few outsiders who succeeded in living among the wild men of Arabia, Shakespear preserved his solitude and his pride. He acted remarkably among them, and was usually too busy to stop and wonder if they approved.

But the last words on the subject were spoken at the final

meeting between Clayton and the king when they went to Jidda in 1927 to ratify the treaty recognizing the complete and absolute independence of the Wahhabi dominions. When the two men had put their signatures to the document, Clayton asked Ibn Saud if he could name the greatest of the Europeans he had met in his life. Without a moment's hesitation he replied: 'Captain Shakespear.'

Selected Bibliography

Armstrong, H. C., *Lord of Arabia* (Arthur Barker, London, 1934)

Atiyah, E., *Palestine Essays*: correspondence between Sir Henry McMahon and Sharif Husain (Copenhagen, 1972)

Bray, N. N. E., *A Paladin of Arabia* (Unicorn Press, London, 1936)

Burton, Sir Richard, *A Pilgrimage to Al Medinah and Mecca* (London, 1893)

Busch, Briton Cooper, *Britain, India and the Arabs* (University of California, 1971)

Carruthers, D., 'Captain Shakespear's Last Journey' in *Geographical Journal* (May/June 1921)

Cheesman, R. E., *In Unknown Arabia* (Macmillan, London, 1926)

De Gaury, Gerald, *Rulers of Mecca* (Harrap, London, 1951)

Dickson, H. R. P., *The Arab of the Desert* (Allen and Unwin, London, 1949)

——, *Kuwait and Her Neighbours* (Allen and Unwin, London, 1956)

Dickson, Violet, *Forty Years in Kuwait* (Allen and Unwin, London, 1971)

Doughty, Charles M., *Travels in Arabia Deserta* (Jonathan Cape, London, 1921, 1936)

Freeth, Zahra, *Kuwait was My Home* (Allen and Unwin, London, 1956)

——, *A New Look at Kuwait* (Allen and Unwin, London, 1972)

——, and Victor Winstone, *Kuwait: Prospect and Reality* (Allen and Unwin, London, 1972)

Gibbon, Edward, *The History of the Decline and Fall of the Roman Empire*, ed. H. H. Milman (Philips, Sampson, Boston, 1852)

Glubb, Sir John, *Britain and the Arabs* (Hodder and Stoughton, London, 1959)

Graves, Philip, *The Life of Sir Percy Cox* (Hutchinson, London, 1941)

Graves, Robert, *Lawrence and the Arabs* (Jonathan Cape, London, 1935)

Hogarth, D. G., *The Penetration of Arabia* (London, 1904)

Howarth, David, *Desert King* (Collins, London, 1964)

Kedourie, Elie, *In the Anglo-Arab Labyrinth* (CUP, Cambridge, 1976)

Kiernan, R. H., *The Unveiling of Arabia* (Harrap, London, 1937)

Lawrence, T. E., *Secret Despatches from Arabia*, ed. A. W. Lawrence (Golden Cockerel Press, London, 1939)

——, *Seven Pillars of Wisdom* (Jonathan Cape, London, 1935)

Lorimer, J. G., *Gazetteer of the Persian Gulf* (Indian Government Press, Bombay, 1913)

Magnus, Sir Philip, *Kitchener, A Portrait of an Imperialist* (John Murray, London, 1958)

Monroe, Elizabeth, *Philby of Arabia* (Faber and Faber, London, 1973)

Murphy, C. C. R., *Soldiers of the Prophet* (London, 1921)

Niebuhr, Carsten, *Travels and Description of Arabia* (Amsterdam, 1780)

Nutting, Anthony, *The Arabs* (Hollis and Carter, London, 1964)

Palgrave, W. G., *Central and Eastern Arabia* (Macmillan, London, 1865)

Philby, H. St J., *Arabia* (Benn, London, 1930)

——, *Arabia of the Wahhabis* (Constable, London, 1928)

——, *The Heart of Arabia* (Constable, London, 1922)

Raswan, Carl R., *The Black Tents of Arabia* (Hutchinson, London, 1935)

Raunkiaer, Barclay, *Through Wahhabiland on Camel-Back*, edited and with an introduction by Gerald de Gaury (Routledge & Kegan Paul, London, 1969)

Sadlier, G. F., *Diary of a Journey Across Arabia* (Bombay, 1866)

Wilson, Sir Arnold T., *Loyalties, Mesopotamia 1914–17* (OUP, Oxford, 1930)

Glossary of Arabic Words

abba, Arab cloak

abd, slave

abu, father of

agal, headdress cord

agheyl, official guide in Ottoman Arabia

akhawat, fee for passage, guide money

allah, ullah, illah, God

allah akbar! God is great!

arfaj, pasture bush, used for firewood

ausaj, thorny bush

bab, gate

birka, birket, cistern, artificial reservoir

boum, sailing ship

burga, burqa, face mask on woman or hawk

dakhala, dakhilak, binding plea for protection, sanctuary

darb, road

dhalul, thalul, fast, female riding camel

dhow, sailing ship

dira, tribal homeland, pastureland

dishdasha, man's white gown

diwaniyah, house, living quarter

dowla, authority or official

Fi aman illah, Go in the peace of the Lord

ghada, succulent tree, delight of camel

ghazu, badawin raiding foray

hakim, wise man, doctor

hamd, praise; also pungent-smelling shrub

hanash, snake

haramieh, thieves

harim, women's quarter

harra, rough desert covered with black volcanic rock

ibn, son of

imam, religious leader

jabal, mountain

jambiyah, dagger

jemader, camel-keeper

Jihad, holy war

kadhi, local magistrate

kaffiya, Arab head-cloth

kaimakam, Turkish governor

kalima, kelam, God's word. Holy slogan of Islam: 'There is no God but God, and Muhammad is his Prophet.' Emblazoned on the flags of Arab princes.

kasr, fort or palace, princely residence

kayf, kayif, pleasurable contemplation, solace

khabra, share; also pond

khanjar, curved dagger

khatib, preacher

kahwa, coffee, coffee-room

leben, buttermilk, soured milk

lisam, litham, badawin face-mask

madrasah, school
majlis, assembly, council
mafrash, carpet for tent floor
maktub, 'It is written'. Badawin response
mashab, *mehjan*, camel stick
mattrah, mattress for guest
mizwada, baggage tent
mutasarrif, overlord. Turkish title
Porte, title given to Ottoman rulers by Arabs, from French satire of Bab al-Ali, high ingate to Sultan's government; thus 'Sublime Porte'.
rafiq, tribal escort or guide
ras, head, headland

raudha, garden
samn, clarified butter
serai, palace
seyf, sword
sharif, noble, also ruler of holy cities
shimal, north wind
suq, market place, bazaar
sura, verses of Koran
um(m), mother of
ulema, learned men
vilayet, Ottoman administrative region
wadi, dry watercourse
wakar al tair, hawk's stand
wasm, cattle mark of tribe

Index

Abdul Aziz ibn Abdur Rahman al Saud, King, *passim*

Abdul Aziz ibn Hassan, *jemader*, *passim*

Abdul Aziz ibn Mitab al Rashid, 61

Abdul Aziz ibn Muhammad al Saud, 57

Abdul Hamid, Sultan, 93, 108

Abdullah ibn Abdur Rahman al Saud, 187

Abdullah ibn Ali al Rashid, 58

Abdullah ibn Faisal al Saud, 58

Abdullah ibn Husain, of Mecca, 21, 208, 212, 220

Abdul Nabi, 63

Abdur Rahman ibn Faisal al Saud, Imam, 58–60, 161, 188, 189, 220

Abu al Kaa, 81

Abu Taiya, 178

Abu Thahir, 99

Adan, 78

Adelboden, Switzerland, 50

Adjusa, Ras, 140

Adriatic, 49

Afghanistan, 37

Agra, district court, 217

Ajibba, 154, 186

Ajlan, Rashidi governor, 59

Ajman, tribe, 73, 82, 87, 124, 133, 207–9, 211–20

Al Ahram, quoted, 97

Al Ats, 18

Aldershot, 114, 193–4

Aleppo, 56

Ali ibn Badr, 155

Ali ibn Husain, of Mecca, 97

Ali ibn Khalifa, 100, 124

Allam, Saad, 10

Allenby, Field-Marshal, Viscount, 221

Amarat, tribe, 176

America, desert Arabs in, 174

Anaiza, 166

Anaiza tribal confederation, 57, 89–93, 176, 204

Anglo-Arab alliance, hope for, 103, 191–2, 196

Anglo-Arab treaty, 196–204, 218

Anglo-Turkish agreements, 67, 126–9, 135, 139, 142, 147, 192

Anthropology: interest in, 138; tribal customs, 164

Aqaba, 19, 182

Arab Bulletin, 23, 218–25

Arab Bureau, 23, 218–25

Arabia, *passim*

Arabia, S.S., 196

Arab revolt, 104–5, 107, 218

Arab-Turkish treaty, 203–4

Ardh, Ras, 140

Arfajiya, 179

Aridh, 17, 57

Arma plateau, 17, 202

Artawiya (Al Artavel), 153, 213

Artemidorus, 100

Asir, 104, 107, 192

Asiyah, 155, 169

Askar, Abdullah ibn, 135, 157

Asquith Government, 63, 187

Atayba, tribe, 163–4

Athens, 49

Audah, Sudair, 159, 186

Audah, Shaikh of Howeitat, 176–9, 184, 188

Austin, Mr Robert, 9

Aylmer, Capt. L., 179, 186

Ayun, 169

Badawin, Al Badu, *passim*

Bagar, 210

Baghdad, 88, 93, 207; railway company, 142

Bahrain, 126, 141–2, 144

Baird, Lt-Col. A. W., F.R.S., 50–54

Baird, Dorothea (Mrs H. B. Irving), 64

Baird, H. Dorothea, *see* Lakin, Dorothea

Baird, Gen. Sir Douglas, 62, 114, 119, 190, 217

Baird, Margaret Elizabeth (née Davidson), 50

Baird, Lt–Col. Niall, 9

Baird, Winifred, *see* Shakespear, Winifred

Balfour Government, 34

Banban, 159, 163

Bandar Abbas, Persia, 36, 38, 39

Bandar-Shuwaikh Lease, 67

Bani, Hilal, 152

Barlow, Capt. C. E., 185

Barrett, Gen. Sir Arthur, 201, 204

Basra, 56, 80, 86, 88, 92, 98, 124, 129, 129, 134, 141–2, 144, 170, 207

Batin, 80, 84, 151, 170, 186

Bawari plain, India, 116, 119

Bayley, C. S., 55

Belhaven, Lord (Lt-Col. R. E. A. Hamilton), quoted, 147

Bell, Gertrude, 186, 205, 220–1

Bengal Cavalry, 62

Bengal Lancers, 32, 117

Bethell, Admiral Sir Alexander, 124

Bibesco, Prince, 44

Biggam, Sam, 131–2

Bir Abbas, 184

Birdwood, Gen. W. R., 145

Bittar, 169–70, 209

Blunt, Lady Anne, 56, 77, 186

Blunt, Wilfrid Scawen, 56, 63, 77, 186

Boat-builders, Kuwait, 120

Boer War, 34

Bologna, 50

Bombay, 30, 34, 40

Bombay-Delhi car journey, 116–17

Bombay Natural History Society, 190

Borghese, Prince, 42

Brighton, England, 52

British Empire, 108–9

British Government, *passim*

Browning, Robert, quoted, 115

Bubiyan Island, 99

Buraida, 130, 144, 167–9, 186, 208

Burgan, 141

Burns, John, 63

Burton, Sir Richard F., 52, 73

Bushire Residency, 37, 38, 41, 56, 65, 110

Butler, Capt. S. S., 179, 186

Caliphate, Ottoman, 104, 107

Campbell-Bannerman Government, 53, 63

Carew, Mrs Barbara, 8, 9

Carruthers, Col. Douglas, 185

Chakdara, S.S., 199

Chamberlain, Austen, 218, 222

Chaudni Chauk, Delhi, 118

Chicago exhibition, 174

Cholera duty, in India, 32

Clarke-Williams, Mrs E., 9

Clayton, Gen. Sir Gilbert, 222, 223–6, 228

Constantinople, 48–9, 57, 110, 122, 174

Copenhagen, 110

Cornwallis, Col. K., 217, 221–3

Cox, Sir Percy Z., *passim*

Craufurd, Brig.-Gen. Sir G. S. G., 9, 96, 125–32

Crewe, Lord, 145, 195

Crowe, F. E., 88, 90

Curzon, Lord, 35, 60, 61, 66, 116, 224

Dahana, sand belt, 100, 135, 154, 186
Dalmatia, 49
Damascus, 57, 129
Darb Zobaida, 170
Dariyah, 57
Dawish, Faisal ibn, 79, 82, 151, 225
Dawson Place Mansions Hotel, London, 187
De Gaury, Lt-Col. Gerald, 10, 217
Delhi, 40
Devonshire Regiment, 32
Dhaffir, tribe, 86, 124
Dhajal, 100
Dibdibba, 80, 149
Dickson, Lt-Col. H. R. P., 24
Dinshawai affair, 63
D'Mello, L. M., 96, 217
Dodecanese, invasion of, 108
Donaldson, Mr Neil, 9
Dora, Iraq, 88
Doughty, Charles M., 52, 56, 74, 77, 138, 167, 220
Durbar, Delhi, 28, 113–19
Dutch Reformed Church, American Mission of, 121, 217

East India Company, 37, 44, 56, 65
Edward VII, king, 113
Egypt, 37, 184, 207
Elgin, Scotland, 52–4, 56, 62
Ellaimiya, 101
Englishman, The, quoted, 116
Enver Pasha, 197

Fahad Beg, Shaikh, 90
Fahd ibn Abdul Aziz al Saud, 161
Failaka Island, 95
Faisal ibn Abdul Aziz al Saud, 161
Faisal ibn Dawish, *see* Dawish
Faisal ibn Husain, 97, 222
Faisal ibn Turki al Saud (Faisal the Great), 57, 58
Falaiji, Abbas al, 167
Fantas, 78
Fao, Iraq, 88, 95, 199
Ferrara, Italy, 50

Fidan, tribe, 176
Flying School, Aldershot, 114
Foreign Office, *passim*
Forestry Department, India, 30
Fort William, 60
Fox-Talbot, family, 30
France: involvement in Arabia, 37, 108
Fraser, Lovat, 79
Freeth, Mrs Zahra, 9

Gara, 81
Geographical Journal, quoted, 185
George V, king, 113–19, 140
Germany, involvement in Arabia, 25, 66, 70, 108
Gerrha, 100, 103
Ghanim, Saqar al, 121, 122, 124
Ghar al Khafa, 100
Ghat, 156–7
Gherra, 102–3
Gibbon, Edward, quoted, 76
Glubb, Sir John B. (Glubb Pasha), 24
Golden Mosque, Delhi, 118
Grand Vizier, chief minister, Constantinople, 61
Greece, 49
Grey, Sir Edward, 25, 63, 70, 108, 110, 142, 196, 222
Grey, Col. W. G., 147, 195, 199, 200–1, 202–5, 211, 214, 216
Guarmani, Carlo, 186

Hadi ibn Saddi, *rafiq, passim*
Hafar, 80, 83, 152–3, 186
Hail, 58, 61, 135, 169, 205
Hajj routes, 182
Halaibah, 84
Hamar, 98
Hamud ibn Subhan, 61, 86
Hanworth, Lady Rosamond, 9
Haraimla, 163–4
Harb, tribe, 207–9
Hardinge, Lord, Viceroy of India, 116 ff
Harma, 134
Harrison, Dr Paul, 121

Hasa, 81, 85, 86, 100, 124–5, 141, 192, 204
Hasi, 159
Hemming, Mr John, 10
Henjam, Persia, 38
Hijaz, 21, 58; railway, 181, 207
Himyarite inscriptions, 102
Hinna, 102
Hirtzel, Sir Arthur, 187, 225
Hithlain, Dhaidan ibn, 86, 123
Hogarth, Dr D. G., 23, 218, 220–2
Hormuz, Persia, 38
Hormuz, Battle of Chains, 153
Hôtel de la Poste, 185
Howarth, David, quoted, 211
Howeitat, tribe, 178–9, 181
Hubara, lesser bustard, 79
Huber, Charles, 77, 186
Humbert, King of Italy, 108
Hunter, Capt. Fraser, 41, 110, 126
Husain, gunner, 209–10
Husain ibn Ali, Sharif of Mecca, 21, 24, 96–8, 100, 104–9, 127, 142, 167, 185, 197, 207, 219–26
Hyderabad, India, 41, 45

Ibrahim, Pasha, 57, 77, 163
Idrisi, Sayid Muhammad al-, 191, 207, 223
Ikhwan, 153
Imperial Cadet Corps, 117
Indian Expeditionary Force, 200
Indian Government, *passim*
Indian Mutiny, 117
India Office, 10, 37, 45, 70, 187, 218
Intelligence activities, 95, 96, 126, 173
Iraq, *see* Mesopotamia
Isfahan, Persia, 43, 44, 56
Islam, protection of, 21, 199
Islamic law, 57
Ismailiya, Egypt, 185
Italy, 108

Jabal Shammar, 18, 58, 169–70
Jabir ibn Mubarak al Sabah, 84, 87, 124, 141
Jacob, Lt-Col. H. F., 221

Jahra, 79, 86, 87, 98
Jambra, 155
Jarab, 210, 212, 220
Jarina, 161
Jauf al Amir, 90, 93, 169 ff
Jauzah al Rashid, 93
Jihad, religious war, 21–4, 196, 199 206–8
Jilai'a, Ras, 140
Jiluwi, Abdullah ibn, 20, 21, 199, 207, *John O. Scott*, S.S., 141
Johnson, Mr, 185
Judi, battle of, 58
Jullunder, India, 32
Jumna, river, 117

Karachi, 41
Karan mountains, 45
Karbala, 90, 174
Karu, 140
Kasr Adhfa, 173
Kasr Ballal, 84, 152
Katif, 141, 158, 192, 204
Keller, motorist, 44
Kemball, Lt-Col. C. A., 87
Key, Mrs Judith, 8
Khabra Dalayil, 123
Khabra Dawish, 123
Khafs, 135, 139, 213
Khalaq, *rafiq*, 78, 82, 83
Khalid, cook; statement of, 213
Khalid, 'Sword of Islam', 153
Khalid, tribe, 101, 163
Khalifa, Abdullah ibn, 168–9
Khalifa, shaikhs of Al Hasa, *see* Ali ibn Khalifa
Khamir, Persia, 38
Khardja hills, 84
Khawaisat, 123
Khazal, Shaikh of Muhammerah, 93, 125, 131, 147
Khurma, 222
King's birthday, celebration, 124
King William's College, Isle of Man, 31, 217
Kitchener, Lord, 23, 60–1, 185
Knox, Col. S. G., 66–7, 77, 84, 85, 97, 100, 126, 186, 195, 214

Niebuhr, Carsten, 74, 110
Nolde, Baron E., 77, 165, 186
Northcote, Lord, 34

O'Conor, Sir Nicholas, 48, 61
Oil: discovery in Persia, 39; indications in Kuwait, 141
Oman, 38, 126
Order of Indian Empire, award of, 211
Ottoman Government, 20, 38, 57-8, 60-2

Padua, 50
Palgrave, W. G., 56-7, 152, 155-6, 161, 163-4, 167, 169, 186
Palmers Cross, Scotland, see Elgin
Pan-Arab movement, 21
Pearl fishing, 89, 126
Peking-Paris car race, 42
Pelly, Col. Lewis, 65, 77, 86, 135, 161, 163, 186
Persepolis, 43
Persia, 36-47
Persian Gulf, passim
Philby, H. St John, 24, 226
Plague duty, in India, 32
Political Agency, Kuwait, 147
Port Said, Egypt, 185
Portsmouth Grammar School, 30
Prayer, in desert, 136
Prostitutes, 88

Qarain, 164
Qasim, 59, 166, 169
Qatar, 141
Quarterly Review, article in, 10
Qulban ibn Towala, 84, 153

Rakhaiya, 86
Rashaida, tribe, 134
Rashid dynasty, see under individual rulers
Raudhatain, 98
Raudhat al Muhanna, 61
Raunkiaer, Barclay, 110-11, 128, 135, 140, 144, 163, 186
Rawaf, Muhammad al, 174-8

Rawalpindi, 32, 34
Red Fort, Delhi, 117
Rees-Jones, Mr G. R., 10
Reinaud, J. L., 163
Ribdi, Ali ibn, 168-73
Riqai, 84, 149-50
Riqai'a, 81
Riyadh, 24, 26, 58, 61, 77 ff
Rome, 50
Royal Danish Geographical Society, 110-11
Royal Geographical Society, 11, 128, 187, 205
Royal Navy, 21
Royal Sussex Regiment, 89
Rub al Khali (Empty Quarter), 18, 110, 164
Russia, involvement in Middle East, 37, 39, 66, 71, 93, 108
Ruwala, tribe, 176

Saada, 79
Saad ibn Abdur Rahman al Saud, 20, 87, 88, 97-8, 103-6, 188, 207
Saba, Sba'a, sub-tribe, 176
Sabaean inscriptions, 102
Sadairi, Saad ibn Abdul Mehsin al, 156-7
Sadlier, Capt. George, 57, 160, 163, 186
Sadun, Dhaidan ibn, 20, 86-7
Safa, 80-3
Sairayat ridges, 155
Saleh ibn Zamil, 166
Salim ibn Badr, 121
Salim ibn Mubarak al Sabah, 121-4
Salisbury Government, 34
Sanam desert, 180
Sandhurst, R.M.C. entrance, 32
Sarif, 209, 212
Saud ibn Abdul Aziz ibn Abdur Rahman al Saud, 161
Saud ibn Abdul Aziz ibn Muhammad al Saud, 57
Saud ibn Abdul Aziz al Rashid, 18, 20, 22, 61, 90, 172, 199, 205, 224
Saud ibn Abdur Rahman al Saud, 186
Saud ibn Faisal al Saud, 58

Kontilla, Egypt, 183–5
Kubbar Island, 127, 134, 140
Kubri, Egypt, 185
Kum, Persia, 44, 45
Kurma, 97
Kuwait, *passim*
Kuwait Agency political diaries, 10

Labba, 173
Lacell, the Misses, preparatory
    school, 30
Lakin, Maj.-Gen. H., 131
Lakin, Mrs H. Dorothea (née Baird),
    8, 51–4, 188
Lamington, Lord, 122
Lansdowne, Lord, 61
Lar caravan route, 38
Larak, Persia, 38
Lawrence, A. W., 223
Lawrence, Col. T. E., 23, 218,
    220–6, 227
Leachman, Lt-Col. Gerald, 89–92,
    128–30, 140, 143, 161, 168, 186,
    217–18
Le Matin, report in, 42
Lewis Pelly, M.V., 95, 120, 125–34,
    146, 149
Locust, 149
Lorimer, Maj. D. L. R., 112
Lorimer, Lt-Col. J. G., 88, 93,
    143–4
Lossie, river, 54, 62
Lowther, Sir Gerard, 88, 110
Lunt, Maj.-Gen. J. D., 8–9
Lut, Persia, 44
Lytton, Lord, 28

Macedonia, 49
McMahon, Sir A. H., 36–7, 53–5, 87,
    139, 143, 219–23
Madina, 21, 208
Madrasah, Kuwait, 121, 131
Mahad ibn Saud, 164
Mail ships, 95, 122, 131
Majmaa, 135, 139, 157, 208
Malham, 163
Mallet, Sir Louis, 25, 38, 142, 197
Manesty, Samuel, 65

Margoliouth, Professor, 103
Markab, Ark of Ishmael, 176
Masjid ar Rashid, 83
Mathi ibn Huzaim, *rafiq,* 123, 1
Maunsell, Lt-Col. F. R., 144, 1
Medjidie, order of, 122
Mesopotamia (Iraq), 21, 37, 199
Mian Mir, India, 32
Montagu Motor Museum, 9
Montenegro, 49
Morley, Lord, 110
Motor car, 40 ff
Mu'amer, Fahad ibn, 167–9
Mubarak ibn Sabah, Shaikh, *pas*
Mudhnib, 166
Muhammad, Prophet, 21, 163
Muhammad V, Sultan, 108
Muhammad Ali, Ottoman Vicer
    57
Muhammad ibn Abdul Aziz al Sau
    161
Muhammad ibn Abdullah al Rashi
    60, 165–6, 220
Muhammad ibn Abdul Wahhab
    Suleiman, 57, 163
Muhammad ibn Abdur Rahman a.
    Saud, 87, 189
Muhammad ibn Sabah, Shaikh, 65
Muhammad ibn Saud, 57
Muhammerah, 95, 145, 199
Multan, Punjab, 30
Muntafiq, tribe, 20, 86, 124, 134
Murphy, Lt-Col. C. C. R., 144
Musaiba, 101
Muscat, 39, 104, 107, 142
Mutair, tribe, 73, 82, 124, 134, 207–9,
    214
Mutasarrif of Najd, 20, 128, 136, 142
Mylrea, Dr C. S. G., 121, 217

Nadir Shah, 118
Nafud, 57, 134, 169 ff
Najd, *passim*
Nakhl, Egypt, 185
Naqab, 182
Natural history, interest in, 138
Natural History Museum, Lond
    189

Saud ibn Saleh ibn Subhan, 172
Sbei, tribe, 148, 159, 163, 207
Schumann, Clara, 50
Sedgwick, Mr Michael, 10
Shaalan, Nawaf ibn Nuri, 175
Shaalan, Nuri ibn, 90, 93, 174–7, 191, 197, 225
Shaalan, Sultan ibn Nawaf, 175, 225
Shahiyah, 90
Shaib al Faisal, 81
Shakespear, Anne Caroline (née Davidson), 29–31, 52–3, 201
Shakespear, Dowdeswell, 28
Shakespear, George Albert, 30, 32
Shakespear, Henry Alexander (Uncle Alex), 51
Shakespear, Lt-Col. Henry Talbot, 8, 30, 32, 62, 119, 190
Shakespear, John, of Brookwood, 28
Shakespear, John, of Shadwell, 28
Shakespear, John Talbot, 28
Shakespear, Col. L. W., 217
Shakespear, Mary, 29
Shakespear, Mary Anne, 28
Shakespear, Maj. Richard Harry Baird, 9
Shakespear, Col. R. P., 10
Shakespear, Sir Richmond Campbell, 28
Shakespear, Thomas, 28
Shakespear, William Henry Sullivan, 29, 30, 52
Shakespear, Winifred (née Baird), 62, 119, 189
Shalwa, hawk, 78 ff
Shamaliyah, 154
Shammar, tribe, fortress, 20, 58, 89–93, 124, 176, 210, 214
Shamsiyah, 160
Shaq depression, valley, 78, 80, 123, 135
Shaqra, 97, 164
Shara, 208, 220
Sharif of Mecca, 58, 62; see also Husain ibn Ali
Shatt-al-Arab, 95
Shaw, George Bernard, 63
Shimal, wind, 80, 150, 169–70

Shiraz, Persia, 43, 56
Shuwaikh, 146, 149
Simla, India, 37, 41, 95
Sinai, 184, 207
Sirr, 165
Sirra, 77, 125
Slade, Admiral Sir E., 141
Sphinx, H.M.S., 38, 127
Spurrier, Mr M. C., 9
Storrs, Sir Ronald, 221
Strabo, 100
Subhan, see Hamud and Zamil ibn
Subhan desert, 83
Sudair, 17, 135
Suez, 21, 185
Suleiman, Abdullah ibn, 156
Suleiman, Mahad ibn, 166
Summan desert, 135
Switzerland, 50–52
Sykes, Sir Mark, 221
Symes, Lt-Col. G. S., 223

Tabuk, 174
Taif, 97
Taima, 169
Taj Mahal Hotel, Bombay, 40
Talib, Sayid, 125–8, 134, 192, 200, 203–5, 212
Tarafiyya, 59, 209
Tehran, 44–5
Thackeray, Emily, 28
Thackeray, Revd Francis, 28
Thackeray, William Mackepeace, 28
Thadiq, 164
Thaj, 101–3, 192, 207
Thalet-at-Fasqah, 81
Thamaniyah, 78
Thamilat al Kaa, 79
Thamilat al Turki, 80
Thessaly, 49
Thomson, Mr Ralph, 10
Tibet, 37
Times of India, quoted, 116, 119, 216
Times, The, of London, quoted, 98, 185, 216
Towala, tribe, 153
Trade routes, ancient, 102
Travel log books, 11, 137

Trevor, Maj. A. P., 141–2, 188, 211
Trieste, 50
Tripoli, north Africa, 108
Tubaik hills, 180
Turkey, *passim*
Turki ibn Abdul Aziz al Saud, 161, 213
Tuwaik, 155–64, 186

Ubaid ibn Ali al Rashid, 58
Umballa, India, 32
Um Janaib, snake, 171
Umm al Kawaisa, 100
Umm al Maradin, 140
Uqair, Ujair, 141, 142–4, 192

Varthema, Lodovico, 182
Venice, 50
Viceroy of India, *passim*
Victoria, Queen Empress, 28
Victoria-Eden Hotel, Adelboden, 51

Wadi ar-Rummah, 153, 166, 186, 209
Wadi Hanifa, 17
Wadi Ithm, 182
Wadi Musa, 182–3
Wadi Sirhan, 24
Wadi Yatun, 182
Wafra, 137
Wahhabi creed, 57, 96, 107
Wahhabi kingdom, 18, 228

Wali Muhammad, servant, *passim*
Wali of Basrs, 66, 147
Wallin, Professor G. A., 77, 186
Wara, 78, 124
War Office, maps, 144, 186
Wasm, tribal marks, 138
Wavell, Field Marshal Lord, 227
Williamson, William Richard, 92
Wilson, Sir Arnold, 129, 131
Wilson, Col. C. E., 219–20, 223
Wingate, Gen. Sir F. Reginald, 185, 223
Wood, Mr J. B., 142
Woolwich, R.M.A., entrance, 32
Worsley, Miss Madeleine E., 9
Wright, Mrs Joan (née Lakin), 9

Yahyah, Imam of Yemen, 191, 207, 223
Yemen, 18, 104, 107, 142, 192
Yezd caravan route, 38

Zamil ibn Subhan, 90–3, 127, 142, 172
Zarag, snake, 171
Zarud, 170
Zeid ibn Husain, of Mecca, 97, 221
Zilfi, 18, 155, 186, 204–6, 214
Zor escarpment, 123
Zor, Ras, 140
Zubaidah (Zobaida), 90
Zubair, 98–9